ESSENTIALS OF CONSUMER BEHAVIOR

Essentials of Consumer Behavior

CARL E. BLOCK University of Missouri at Columbia

KENNETH J. ROERING University of Missouri at Columbia

**Based on Engel, Kollat, and Blackwell's:
CONSUMER BEHAVIOR**

The Dryden Press
Hinsdale, Illinois

Copyright © 1976 by The Dryden Press
A Division of Holt, Rinehart and Winston

All rights reserved

Library of Congress Catalog Card Number: 75-21321
ISBN: 0-03-089703-3

Printed in the United States of America
6 7 8 9 032 9 8 7 6 5 4 3 2 1

Editorial-Production services provided by
COBB/DUNLOP, Inc.

To Joyanne and Betsy

Contents

Preface

This is a textbook for students taking their first course in consumer behavior. Consequently, no special preparation is necessary, although a basic appreciation of our business system and of the interests of the marketing manager are assumed. This latter assumption is made because historically students of business and of marketing most specifically have shown the greatest interest in the formalized study of consumer behavior. Furthermore, it is anticipated that this will continue.

The book is written so that it can be used by those who will have no opportunity to pursue further formal study of the subject as well as by those who plan to take additional courses in consumer behavior or in closely related areas.

Our purpose in writing this book was to provide the beginning student with a clear, interesting and systematic treatment of what is known about consumer behavior. To be consistent with this purpose a book must include the major trends, their theoretical origins and the principles they sustain without the inclusion of an exhaustive literature review.

The most efficient and expeditious way to achieve our purpose was to use the comprehensive model developed by Engel, Kollat, and Blackwell and to creatively modify the rich synthesis of the theoretical and empirical research included in the second edition of *Consumer Behavior*. The resulting essentials book eliminates some topics, simplifies others, adds new topics, draws more of the managerial implications out of the various topics and, hopefully brings to life consumer behavior from the perspective of the marketing decision maker and other interested individuals.

We have concentrated on the fundamental areas within consumer behavior and deliberately omitted extensive summaries of empirical studies, theoretical refinements, and methodological issues in the belief that these are more properly suited to a more advanced book. As with most textbooks little of the work is original, rather it is the domain of all who seek to understand consumer behavior. In short, we have attempted to relate the results of scientific research to the real, immediate problems of the marketing decision maker. While the in depth evaluation of complex theoretical and methodological issues is necessary for the development of an understanding of consumer behavior, the near exclusive reliance on such issues is inappropriate for the student preparing for a career in the business world. Furthermore, the relevance of consumer behavior analysis to nonbusiness organizations is explicitly recognized by the use of various examples throughout the book.

The book has been organized into five major sections. Part I: *Introduction and Overview* sets the stage for the remainder of the text. It introduces the subject of consumer behavior and discusses its importance as a discipline. Particular attention is given to the development of a conceptual basis for the systematic study of consumer behavior. It is at this point that the Engel, Kollat, and Blackwell decision process model is presented.

Part II: *Analysis of Group Influences on Consumer Behavior* focuses on the major components of the social setting that come to bear upon individual behavior. In this section the family is studied as a decision making unit as well as a source of influence on individual behavior.

Part III: *Analysis of Individual Influencing Forces on Consumer Behavior* gives attention to what are often called internal state variables. These include those factors that are unique to an individual that influence his or her functioning as a consumer. These include personality, learning, evaluative criteria and attitudes.

Part IV: *Analysis of the Consumer Decision Process* deals with the way in which individual consumers make decisions given their social setting and internal state variables discussed in parts II and III. Specifically included are problem recognition, the search process, assembling of relevant information, evaluation of alternative actions, the act of purchasing, and the postpurchase evaluation process.

Part V: *Directions in Consumer Analysis* is the concluding section. It focuses on several major areas of application of the knowledge of consumer behavior to marketing decision making and on exploring future prospects for the continued development of consumer behavior as an important applied discipline.

At the end of each chapter three aids to furthering the understanding of the material have been provided. First, summaries have been included which highlight the important chapter concepts. A series of eight to ten questions and topics for discussion follow each chapter summary. Most of these questions cannot be dealt with by simply going back to one page in the chapter and noting the answer. Finally, two short cases called "situational problems" are provided. These offer a unique opportunity to apply the chapter material in a realistic setting.

We want to acknowledge our debt to the authors of *Consumer Behavior*, Jim Engel, Dave Kollat, and Roger Blackwell. Their interest and encouragement in writing the *Essentials of Consumer Behavior* was indeed critical. This book also benefited materially from the comments and suggestions of the many reviewers, especially Paul Green of the University of Pennsylvania, and Philip Kotler of Northwestern University. We are also indebted to all of the following individuals who cared enough about the books available in consumer behavior that they willingly took the time necessary to read the manuscript and make suggestions for its improvement:

Beverlee B. Anderson, University of Cincinnati
Robert L. Anderson, University of South Florida
E. H. Bonfield, University of Alabama
Peter L. Gillett, Virginia Commonwealth University
Lawrence M. Richard, Wayne State University
Terence A. Shimp, Kent State University
Thomas J. Stanley, State University of New York at Albany
M. Venkatesan, University of Iowa
Robert B. Woodruff, University of Tennessee
William G. Zikmund, Oklahoma State University

We want to give special recognition to our wives whose encouragement, advice, editorial comments and typing assistance were lovingly given. Despite the numerous contributions made by others to the book's completion, we alone must assume the responsibility for the errors and shortcomings.

C.E.B.
K.J.R.

PART I

INTRODUCTION

OUTLINE

1

The Scope
of Consumer
Behavior

The field of consumer behavior is one of the exciting frontiers open to serious students of the social sciences. It is a dynamic area, the essence of which is crucial to decisions made by business management, public agencies, nonprofit organizations, and publicly elected officials. Those responsible for managing the marketing programs in modern business firms have been the most interested and persistent group to pursue the study of the consumer. It would be difficult, if not impossible, for a business to survive today without giving at least some attention to consumer behavior. For instance, how else but with an awareness of consumer interests and a sensitivity to likely market behavior could management make decisions with respect to the following:

A typewriter with a modified version of the standard keyboard is being introduced by SCM. It is a simplified keyboard aimed at junior-high-school students who want to teach themselves to type for personal use.[1]

Krazy Kar, a hand propelled riding toy manufactured by Marx Toy Company, was not well received in the general toy market but now may have a new lease on life: It appears to have special benefits for use in the rehabilitation of handicapped children.[2]

Foods formerly restricted to relatively limited ethnic markets are now a part of everyday meals on American tables. The kosher hot dog and pickle, for example, have wide appeal as do many Mexican, oriental, and Italian foods. Aggressive marketing efforts have stimulated sales of these and other ethnic foods to the extent that estimated sales are over $6.5 billion annually.[3]

The relevance of consumer behavior to nonbusiness applications exists whether or not those involved in such fields recognize it or are knowledgeable in the subject. For example, many dedicated legislators believe they have consumers' interests in mind when they propose new protective regulations. But, do these legislators accurately perceive what is truly in the consum-

[1]"The Keyboard Whose Time Has Come—Maybe," *Sales Management,* 114 (February 3, 1975), p. 3.
[2]"Marketing Observer," *Business Week* (July 28, 1975), p. 43.
[3]N. Giges, "Ethnic foods lose 'foreign' accents, but economy is slowing their growth," *Advertising Age,* 46 (July 21, 1975), p. 3.

ers' best interest, given actual buyer behavior patterns? Unfortunately, nearly all such public policy information is developed, reviewed, and enacted by individuals with a wide range of personal interpretations of consumer behavior, few of which have been systematically developed and empirically verified.

A case to consider is the inferior quality of service to which the uninformed consumer, seeking the repair of his television set or automobile, has often fallen victim. As a result of growing concern, a number of people have proposed various ways of ensuring that the consumer receive appropriate service at an equitable price.

It is apparent that there are a number of market-oriented considerations and constraints that must be kept in mind when services such as these are the focus of attention. At the outset it is staggering to realize that these are services provided by thousands of companies through hundreds of thousands of their employees for millions of U.S. households. In the case of auto repair, the service may have a direct effect on the safety of the individual buyer as well as those who share his car and the highway with him.

A bill designed to cope with the deceptive practices in both of these service industries was recently introduced in one midwestern state legislature. A brief summary of this bill follows:

> Truth in Repair: All persons in the business of repairing television sets or motor vehicles would be required in transactions where the estimated costs of repair will exceed $35.00 to provide the consumer with a written estimate of the cost of repairs broken down into goods and services, and labor. The repair shop cannot exceed that estimate by more than 10 percent without the prior written permission of the consumer. If it does, the consumer is liable only for the estimated price plus 10 percent. Furthermore, all parts replaced must be retained by the repairman and offered to the consumer.[4]

There is no question that this is well-meaning legislation and that if passed it may have a substantial impact on the television and automotive repair business. However, it also illustrates the

[4]Consumer Protection Division, Office of the Attorney General of Missouri, Information Release to the Press on House Bill 381: Truth-In-Repair, Spring, 1975.

assumptions about consumer behavior that were made by the authors of the bill. These include the following:

1. Comparative shopping for repair services will be fostered.
2. The consumer will use the information provided as a basis for selecting service establishments that offer the desired service at a fair price.
3. Consumers will use the provisions of the bill to examine which parts have been replaced and the work done, then decide whether quality services have been rendered at a fair price.

If passed, this bill is likely to increase the cost of doing business for television and automotive service establishments. Furthermore, if the intended results of the regulation are not obtained, the consumer may actually end up paying more for existing service. Therefore, it is extemely important to explicitly identify the assumptions about consumer behavior underlying such proposed legislation and to apply existing knowledge to the desired results in an attempt to test the validity of those assumptions.

This legislative bill is just an illustration of the widespread need for accuracy in the assessment of consumer behavioral patterns. This example notwithstanding, it appears that consumer analysis will continue to find its greatest use in the area of marketing in the foreseeable future.

The Field of Consumer Behavior

History shows that every human community develops some means by which it produces and exchanges goods and services to meet its members' needs. In the most primitive societies this process is simple and often involves a barter system. However, in the industrially advanced areas, such as those of North America, Japan, Australia, and Europe, the production and distribution system is complex, and the available range of goods and services is wide. Consequently, a full understanding of consumption decisions in these geographical areas would require the study of every aspect of a person's entire lifetime of experiences. Also, in the broadest sense, consumer behavior and human behavior would be nearly identical fields of study because the consumption of economic goods pervades almost every activity in which humans are involved. For practical reasons the field must be limited to include only a portion of human activity.

DEFINING CONSUMER BEHAVIOR

Before more is said about consumer behavior, it is appropriate to define the scope of the subject as it is treated in this text. Therefore, the following definition is included here to set boundaries. Consumer behavior is defined as:

> ... the acts of individuals directly involved in obtaining and using economic goods and services, including the decision processes that precede and determine those acts.[5]

This definition has three key parts: (1) "The acts of individuals ..." This includes such activities as travel to and from stores, in-store shopping, actual purchase, transportation, use, and evaluation of both goods and services available in the market. (2) " ... individuals directly involved in obtaining and using economic goods and services ..." This statement identifies the focus of this book—the ultimate consumer. That is, it concentrates on individuals purchasing goods and services for personal consumption by themselves and/or for some other similar unit such as their family or a friend. This latter context would include the homemaker acting as the family purchasing agent as well as someone buying a gift for another person. This part of the definition of consumer behavior also notes that the text does not deal specifically with individuals purchasing for business or institutional usage, even though many of the topics are equally relevant to such activities. (3) " ... including the decision processes that precede and determine these acts." This statement is included to recognize the importance of the purchase activities of consumers that directly affect their observable market action, for example contact with salesmen, media and advertising exposure, informal explorations with friends, the formation of evalu-

[5]J. F. Engel, D. T. Kollat, and R. D. Blackwell, *Consumer Behavior,* 2nd ed. (New York: Holt, Rinehart and Winston, Inc., 1973), p. 5.

ative criteria, and the overt acts of identifying and considering alternative purchase decisions.

AN APPLIED DISCIPLINE WITH INTERDISCIPLINARY ROOTS

The systematic study of consumer behavior has been interdisciplinary from the very start. In fact, some of the first marketing scholars to focus attention on the behavioral dimensions of consumer actions were themselves trained in such disciplines as psychology and sociology. One of the major reasons why consumer behavior is such a rich field of study today is that it continues to rely on both the theoretical and empirical work of a number of other disciplines. For instance, social psychology provides insight into individual behavior in social settings. The work of anthropologists, economists, political scientists, statisticians, and philosophers also makes contributions to the understanding of consumer decision making.

Despite continued borrowing from other fields, consumer behavior has emerged as an applied discipline much like medicine. In the practice of medicine, the physician uses techniques developed through an understanding of the physical and biological sciences. In the case of the consumer analyst, he or she must be ever aware of the empirical and theoretical underpinnings of the behavioral sciences that support this work.

The study of consumer behavior as an applied field presents some difficulties, the most bothersome of which are set forth in the next section.

Problems Common to the Study of Consumer Behavior

Everyone has expectations as to how people will act under various circumstances, and most people even engage in predicting the behavior of those in whom they have an interest. For instance, most of us are rather good at predicting who will remember us on our birthday with a gift, and we are probably able to forecast the type of gift that we will receive. This suggests that everyone has a set of propositions or theories of human behavior, whether recognized or not, that have been developed over his or her lifetime and that, in addition, these propositions are called upon quite often in everyday life as practical aids to living.

Of course, these behavioral propositions are not used only for predicting behavior; they also can be used as an aid to the planning of personal actions. For instance, most of us at some time have tried to influence and shape the anticipated behavior of other people. Frequently, this is to make their future actions more consistent with our own desires. For example, it might be possible to get a friend or family member to be supportive of a desire to move out of a dormitory or to buy a new car. These attempts at influencing people can take on any number of forms but often include carefully selected comments or gestures that are made at "choice" times. As a result of this constant awareness of others, many individuals are tempted to conclude that they really know quite a lot about people, such as their make-up and what can be expected from them. And in some respects, this is true—most of us have a great deal of experience with people because we are social beings by nature. However, this is where some of us begin to get into difficulty. What follows is an attempt to identify the most prevalent and bothersome difficulties that face those who are beginning their study of consumer behavior. These are discussed under the topical headings of myopic view, oversimplification, and the logic trap.

MYOPIC VIEW OF BEHAVIOR

There is a great temptation to define the world in terms of personal experiences, that is, from a personal perspective. Although many of us possess a keen insight into our close associates, we often have not had the benefit of long-term exposure to the behavior of many people with whom we eventually must deal or who are of major concern to us, that is, we lack real breadth of experience. Consequently, we are not very good at explaining or predicting actions of these unfamiliar individuals.

An example of a myopic view would be the observation that because you personally enjoyed a local nightclub in your hometown, the college community where you go to school would be an ideal location for a similar facility. The implication is that you are a typical student whose interests are shared by a sizable market segment in the college community and, therefore, that such a nightclub would be a profitable business venture. This observation may or may not be correct; it is open to study.

The serious study of consumer behavior requires a constant questioning of the *representativeness* of personal experience and observation and a desire to broaden one's understanding of behavioral processes.

OVERSIMPLIFICATION

Another problem that many people have is that they oversimplify things, particularly the explanations and/or solutions to complex problems. For instance, to many people today U.S. inflation and world overpopulation have relatively simple solutions. Reliable sources suggest that this is hardly the case. Consumer behavior has not been spared this urge to oversimplify. We have all heard people classify someone as a status-seeker or show-off. Such labels are sometimes used to explain a particular purchase. For instance: "It's just like Mary to buy that kind of a dress; she is always seeking attention." The implication is that Mary's purchasing behavior is easily explained by this one characteristic.

One way of substantiating this observed tendency toward oversimplification in consumer behavior is to ask yourself what led to your making a particular purchase such as a new suit or a piece of stereo equipment. Then, having noted your response, try to write down the actual series of events and steps that you went through in the process leading to the purchase. Also include a description of your behavior that followed the purchase that was related to the use or to the evaluation of the item. Obviously this is a rather challenging task—one that most would dismiss as nonsense or not worth the time involved. Nevertheless, as individuals who have an interest in consumer behavior, you must be willing to recognize the likelihood that much of what may influence observable market behavior has too often gone unrecorded and, therefore, has not been analyzed.

Tucker, in *Foundations of a Theory of Consumer Behavior,*[6] made just this observation. He attempted to call attention to the fact that an understanding of consumer behavior must start with a fundamental appreciation of consumer actions on a microlevel. Therefore, in a very real sense, to expect even limited success in coming to understand consumer behavior at this stage, each student must consciously decide to be more observant of his own behavioral patterns as well as those of others. This must be done while keeping in mind the previous warning about myopic views. A decision must also be made to be hesitant in making broad generalizations.

Yet, to a large extent, generalizations will make up a substantial part of what is presented in this book, but these must be made with care and only after close and insightful observation. It is also helpful to recognize that much of what is stated as a behavioral proposition will have to include some explicit qualifications as to the circumstances under which it applies.

THE LOGIC TRAP

Although intuitive reasoning and logic are useful to everyone in making and evaluating conjectures or assumptions about behavior, they are simply not a substitute for empirical investigation as a means of broadening understanding and of validation. It would be like assuming that because some consumers have been known to use price as a guide to the quality of a product, the highest priced brand will gain the largest market share.

Too frequently the behavioral patterns that are expected to logically occur under some well-prepared marketing plan do not materialize. This is probably due less to consumers being illogical in their actions than it is to a lack of comprehensiveness in behavioral theory. An old parable, well known in the Middle East, captures the essence of the "logic trap" in a different context, but it is a good warning to keep in mind. In many ways, the number

[6]W. T. Tucker, *Foundations for a Theory of Consumer Behavior* (New York: Holt, Rinehart and Winston, Inc., 1967).

and nature of the variables affecting the consumer in the market make the analyst feel as though he is in the Middle East.

> One day in Iraq a field caught fire. All the animals and insects began to dash for the river. Just as a camel was about to slip into the stream and swim to safety he was accosted by a scorpion. "Please," pleaded the scorpion, "I can't swim. If I stay here in the field, I will die in the fire. But you can swim. Won't you please ferry me to safety on your back?" "Oh, no," snorted the camel, "You will surely sting me, and I will die." "Why should I do a stupid thing like that?" countered the scorpion. "If I sting you and you die, I'll drown. That doesn't make sense." So the camel, a logical beast, gave in. The scorpion clambered aboard, and the camel, bearing his lethal burden, began to swim across the river. Midway across, the scorpion stung the camel. As the camel sank, he groaned, "Why, why?" The scorpion, giving a final shrug before he too went below the surface, answered: "This is the Middle East."[7]

Providing a warning about the most prevalent difficulties that arise in studying consumers does not necessarily prevent their occurrence, but hopefully it builds some resistance to one's susceptibility to their lure. The decision process approach, which is discussed in the next section, provides a very helpful conceptual basis for systematically studying the consumer.

The Decision-Process Approach

The decision-process approach to analyzing consumer behavior has emerged in recent years and is the approach taken in this book. Using this conceptualization, a purchase is viewed as simply one stage in a particular course of action undertaken by a consumer. In order to understand the act of purchasing as a distinct stage in the buying process, it is necessary to examine the events that precede and follow the purchase.

The decision-process approach provides an analytical framework for studying consumer behavior, that is, it provides a frame of reference for the identification of relevant factors or processes

[7]T. L. Cross, *Black Capitalism* (New York: Antheneum, 1969), p. 21.

and their relationships. It also takes care not to imply relationships for which there is little supporting evidence. As propositions are tested and validated or rejected, knowledge is accumulated, and by this means the analyst is encouraged to move beyond the mere description of specific observable behavior that has immediate importance.

By building on past personal experience and the experience of others, the consumer analyst's knowledge is accumulated. However, if no analytical framework were used, no such systematic accumulation would occur. An example of this kind of failure would be the company that learns which of four ads it has developed for a campaign is most effective in attracting consumer attention but does not discover what qualities gave the advertisement the features that attract the attention. As a result, subsequent campaigns would benefit little from prior experience.

The decision-process approach that provides the framework used in this book is based upon the Engel, Kollat, and Blackwell model.[8] Essentially, this framework: (1) identifies and defines the structural variables involved in consumer behavior and (2) indicates the relationships that exist among the identified variables in so far as these relationships can be determined. As used here, a *variable* is a factor or influence that enters into the measurement and prediction of consumer behavior.

The Practical Importance of Consumer Behavior

Despite what has been stated earlier in this chapter about the relevance of consumer behavior, some questions may remain as to what specific practical benefits can come from an intensive study of the subject. One very practical reason for the concentrated study of consumer behavior is to better understand *macromarketing* problems—how a society meets the needs of its people as an aggregate. This involves the study of issues related to broadly based problems of resource allocation, which can take any number of forms. Examples include the preparation of an equitable plan for the allocation of a scarce resource, such as

[8]J. F. Engel, *et al.,* p. 58.

crude oil, among alternative users or the development of a comprehensive strategy for the distribution of surplus food commodities among the poor. Those who have had the greatest interest in consumer behavior for macromarketing reasons have most often included government officials, urban planners, economists, administrators of social agencies, and others primarily responsible for the social welfare of a nation.

The concern for solving *micromarketing* problems has motivated others to study consumer behavior. Micromarketing focuses on the problems of administering specific units or entities in any economy, for example, a hotel, supermarket, amusement park, or consumer goods manufacturing plant. The day-to-day concerns of the marketing manager or product manager are primarily those of a micromarketing nature. A typical problem is the allocation of the advertising budget among various media alternatives to maximize effective exposure among important consumer groups. Another is the decision as to the selection of packing materials that provide adequate physical protection for the product and yet are attractive to the consumer.

What follows is the identification of three key thrusts that draw attention to the variety of practical applications of the knowledge of consumer behavior in both a macro and microsetting. The first considers one of the most widely used ways of utilizing the analysis of consumer behavior in marketing planning—the evaluation of new market opportunities. The second and third topics that follow focus on applications that are less widespread but represent new and promising opportunities for applying what is known about consumer behavior. These latter two directions include demarketing and metamarketing.

EVALUATING NEW MARKET OPPORTUNITIES

An important reason for studying consumer behavior is the evaluation of consumer groups with unsatisfied needs or desires. To be successful, an organization must not only recognize unmet needs but also understand whether there are clusters of such needs that can be profitably served and what organizational response is required for success in selling to these clusters. Firms that organize their resources capably and flexibly toward unmet needs are sometimes described as consumer-oriented or operating under the "marketing concept."

Evaluation of new markets varies in difficulty according to the affluence and sophistication of a country's economy. In the case of an emerging nation, evaluating new markets may be simply a process of determining how much economic power can be generated and how quantities of basic commodities and services— food, housing, medical care, and so on—can be supplied. When most of the citizens do not have enough basic food to eat, it is not difficult to locate new market opportunities. The best market opportunity is simply the provision of more food, probably of the same types already being consumed. Until a society reaches a point where a significant number of its members are above a subsistence level, the determination of new market opportunities is fairly obvious.

In an affluent, industrialized society the most attractive new market opportunities do not ordinarily arise by simply providing more of what is already being consumed. New market opportunities arise because of other reasons, and these reasons make prediction of consumer response somewhat more difficult. Two illustrations follow.

Through geographic mobility new market opportunities arise. As consumers move from one area to another they must reestablish patronage patterns. Financial institutions must be selected; groceries, medical supplies, auto repairs, and gasoline must be purchased in a new setting. In many cases some of their familiar brands will be less convenient to obtain, and some others will not even be available. The consumers' needs and desires in this new environment provide opportunities for local businesses as well as for manufacturers of brands of merchandise available in the new community.

The increasing number of women in the labor force has nurtured new market opportunities. Simply the scarcity of time at home for working women has contributed to the growing interest in convenience foods and even in eating out. Commercial banks, savings and loan associations, and insurance companies have begun to recognize the importance of women as a significant market segment. For example, many women now desire to have salary continuation insurance and life insurance tailored to their professional needs. They also want to establish credit and in some cases borrow money on their own for various personal and family needs.

DEMARKETING REQUIRES INFORMED DECISION MAKERS

For the last thirty years in this country a major emphasis has been placed on stimulating consumer demand for nearly all goods and services as a means of raising the general standard of living, and for many much has been accomplished during this period. As a result of this effort and the fact that we have become accustomed to the fruits of the labor expended, it is particularly difficult to face the shortages that are beginning to appear. Nevertheless, within recent years the American public has come to realize that constant increases in consumption cannot continue indefinitely. In fact, it is now quite clear to most that there is a limit to the amount of gasoline and heating oil that will be available, particularly the amount that will be available at prices paid in the early 1970's. Of course, the list of such shortages seems to grow weekly with no true relief in sight.

Such recognized scarcity has already called for some *demarketing,* that is, the orderly reduction of demand among consumers for selected goods and services. Each of the actions taken to directly encourage conservation of resources or directed toward diverting demand from goods requiring scarce commodities to others that rely on those that are more plentiful is undertaken with specific consumer response patterns as the desired outcome. Unfortunately, there is evidence to suggest that stimulating widespread interest in conservation of scarce resources will be considerably more difficult than nurturing greater personal consumption. Therefore, now possibly as never before, accurate information about consumer behavior is needed.

METAMARKETING OFFERS NEW CHALLENGES

Metamarketing is the application of marketing technology to problems facing the nonprofit sector, particularly on a microbasis, in other words, problems relating to such groups as professional associations, political parties, local municipalities, religious denominations, libraries, the arts, and public school systems. Increasingly such groups are seeking information about their constituencies—composition, interests, opinions, activities, and willingness to support various issues. The situation described in the next paragraph illustrates the kind of issues that are gaining attention.

As a result of the growing concern with alcoholism in this country, a number of efforts have been launched to combat the problem. In California, for example, the California Office of Alcohol Program Management proposed to fight alcoholism with a media campaign modeled after the liquor industry's own marketing strategies and financed with a tax on a variety of alcoholic beverages. The plan is to spend $4 million during a five-year period on a prevention campaign aimed squarely at young people and minorities. In making the proposal, the COAPM drew specific attention to what they called the excellent market research which the liquor industry had done in identifying these groups as target markets for alcoholic products. However, a spokesman for the Distilled Spirits Institute, the liquor industry trade association, reportedly was quick to point out that: "You just can't use marketing research as the basis for a public health program."[9]

Certainly this trade association spokesman was wrong. There is no reason to believe that information about consumer behavior is any less valuable to groups like COAPM than it is to business. Furthermore, one of the newest challenges to students of marketing is the whole metamarketing area.

QUESTIONS FOR ANALYSIS

To further illustrate the scope of consumer behavior, listed below are a few of the many questions that the consumer analyst might focus upon. The answers to these questions have relevance for a wide variety of decision makers. At this time it may be helpful for you to think about each of the questions and to record your immediate responses to those that are most interesting. Then, put these answers aside until you are at least half to two-thirds

[9]"A tax on alcohol to tout temperance," *Business Week* (February 10, 1975), pp. 29, 32.

of the way through the book. At a convenient time come back to this same list and again make note of your answers. It will be very interesting to compare the change in your responses.

1. Is buying behavior generally a logical process with important identifiable sequential steps?
2. What are motives and how significant are they in the arousal of buying behavior?
3. Do consumers seek to maximize the expected value in the goods and services they purchase?
4. How do people learn to become consumers?
5. How important is "time" in the buying process?
6. What is persuasive communication?
7. Do consumers like advertising?
8. Is social class the same as life-style?
9. Are the purchasing patterns of black consumers significantly different from those of white consumers?
10. Can market segments be identified by variation in life-styles?
11. How can brand awareness be created?
12. Do personality differences correlate strongly with brand choice?
13. Are most consumers' store patronage patterns similar across product groups?
14. Are today's youths more rational consumers than their parents?
15. How do consumers form priorities among product groups?
16. Is the family a major buying unit in the United States?
17. How are group purchasing decisions made?
18. Should salesmen who have personalities similar to those of their customers or personalities substantially different from customers be recruited?
19. Do some people consistently try new products or services before other segments of the population?
20. What is the concept of store image and how important is this to a firm?

Summary

Consumer behavior is defined as those acts of individuals that are directly involved in obtaining and using economic goods and services, including the decision processes that precede and determine those acts. As a field of study consumer behavior relies heavily on theoretical and empirical work from other disciplines such as psychology and sociology. New students of consumer behavior are often faced with three difficulties: (1) taking a myopic view of behavior and expecting their personal experiences to be representative of the experiences of the majority, (2) oversimplifying the solution to complex behavioral problems, and (3) assuming that a logical explanation for a proposition about behavior is correct without any supporting empirical investigation.

In analyzing consumer behavior this text uses the decision-process approach which examines the events that precede and follow the purchase. The study of consumer behavior is very practical for two major reasons. One is that it affords a better understanding of macromarketing problems—or, how a society meets the needs of its people as an aggregate. The other is that it can aid in solving micromarketing problems—or, in the administration of specific units in an economy. Three key applications are: (1) the evaluation of new market opportunities, (2) the demarketing of goods and services, and (3) metamarketing. Through metamarketing the study of consumer behavior also is becoming a valuable asset to many areas outside of the business world.

The two sections that follow are entitled "Questions and Issues for Discussion" and "Situational Problems"; both will conclude each chapter of the book. They are designed to serve as a means of reviewing the material presented in the chapter and to facilitate the understanding of new information in the context of consumer behavior. The questions that are included in the next section are intended to be thought-provoking; therefore, most cannot be answered by looking back into the chapter for a word or brief phrase. However, once you have studied the chapter you will be ready to use these questions to spark your ideas and insights. This section should serve as a basis for personal study, classroom discussion, or reviewing for an examination.

The section called "Situational Problems" includes two short cases. Each focuses on a different aspect of consumer behavior. They are more likely to provide insight into consumer behavior when they are discussed among members of a class or some other group.

QUESTIONS AND
ISSUES FOR
DISCUSSION

1. Consumer behavior is nothing more than applied psychology. Discuss.
2. Most successful small businessmen have never taken a course in consumer behavior nor formally studied the subject. How can this be true?
3. Little or no experience exists in the application of knowledge of consumer behavior to the problem of demarketing; therefore, little success can be expected. Discuss.
4. Public agencies such as HEW and DOT should never spend part of their budgets on consumer analysis. Discuss.
5. Providing for the consumers' best interests cannot be accomplished by a firm while attempting to realize maximum profit. Discuss.
6. Most government services are basically free, that is, they are not obtained by direct payment by the user. Therefore, consumer purchase patterns of such services cannot be studied in a meaningful manner. Discuss.
7. Although everyone is a unique person, there are sufficient similarities among people that make it possible to systematically study human behavior. Discuss.
8. Most consumers can be classified into one of several categories identified by descriptive labels, such as conservative or aggressive, making easy prediction of their market behavior possible. Discuss.
9. A motorcycle manufacturer who has carefully studied consumer interests and buying patterns in the United States should have little difficulty in applying these findings in other industrialized countries. Discuss.

SITUATIONAL
PROBLEMS

Case 1
The Batton Company manufactures wheel bearings for the automotive industry. Their bearings are used as original equipment by

two of the major U.S. automobile manufacturers. It has just been discovered by Batton's new marketing manager that the company has never made any attempt to determine how satisfied car buyers are with the Batton wheel bearings.

Why would the new marketing manager even bring up this issue?

How are other Batton executives likely to respond to his discovery?

Case 2

The Master Dance Company is a local nonprofit group that is made up of people interested in modern dance. The organization's objective is to promote interest in modern dance. The members offer free class lessons to local youngsters and produce an annual dance program. Members donate their time and have been successful in generating considerable community interest. All financial support has come from donations and the revenue from their annual dance program. Recently a group of local musicians has begun organizing a community symphony. They have proposed that one half of the necessary operating funds be raised by donations and that the city match these funds from the Parks and Recreation Department's budget. Upon hearing of this proposal, the Master Dance Company asked for funds from the city. This situation has become a sensitive local issue.

How should the Parks and Recreation Department administrator determine what is in the best interest of the public in this situation?

2

A Conceptual Basis for Consumer Behavior

Although consumer behavior is complex, the identification of a few basic relationships that capture the essence of modern social science theory can serve to introduce the subject. Furthermore, since consumer behavior is a part of all human behavior, any theory of consumer behavior must be consistent with what is basic to human behavior.

Lewin offers a conceptual view that summarizes the essence of contemporary thinking and portrays human behavior as the result of the interaction among components of what is viewed as one's life space.[1] This can be represented as follows:

$$B = f \text{ (life space)}.$$

Or, stated another way,

$$B = f (P, E).$$

The life space consists of the total "facts" that psychologically exist for an individual at a given moment. The life space is really the totality of the individual's world as he perceives it, and in such a context, a thing exists only if it has demonstrable effects upon behavior.

In the latter formula, (B) represents behavior, (f) function, (P) person, and (E) environment. This expression states that an individual's behavior is the result of the interaction between the individual and his or her environment. The behavior that is being referred to is broad and involves all human actions including buying behavior. The (P) person in the formula is composed of at least two distinct dimensions. One is heredity, that is, to a large extent individuals are a genetically determined entity. For example, some physical characteristics that may set very real limits on one's activity are inherited and cannot be altered. However, at birth humans also begin to acquire information and, thus, learning is another major dimension of the (P) person in Lewin's model. The (E) environment component recognizes the influence of both the near physical and social settings on behavior.

[1] H. H. Kassarjian, "Field Theory in Consumer Behavior," in *Consumer Behavior: Theoretical Sources,* S. Ward and T. S. Robertson, eds. (Englewood Cliffs, New Jersey: Prentice-Hall, Inc., 1973), pp. 124–130.

An illustration of the importance of the social setting is evident in the observation often made today that contemporary man appears to be more "other directed." This uses Reisman's terminology to indicate that people rely more on immediate social stimuli as behavioral cues today then they have done historically. But, of course, this does not deny the impact of the other components on a person's life space.

The life space has also been called a person's psychological field. Figure 2.1 expands upon what is summarized in the Lewinian formula and offers another means of conceptualizing what it is that shapes human behavior.

As Figure 2.1 indicates, a person is moved by basic needs that are internal and exist largely apart from his environment. In this sense, man is similar to many animals. However, as a human being he has a considerable capacity to call upon past experiences and observations as well as to anticipate the future. In addition, man as a social being is profoundly influenced by other people and, of course, is affected by the physical environment as are other forms of life.

By perceiving a person as being subject to compound and sometimes conflicting motivational determinants, it is possible to recognize the complexity of the forces underlying behavior. Each individual must adapt to his unique psychological field, and to

FIGURE 2.1
A Person's Psychological Field

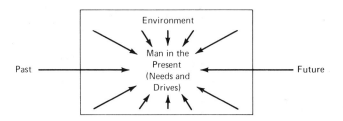

Source: James F. Engel, David T. Kollat, and Roger D. Blackwell, *Consumer Behavior,* 2nd ed. (New York: Holt, Rinehart and Winston, Inc., 1973), p. 21. Reprinted by permission of the publisher.

him, as mentioned earlier, this field is reality. He will establish forms of behavior that permit a workable and meaningful pattern of adaptation to his perception of the world. Despite individual uniqueness and the complexity of the forces that affect people, an orderly study of human behavior is possible. The next section discusses the methods used to facilitate the orderly study of behavior and to increase the likelihood of obtaining useful results.

The Orderly Study of Human Behavior

In trying to explain human behavior, social scientists have offered what appears to be an endless number of models of man. *Model* is used here to refer to any simplified representation of some occurrence or phenomenon.

Models come in several varieties, but two are used most often in the analysis of human behavior. These are the *analogue model* and the *mathematical model.* An analogue model describes various properties of something by using a different set of properties, for example, a road map. Nearly all the models used in this text are of the analogue type. Mathematical models use mathematical relationships to represent something else. These are being employed increasingly in the study of human behavior. One of the primary appeals of the mathematical model is the precision with which relationships can be shown.

Fundamentally, models aid understanding through simplification. Also, a model can continue to be useful in supplying helpful insights even though it may at times yield some conclusions that are incorrect. For instance, the organization chart of a business firm is an analogue model of a particular entity. As such, it provides a simplified overview of the key divisions and positions and the interrelationships among these units. Ordinarily this will show such things as the formal lines of authority and whether the firm's marketing effort is organized by geographic area or product groups or, possibly, some combination. However, this model of the firm does not typically reflect the true power structure and, in fact, it may lead some observers to draw incorrect conclusions about the firm. Nevertheless, the organization chart can be a useful vehicle for analysis.

The various models of man that have been developed represent alternative hypotheses or theories of human behavior. A *theory* is an explanation of a set of phenomena. This includes the identification of important variables and an indication of their interrelationships. The logical structure of a theory is such that the conclusions derived from it can be interpreted as empirical hypotheses and confirmed or refuted by appropriate testing.

It is not uncommon to hear the comment: "Don't be so theoretical; be practical." Actually, there is nothing more practical than a good theory, that is, a valid theory that focuses on a set of important circumstances. A good theory also builds on the validated hypotheses of previous research and itself becomes a foundation for further investigation. It thereby eliminates the need to expend valuable resources to rediscover what is already known, or as some might say, it eliminates the need to "reinvent the wheel" each time a new project is undertaken.

What is generally sought by scientists in most areas is a comprehensive or grand theory of the focus of their discipline. This would provide a complete explanation of all the forces under study in the field. For example, a comprehensive theory of sociology would identify all the key variables at work in personal interaction and explain their relationships, including the influence of each upon the others. Such a complete theory would make it possible to be accurate in predicting the outcome of a set of circumstances knowing the values of the key variables. Although such comprehensiveness is sought, most of what has appeared as theory in the behavioral sciences is more precisely labeled as partial or middle range theory, such as Festinger's cognitive dissonance, Maslow's hierarchy of needs, learning theory, and bargaining theory.

The various models used as representations of such theories or simply as clusters of hypotheses have come from numerous sources. What follows in the next two sections of this chapter is a brief capsulization of how people as consumers have been viewed, first in economic theory and then in marketing.

Economic Perspectives of the Consumer

The role of the consumer differs in microeconomics and macro-economics; therefore, it is necessary to review each of these areas separately.

A MICROECONOMIC PERSPECTIVE

The classical economist of the nineteenth century postulated a view of consumer behavior that is still present in contemporary theory, although it has been modified. The basic assumptions are that an individual has complete knowledge of his wants as well as all available means of satisfying these wants. In addition, personal preferences are assumed to be independent of the environment at the time in which choice is made as well as unlimited, insatiable, and consistent. The buying decision, then, is simply one of careful allocation of resources to maximize utility or satisfaction. The maximization of utility is thus considered to be the only impetus to buying behavior, and the result is an explicit and elegant theory that lends itself to manipulation using various quantitative techniques.

The classical economist viewed man as behaving in a rational mechanistic manner with largely the same reactions to a given situation over time. In reality, of course, behavior is seldom predictable to this extent, and little or no attention was devoted to validating the empirical reality of these assumptions. A prime example of this deductive approach is the long-standing assumption that expenditures vary directly with income, increasing as income increases or decreases.

The assumed income-consumption relationship has been challenged by reliable survey evidence, and this is one example of how microeconomic theory has undergone revision to make it more consistent with reality. The Survey Research Center at the University of Michigan has demonstrated that willingness to purchase consumer goods does not bear an invariably direct relation to income; in fact, purchase of durable goods can decline in a period of high and rising incomes. It is recognized that buyers can anticipate the future and that attitudes such as optimism or pessimism concerning one's financial condition in the future can profoundly affect the decision to buy.

The real criticism of the classical economist does not lie in this assumption of rational behavior, because maximization of utility (i.e., value) is a reasonable initial approximation to the fundamental motives underlying buying behavior. The weakness of the classical view for the purposes of systematically studying consumer behavior is its tendency to embrace economics in a moralistic or normative perspective that circumscribes what is so-called "sensible" consumer behavior.

Despite this limitation it would be an error to include a section on microeconomics without mentioning some of its more positive contributions to the study of consumer behavior. The rigor and exactness of economic theory itself sets a challenging goal for behavioral scientists to strive toward. Furthermore, some of the most comprehensive models of consumer behavior yet developed rely upon concepts used earlier by economists. For example, the study of indifference curve analysis, which incorporates an identification and ranking of consumer wants, is also fundamental to the contemporary models of consumer behavior. In addition, some economists today take a view of the basic components of individual decision making similar to that of the modern consumer analyst, as the following quotation from *Man and Economics* by Mundell illustrates:

> The act of choice is the action of making a decision. A chooser is a decision maker. He confronts aspirations with limitations, preferences with opportunities, intentions with resources.
>
> The act of choice integrates the psychological categories of wants, desires, and preferences with the objective categories of resources, goods, and opportunities. Wants (which are passive) produce desires (which are active), and desires are transformed into preferences; resources produce goods, and goods are transformed into opportunities. Preferences are joined with opportunities in the act of choice.[2]

[2]R. A. Mundell, *Man and Economics* (New York: McGraw Hill, 1968), p. 8.

A MACROECONOMIC PERSPECTIVE

Generally, the economist is not directly concerned with the buying choices of individuals, but rather focuses on the choice patterns of large groups over time. Here, the economist's interest may lie in the patterns of behavior pertaining to major decisions such as the allocation of portions of income to savings, that is, the propensity to save versus spend or, in other cases, to the spending on major categories of goods such as consumer durables (e.g., freezers and washing machines). Some economic studies of aggregate demand focus on specific goods like beef, sugar, coffee, automobiles, and housing.

Economists employed in both the public and private sectors have spent considerable time in demand analysis and forecasting. Their theories of aggregate demand are constantly put to the test of empirical relevance and validity, particularly by government. Business firms can use such statistical studies of demand in making sales forecasts. However, one major drawback is that these studies cover industry demand—the demand for automobiles, refrigerators, new houses, and so forth—produced by all of the firms in each of the industries studied. The demand for the products of any one firm depends critically upon its market behavior, which includes such factors as its promotion and general reputation as well as the specific environmental circumstances it faces. Nevertheless, the management of many businesses actively seeks the evidence available from aggregate demand analysis of their own industry. Some businesses even employ their own economists and spend a considerable amount of money in developing econometric models for forecasting demand.

The consumer analyst should not overlook the substantial information base produced from the aggregate demand analysis of economists. Both time-series and cross-sectional, economic data-based studies have contributed much to marketing thought by helping to clarify the relationships between purchasing and numerous underlying variables.

Consumer Analysis in Marketing

Marketing thought has undergone dramatic changes because of the post-World War II infusion of behavioral science concepts, and many of the earliest views of buyer behavior have had to yield to new information. As a result, contemporary thought is a blend of the old and the new. But for purposes of clarity, it is helpful to discuss both the traditional viewpoint, because of its historical contributions, and the more recent modifications that have come from psychology and sociology.

EARLY ATTEMPTS TO UNDERSTAND BUYER BEHAVIOR

In approaching the subject of why consumers do what they do, the earliest marketing studies explained causation through the use of the term "motive." In other words, motive or internal urges assume the entire burden of explanation for a consumer's actions. Classifications of motives quickly became extensive, and many analysts advanced lengthy lists. One leading psychologist, for example, listed approximately 30 motives that were presumably common to all individuals.[3] These included such underlying forces as hunger, sex, love, and curiosity. Other more general categories of motives also emerged. The following have appeared most frequently in marketing literature: (1) primary and selective, (2) rational and emotional, (3) patronage and product, and (4) conscious and dormant. These are not necessarily mutually exclusive.

Because some of this thinking remains and because it can be useful in a modified form, it is worth considering the substance of each of these four kinds of motives. They are discussed in the following paragraphs in the order listed above.

Primary buying motives are ordinarily defined to be those that lead to the purchase of a general class of product or service. For instance, one may buy skim milk because of its nutritional value and low fat content rather than purchase some other beverage. These criteria are considered to be a result of primary motives,

[3]H. A. Murray, *Explorations in Personality* (New York: Oxford University Press, 1938).

that is, those fundamental to distinguishing among classes of products. The reasons for buying one brand of skim milk, like Weight Watchers, over Sealtest would be referred to as *selective* buying motives.

Rational and emotional motives are somewhat more difficult to define and distinguish. In general, this dichotomy seems to be based on the extent to which external and measurable functional product features are the purchase decision criteria as opposed to personal feelings. When rational motives are cited, these usually include economy, efficiency, dependability, and durability. Emotional motives are often assumed to include pride, status, pleasure, uniqueness, and showiness. Another distinction often implicit in the rational/emotional classification scheme is that rational purchases take more time and effort. This effort may be measured in terms of time spent searching, number of stores visited, and number of alternative products or brands considered. Consequently, this leads one to label impulse buying as essentially emotional, which may not be the case.

Patronage and product motives refer to the variation in reasons for selecting a source from which a product may be purchased and the reasons for selecting the good itself. For example, major motives for selecting a supermarket might be its convenience, general price level, and the quality of its meats. These would be considered patronage motives. Product motives are the reasons for selecting one product over another or one brand instead of another. These often include such product features as color, quality, availability, and price.

Yet another classification of buying motives is *conscious or dormant.* Conscious motives are generally considered those reasons for action that a person is readily aware of and, therefore, they need not be aroused by a sales person or advertisement. Using this perspective, dormant motives are hidden from self-awareness and need to be aroused. An example of such motives might be the unexpected attractiveness or feeling of comfort one has upon being shown a new home by a real estate salesperson and not knowing why. Some who have nurtured an interest in motivational research have done so because they felt that many human motives are deeply rooted and dormant and can only be discovered through clinical probing. One only has to turn to some of Vance Packard's work, such as *Hidden Persuaders,*[4] for vivid illustrations.

Although these early views are appealing, particularly because of their simplicity and surface logic, they suffer from significant weaknesses. To a large extent, they represent armchair reasoning. That is, they are personal opinions and, in most cases, lack sufficient substance and specificity for empirical validation. In addition, some have been stated so often with conviction that they have been assumed to be true.

Another weakness common to some of these views about consumer behavior is that their simplicity has obscured other variables. For example, in focusing upon motives as the principal explanatory factor for consumer actions, much has been overlooked. It is now known that behavior can be substantially influenced by other variables such as personality, time pressure, perceived risk, and the views of others. In other words, the use of motive as the sole variable intervening between stimulus and response is a gross oversimplification of the kind referred to in Chapter 1.

The rational/emotional dichotomy is particularly bothersome even though it is still appealing to some analysts. As used in marketing literature, it erroneously contends that objective purchase criteria are purposeful while subjective purchase criteria, such as beauty, prestige, and love, are not. It would probably serve consumer behavior research best if the rational/emotional distinction was avoided.

RECENT CONTRIBUTIONS TO THE STUDY OF CONSUMER BEHAVIOR

Only within the last ten years has real progress been evident in developing integrative-comprehensive theory in consumer behavior. The works of Engel, Kollat, and Blackwell; Howard and Sheth; and Nicosia exemplify this effort. These represent specific attempts at identifying all the significant variables that shape consumer action and the interrelationships among these factors.

[4]Vance Packard, *Hidden Persuaders* (New York: McKay, 1957).

These are truly unique accomplishments and have made several noteworthy contributions:[5]

1. They have brought to light the limitations of the attempt to transplant various behavioral theories developed in other disciplines such as psychology and sociology without appropriate modification.

2. Through persistent efforts to formulate comprehensive theories, consumer analysts have gained much self-confidence. Although considerable work remains, there is a feeling of having made some progress.

3. This developmental process in an applied discipline such as consumer behavior has also fostered a demand for comprehensive theory that is grounded in reality—based upon realistic assumptions and verifiable propositions.

Nevertheless, much remains borrowed from other behavioral sciences. Therefore, as a prelude to discussing comprehensive theory development in consumer behavior, it is helpful to briefly trace the developmental process that has been taking place in the study of human behavior. It shows that the accomplishments of the last ten years in the discipline of consumer behavior were not revolutionary occurrences but evolutionary steps in the study of human behavior.

This evolutionary process has been summarized well by Thompson and Van Houten.[6] They describe three classifications or models of man which are representative of the theoretical development that has taken place in the study of human behavior. Their model groupings include: (1) conflict models of man, probably the oldest, (2) machine models of man, and (3) open-system models of man that include the emerging comprehensive theories referred to earlier. Each of these will be discussed briefly in the remainder of this section.

[5]J. N. Sheth, *Models of Buyer Behavior: Conceptual, Quantitative, and Empirical* (New York: Harper & Row, Publishers, 1974), pp. 394–395.

[6]J. D. Thompson and D. R. Van Houten, *The Behavioral Sciences: An Interpretation* (Reading, Massachusetts: Addison-Wesley Publishing Company, 1970), pp. 4–13.

Conflict models of man in their simplest and most primitive form describe human behavior as the result of the struggle between good and evil. The individual is shown basically as a medium through which these forces emerge. Consequently, man is viewed as essentially an innocent bystander and not responsible for his actions.

The most recent conflict models continue to focus on the struggle between opposing forces that are, however, not necessarily good and evil. For substantiation, Freud's work can be cited: The lines of conflict are laid early in life in what he called the three basic components of personality: the id, the ego, and the superego. The id is the genetically implanted component containing basic cravings or instincts—all that exists at birth. The ego and superego gradually develop and help the individual satisfy these id urges while relating to his environment; hence, the basis for the conflict or struggle.

Conflict models have come principally from clinical psychology. Some of their most prominent authors include Horney, Jung, and Menninger. To a large extent the theories underlying these models have not met the test of rigorous empirical testing and validation. Nevertheless, they have made a contribution in the developmental process of studying human behavior. A number of direct references have been made to these works in consumer behavior. For instance, Lasswell's concept of the "triple appeal" approach to political propaganda formulation relies on Freudian psychoanalytic theory, and Myers and Reynolds suggest that it is applicable to advertising.[7] Lasswell contended that to be effective a message should arouse id impulses toward such basic drives as hunger or sex, for example, while appeasing the superego by suggesting that the id impulses are justified in some way. Also, the ego should be reached by emphasizing the logic of the proposed action. Cohen's development of the CAD scaling technique for the measurement of personal orientation and behavioral tendencies relies heavily on the work of Horney.[8] Cohen uses Horney's tripartite interpersonal model to help explain a person's perception of his social environment and his action

[7]J. H. Myers and W. H. Reynolds, *Consumer Behavior and Marketing Management* (New York: Houghton Mifflin Company, 1967), pp. 91–93.

[8]J. B. Cohen, "An Interpersonal Orientation to the Study of Consumer Behavior," *Journal of Marketing Research,* 4 (August, 1967), pp. 270–278.

tendencies toward the objects in his life space. The CAD instrument includes three sets of scales, thereby providing a means of measuring a person's compliance, aggressiveness, and detachment. Its use enables the analysts to place individuals into three groups that reflect their most predominant response to others: (1) those who generally move toward other people are considered compliant; (2) those who ordinarily move against others are classified as aggressive; and (3) those who typically move away from people are characterized as detached.[9]

Machine models of man focus upon the S-R sequence, meaning that man is essentially Pavlovian. In their most basic forms these models view a person simply as a physiological machine that responds to genetically implanted drives and environmental stimulation. However, the most complex machine models also recognize the importance of acquired drives. These are drives (needs) which do not exist at birth but are learned throughout life.

In the most simplistic versions of machine models, man has drives for biological nourishment and physical safety in relating to his environment—self-preservation in the most basic sense. However, in the more complex models it is recognized that people acquire the need for social acceptance, self-confidence, and self-fulfillment. The basic logic of this grouping of models is that responses to stimuli are elicited by the expectation of a reward such as satisfaction or pleasure. When the reward is received, the behavior is said to be reinforced and more likely to reoccur under similar need states and environmental circumstances than unreinforced experiences.

The machine models have ordinarily been associated with the behavioral school of psychology which includes the works of such well-known figures as Pavlov, Hull, Spence, and Skinner.

Although many modern theories of human behavior, particularly those in the consumer behavior area, have borrowed extensively from the S-R theoretical framework, a person is much more than what machine models represent. This awareness has led in another theoretical direction that goes considerably beyond the scope of what the machine models basically represent. This

[9]J. B. Kernan, "The CAD Instrument in Behavioral Diagnosis," *Proceedings 2nd Annual Conference,* D. A. Gardner, ed. (College Park, Maryland: Association for Consumer Research, 1971), pp. 307–311.

development is what Thompson and Van Houten call open-system models of man.

The *open-system model* is an emerging conceptual category of models and, therefore, is not yet highly refined in terms of its boundaries. There are, however, identifiable features that help describe its nature. The most salient feature is that it takes a transactional view of human behavior, meaning that man is no longer largely considered a passive participant in his life space reacting to stimuli. He is viewed as pro-active. People can and do take initiative.

A second feature of open-system man is that his behavior is purposive. Such a person is capable of having goals or aspirations and of consciously working toward these. Purposive behavior of this type requires such cognitive processes as thinking, planning, and decision making. It also recognizes that deferred gratification is a part of an individual's problem-solving capabilities.

A third feature of this perspective of man is concern for his mental content and how it is acquired. It is assumed that mental content is only understandable in terms of its meaning for the person, and for something to have meaning, it must be perceived and interpreted. Considerable attention has been given to selective perception in consumer behavior, a concept directly related to this dimension of one's being.

Another major emphasis of the open-system model is that man is social. Human activities are often carried out with other people or at least with others in mind. This includes transactional-oriented involvement as well as the use of reference groups. Thus, Thompson and Van Houten characterize open-system man as:

> . . . purposive, as interdependent with the physical and social environment, and as actively involved in transactions with that environment as he pursues his goals. This requires not only that man develop mental processing capabilities—for thinking, deciding, and so on—but also that he acquire information and beliefs which allow him to 'know' the persons and things in his environment and to cope with them.[10]

[10]Thompson and Van Houten, p. 13.

Contributions to this emerging view of human behavior have come from a number of disciplines and individuals too numerous to mention. Certainly consumer behavior theorists have had an input. The work of Lewin, as reflected in his field theory referred to earlier in this chapter, has had a significant impact. Also, a major impetus to his perspective has come from the work done in Gestalt psychology and social psychology.

The following section includes a discussion of two of the three major models of the integrative-comprehensive theories of consumer behavior referred to earlier. These are the Nicosia model and the Howard/Sheth model. The Engel, Kollat, and Blackwell model is presented in Chapter 3. All three of these are open-system models.

Integrative-Comprehensive Models of Consumer Behavior

NICOSIA MODEL

Francesco Nicosia, a leading scholar in the field of consumer behavior, published one of the earliest integrative-comprehensive models.[11] The basic components of his model are reproduced in Figure 2.2. Nicosia uses a flowchart to designate the basic elements of the decision process and the relationships that exist among these elements. Figure 2.2 shows the consumer decision process as consisting of four fields. Field One (Source of Message to the Consumer's Attitude) includes the output of an advertising message from a business firm where the consumer recipient was previously unfamiliar with the advertised product. The message from the firm (Subfield One) serves as an input to the consumer's space (Subfield Two), which is composed of his psychological attributes. A message that is received and accepted by the individual fosters the development of an attitude toward the product or service. This attitude then becomes an input into what is called Field Two. Field Two represents the process of searching and evaluating the product referred to in the

[11]F. M. Nicosia, *Consumer Decision Processes: Marketing and Advertising Implications* (Englewood Cliffs, New Jersey: Prentice-Hall, Inc., 1966).

FIGURE 2.2
Summary Flowchart of the Nicosia Model of Buyer Behavior.

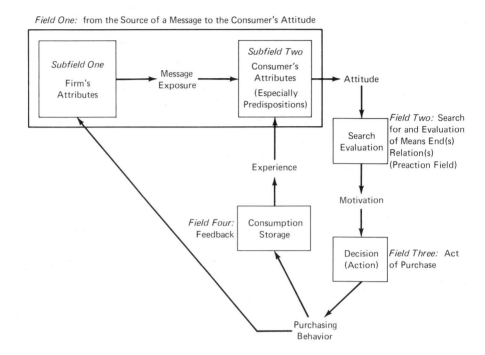

Field One: from the Source of a Message to the Consumer's Attitude

Source: F. M. Nicosia, *Consumer Decision Processes: Marketing and Advertising Implications* (Englewood Cliffs, N. J.: Prentice-Hall, Inc., 1966), p. 156. Reprinted by permission of the publisher.

message as well as the consideration of alternatives available in this product category. The actions that take place in this field may or may not result in a motivation to buy the product in question. When the motivation to buy the product does result, it serves as an input into Field Three (Act of Purchase), which transforms this intention to buy into a purchase decision. If purchase behavior results from Field Three, it serves as an input into Field Four, the storage or use of the product. Purchase behavior also provides feedback—sales results to the business firm and the consequences of the purchase to the buyer's memory.

Nicosia made a substantial and much needed contribution to the field of consumer behavior by incorporating a wealth of research findings from many sources into his theory. Nevertheless, there are a number of difficulties that inhibit the application of the theory represented by his model. First, many of the assumptions, qualifications, and limitations with respect to the model's under-pinnings are not explicit. Thus, the reader is faced with difficulty in differentiating areas where substantial knowledge exists from those areas in which future research is needed. Furthermore, the lack of clarity in specifying the interrelationships of the model results in considerable confusion as to its relevance to the deci-sion-making process of the typical marketing manager.

HOWARD/SHETH MODEL

John Howard proposed the first truly integrative model of buyer behavior in 1963.[12] Howard's model was based on a systematic and thorough utilization of learning theory. Perhaps the major contribution of the Howard model was the distinction drawn be-tween extensive problem solving, limited problem solving, and automatic response behavior. A major contribution in its own right, this model drew attention to the need for an interdisciplinary approach to clarification of the conceptual basis for such a model and to the need for extensive development of practical implica-tions of buyer behavior models.

The results of the combined efforts of Howard and Sheth provided much of the needed clarification and elaboration of the earlier Howard model. The Howard/Sheth model was essentially an attempt to explain brand choice behavior over time.[13] In the development of their model, Howard and Sheth assume that brand choice is not a random but rather a systematic process and that buyers attempt to make logical decisions, that is, reasonable within the limits of their cognitive and learning capacities and with the further constraint of limited information.

The Howard/Sheth model consists of four sets of constructs or variables: (1) input variables, (2) output variables, (3) hypothet-

---

[12]J. A. Howard, *Marketing Management: Analysis and Planning* (Home-wood, Illinois: Richard D. Irwin, Inc., 1963).
[13]J. A. Howard and J. N. Sheth, *The Theory of Buyer Behavior* (New York: John Wiley and Sons, Inc., 1969).

ical constructs, and (4) exogenous variables. A simplified diagram of this model appears in Figure 2.3.

Each of the variables included in the model and the probable linkages are described in considerable detail in the Howard/-Sheth book, *The Theory of Buyer Behavior,* and it is not possible to indicate in a few paragraphs the richness of their theory. However, the essence of the model, that is, the way Howard and Sheth characterize the buying process can be described briefly.

Howard and Sheth contend that when the buyer is interested in purchasing something, he actively seeks information from his commercial (significative and symbolic) and social environment. The buyer's perceptual processes limit the information received and modify it so that it is consistent with his own frame of reference. In addition to the process of searching for information, the

FIGURE 2.3
Simplified Description of the Howard/Sheth Model of Buyer Behavior.

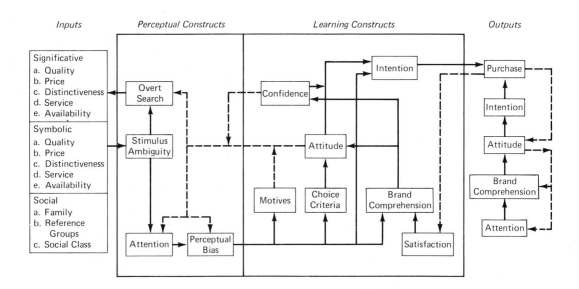

Source: J. A. Howard and J. N. Sheth, *The Theory of Buyer Behavior* (New York: John Wiley and Sons, Inc., 1969). Reprinted by permission of the publixher.

buyer draws from his learning constructs, such as attitudes and motives. The choice criteria the buyer has developed enable him to choose a brand that has the greatest potential for satisfying his motives. When a buyer's experiences with a brand are satisfactory, the evaluation of it increases and the likelihood of his purchasing that brand of product again increases. If the buyer repeats the decision a number of times, routinized purchase behavior develops. Whether or not a person actually buys a given alternative, however, is a function of the comprehension of brand attributes, attitude toward the brand, confidence in the purchase, and individual intention. Furthermore, the exogenous variables help explain individual differences through such factors as financial status, time pressure, and social class.

The great strength of this model lies in the fact that a multiplicity of variables are linked in a precise way. The relationships hypothesized in the model at times approach the rigor of fully developed theory. The work of Howard and Sheth has stimulated and enriched the thinking and research of nearly every student of consumer behavior and promises to do so in the future.

Despite its many contributions, a number of weaknesses are evident in the model, and these serve to illustrate the work that lies ahead for the consumer analyst. First, the distinction drawn between hypothetical and measurable variables, while conceptually laudable, serves to introduce unnecessary complexity. A reduced form of the model has been subjected to empirical verification and, therefore, is much more concise in the variables it includes and in the relationships specified among these factors. Furthermore, the empirical research undertaken for purposes of validation has indicated the need for modifications and extensions of the model. In general, the research has shown that the amount of variation in behavior explained by the model is quite low, although it is in the predicted direction. In addition, some variables that were originally included were found not to be related as hypothesized, while others not specified should have been included. The number of attempts to validate the model has been quite limited; therefore, such efforts must be continued. In conclusion, it is fair to say that the empirical research to date seems to provide considerable support for the model generally, but it has demonstrated the need for extensive revision.

The presentation and discussion of the Engel, Kollat, and Blackwell model will follow in Chapter 3. This integrative-comprehensive model will then serve as the conceptual framework for the remainder of the text.

SUMMARY

The study of human behavior is best done in an orderly fashion in order to produce the most useful results. To facilitate this effort numerous models and theories have been developed to simplify and explain complex phenomena.

The economist sees the consumer from both microeconomic and macroeconomic perspectives. The consumer in microeconomic theory has complete knowledge of his wants and all the means for satisfying these wants, and his buying decisions attempt to maximize his satisfaction. In macroeconomics, consumers are viewed in the aggregate, and product demand is viewed on the industry level instead of on the company level.

The marketer first attempted to explain buyer behavior through numerous motives. Those appearing most frequently in marketing literature are primary and selective, rational and emotional, patronage and product, and conscious and dormant. The use of motive as the sole variable between stimulus and response is a gross oversimplification however.

Recent contributions to consumer behavior have developed through an evolutionary process that Thompson and Van Houten have categorized into three groups: (1) conflict models of man, (2) machine models of man, and (3) open-system models of man. Conflict models of man describe human behavior as the result of the struggle between good and evil in which man is viewed as essentially an innocent bystander and not responsible for his actions. Machine models of man focus on the stimulus and response or Pavlovian type sequence. The most salient feature of open-system models is that they take a transactional view of human behavior in which man is viewed as pro-active. Three major open-system models are the integrative-comprehensive models of Nicosia; Howard and Sheth; and Engel, Kollat, and Blackwell.

Nicosia's model uses four interrelated fields to explain the consumer decision process. Field one follows from the source of a message to the consumer's attitude. Field two includes searching and evaluating the product. Field three is the act of purchase. Field four includes consumption or storage of the product and a feedback to the business firm. The Howard/Sheth model, the first truly integrative one, explains the consumer decision process through four sets of variables: (1) input variables, (2) output variables, (3) hypothetical constructs, and (4) exogenous variables. Significant strengths and weaknesses can be attributed to both of these models. The Engel, Kollat, and Blackwell model is discussed in the following chapter.

QUESTIONS AND ISSUES FOR DISCUSSION

1. How much does the life space of most individuals change over time? Which component, P or E, changes more?
2. The classical economist viewed man as behaving in a rational, mechanistic manner. Are there individuals whom you know who appear to fit this model? If so, is this behavior pattern evident in most of these persons' actions or just in the buying of certain kinds of products?
3. In a total sense, which is more reasonable to conclude, that economic theory has helped or hindered the contemporary study of consumer behavior?
4. Identify one or two of your personal propositions or theories about consumer behavior, such as how price affects a product's image. What are these propositions based upon?
5. What does it mean to say that a theory is grounded in reality? Why should this be important in the field of consumer behavior?
6. Make two lists, one of ten rational motives and the other of ten emotional motives. How could this information help in developing advertising for a product such as a woman's dress coat?

7. What difference could it make to the marketing manager of a fishing equipment manufacturer to know, for example, that a large proportion of the readers of *Field and Stream* magazine are essentially "detached" according to Cohen's CAD measure, that is, they want to put emotional distance between themselves and others?

8. Open-system man has been characterized as purposive. Give an example of purposive action in consumer behavior. Does this characteristic of human behavior simplify or complicate the study of the consumer?

9. The use of integrative-comprehensive models makes the study of consumer behavior unnecessarily difficult by including many variables that are only influential in unusual circumstances. Discuss.

10. The systematic study and analysis of the consumer will likely lead to insights that will permit business to use their resources to control consumer buying behavior. Discuss.

SITUATIONAL PROBLEMS

Case 1

The owner of the College Campus Bookstore has set as her major objective for the next year the increase of the store's profit by 25 percent. To accomplish this goal she is expanding the store's line of school supplies, sundries, and gift items. Two part-time clerks have also been added to help during the busy periods. After hearing about the plans, one of the senior clerks who has worked in the store for over 20 years made the following comment: "College students are all alike when it comes to buying textbooks and supplies. They are strictly interested in price, that is, they search out the lowest price on every item they need. Therefore, we cannot expect to attract more business unless we offer discount prices on the new items."

What is the senior clerk's theory of student buyer behavior? Of what help is this theory to the store's owner?

Case 2

The Zero Tool Company produces a line of hand power tools for home use that includes circular saws, drills, and sanders. These have been sold under the E-Z Use brand for over ten years. It has recently come to the attention of the Vice-president of Marketing of Zero Company that the Standard Tool Company, an old established industrial power tool manufacturer, has introduced a line of tools for home use similar to those sold by Zero. Standard's new line is being marketed under the brand name of Easy Tools. The management of Zero Company believes that these two brand names are too similar. Therefore, the Zero Company has taken legal action to prevent the Standard Tool Company from using the Easy Tool name.

What is the primary issue of concern to the Zero Company management?

How could a consumer analyst assist Standard Tool's management in this case?

The Consumer
Decision Process

The preceding chapter drew attention to the importance of theory development in studying consumer behavior and to how this orderly study may be pursued. Special emphasis was given to the contributions made by other disciplines. This chapter provides an overview of the consumer decision process and, in so doing, lays the conceptual foundation for the remainder of the book. First, a discussion of the decision process approach and the implications it has for the study of consumer behavior is presented. This is followed by a description of the comprehensive decision model developed by Engel, Kollat, and Blackwell which serves an integrative and organizational function for the remainder of the book. Since most of the following chapters focus on a limited portion of the model, it will be helpful to refer to this chapter from time to time to retain the focus of the over-all structure.

Approaches to the Study of Consumer Behavior

As pointed out in Chapter 2, the study of consumer behavior is characterized by research that makes use of the theories and concepts borrowed from various behavioral science disciplines. Examination of the history of the behavioral sciences reveals that there are essentially two basic ways to study consumer behavior empirically: (1) the distributive approach and (2) the decision-process approach.[1] The distributive approach focuses on behavioral outcomes, that is, on the purchase act rather than the purchase process. The decision-process approach describes the way consumers actually make decisions, including the impact of various influences on the purchase process.

DISTRIBUTIVE APPROACH

The empirical research on consumer behavior has historically utilized the distributive approach.[2] Consequently, consumer be-

[1]R. A. Dahl, M. Haire, and P. F. Lazarsfeld, *Social Science Research on Business: Product and Potential* (New York: Columbia University Press, 1959), pp. 103–104.
[2]R. Ferber, "Research on Household Behavior," *American Economic Review,* 52 (March, 1962), pp. 19–63.

havior has been conceptualized and studied as an act rather than as a process or series of interrelated acts. Researchers utilizing this approach attempt to determine the relationship between the outcome of consumer decision making and a variety of independent variables such as income, social class, race, and marital status.

Advantages of the Distributive Approach

The distributive approach has been frequently used because it has a number of advantages. The major advantage is that research utilizing this strategy is relatively simple and typically less expensive than other alternatives. Furthermore, it has been very useful in those instances where the independent variables under study are highly correlated with the purchase of a product. The distributive approach has proven to be somewhat useful in estimating market potential and in making media selection decisions.[3] For example, if the purchase of a particular make of automobile such as a Porsche is found to be related to a certain age group, then the number of people who are in that age group might be an excellent estimate of the potential buying units for Porsches. Also, to the extent that people in this age group have distinctive media viewing habits, the advertising strategy for Porsche may be made more successful by selecting media consistent with these viewing patterns. Clearly, the distributive approach to studying consumer behavior can be very appropriate in certain situations.

Limitations of the Distributive Approach

There are also a number of limitations inherent in the distributive approach. The foremost difficulty is that this approach can, at best, provide only a partial or incomplete explanation of consumer behavior. Consumer analysts now agree that the act of buying a particular product is only a fraction of the relevant consumption behavior, that is, it is important to recognize that the decision to purchase a specific product is preceded by some pattern of conscious and subconscious actions that are a part of decision making. Unless purchase acts (outcomes) are related to

[3]J. A. Patterson, "Buying as a Process," *Business Horizons* (Spring, 1965), p. 59.

these broader processes—and they seldom are—both the decision and the correlates of the decision may be misleading in the sense that they may be true only if certain mixtures of predecision processes take place. Furthermore, the distributive approach does not provide the marketing manager with any insight into why the relationship between an independent variable and purchase decisions exists. Because this approach fails to provide information on the sequence of events culminating in a purchase act, it is of limited value in developing effective marketing strategies or in evaluating existing business practices in terms of their relationship to consumer needs. Clearly then, if analysts are to understand, explain, and predict consumer behavior, an approach is needed that is more probing than the distributive approach.

DECISION-PROCESS APPROACH

The decision-process approach to the study of consumer behavior focuses on the means by which consuming units reach a purchase decision. The configuration of this decision process consists of five processes linked in a sequence: (1) problem recognition, (2) alternative evaluation-internal search, (3) alternative evaluation-external search, (4) purchase, and (5) outcomes. This conceptualization describes the behavioral processes that are operative from the time the consumer recognizes that some decision is necessary to the point at which there is some postpurchase evaluation of the particular purchase made.

Reflect for a few moments on a recent purchase that you have made. Perhaps you have bought ski equipment, stereo components, a cassette recorder, a pair of slacks, or an automobile. When did you recognize the existence of a desire for this item? Did you evaluate a number of alternative brands or models prior to your decision? Were you satisfied with your final choice? In your recall of the purchase you probably identified a number of exceptions to the five-stage decision process specified previously. First, you may not have been aware that you were passing through these phases. Indeed, most consumers do not consciously state, "I have a problem or a personal desire" or "Now that I have recognized a desire, I had best evaluate the alternatives for satisfying it." Secondly, you may have omitted one or more of the five decision processes. Finally, you may have observed that your decision process had a time dimension, that is, the decision to purchase may have evolved over several months or, in some instances, the entire process may have involved only a few seconds. It is not that the exact replication of the five processes within a specific time frame is strictly followed but that a similarity in decision patterns does exist among consumers. The decision-process approach to studying consumer behavior has several distinct advantages as well as limitations.

Advantages of the Decision-Process Approach
The decision-process approach has some distinct advantages over the distributive approach. The decision-process approach, as the name implies, views consumer behavior as a *process* and is as concerned with how a decision is reached as it is with the decision itself. Furthermore, the decision approach involves a sequence of processes including the steps that generally precede the decision, the decision itself, and the course of action that follows the decision. This approach is a more extended and elaborate means of studying consumer behavior than is the distributive approach; therefore, it can ordinarily provide the marketing manager with more relevant information. The identification of the various stages of consumer decision making and the factors that influence the individual at each stage can contribute to the development of more effective marketing strategies and appropriate public policy for the regulation of business practices.

Limitations of the Decision-Process Approach
There are a number of limitations associated with this approach to studying consumer behavior. In particular, the fact that this approach is a relatively recent development means that less empirical research has been conducted using this perspective than researchers would like. Furthermore, the research that has been done from the decision-process approach has revealed a considerable amount of variation among consumers in their decision-making behavior. These variations are thought to result from the complexity of interactions arising from the fact that consum-

ers live under many different circumstances.[4] Another difficulty is that very little research has included more than one phase of the decision process, and therefore, little is known about the relationship among phases or the influence of one phase on another. For example, there are uncertainties as to exactly how internal search leads to external search or what amount of external search typically precedes the purchase decision. Nevertheless, all the stages in the decision process should be included even though some of them do not always occur and the relationships among those that do are not yet fully clear. Finally, despite the fact that there are a number of problems involved in the conceptualization and study of consumer behavior from the decision-process approach, it is increasingly recognized that the advantages outweigh the limitations.

Decision-Process Model of Consumer Behavior

As mentioned earlier, the decision-process model of consumer behavior presented in this chapter was developed by Engel, Kollat, and Blackwell. In order to convey the fact that many processes intervene or mediate between exposure to a stimulus and the final outcomes of behavior, the term "multimediation" can be applied to the model. This serves as a reminder that many factors affect the outcome. An overview of the model is presented at this point. A more complete development of the individual components will follow in later chapters along with the identification of the empirical foundations for the model.

Although the issue as to whether this is the best model remains open, the model does fare well relative to the following criteria: (1) it is consistent with existing knowledge; (2) it makes intuitive sense; and (3) accurate predictions of consumer behavior can be deduced from the model.

The decision-process model consists of four basic components. They are: (1) the central control unit or significant psycho-

[4]D. H. Granbois, "The Role of Communication in the Family Decision Making Process," *Toward Scientific Marketing,* S. A. Greyser, ed. (Chicago: American Marketing Association, 1963), pp. 44–57, at p. 48.

logical variables that help explain a consumer's motivation and behavior; (2) the consumer information processing component, that is, the perception and internalization of incoming stimuli; (3) the consumer decision process, whereby a problem is recognized and possibly continues into the search, purchase, and outcomes; and (4) the constraints on the consumer decision process or the effect of such factors as income and social pressures on behavior.

CENTRAL CONTROL UNIT

The major elements of the central control unit (CCU) of a consumer, sometimes referred to as his psychological make-up or "black box," are presented in Figure 3.1. The CCU is the individual's psychological command center in that it includes both memory and the basic facilities for thinking and directing behavior. In order to understand the nature of the CCU as it applies to consumer behavior, Figure 3.1 presents its primary elements as being information and experience, evaluative criteria, and attitudes, each of which is affected by personality. These four elements interact to form a fifth element—the filter—through which incoming stimuli are processed. Each of these elements has a unique function that will become apparent shortly.

Stored Information and Experience
As the consumer engages in consumption and its related activities, he or she learns from these experiences and, therefore, some of this information is retained. This stored information from prior experiences enables the consumer to respond to stimuli more directly because previously processed information is available. This information can be stored in an organized or unorganized manner in either conscious or unconscious memory.

This component of the CCU is of particular importance to those interested in influencing consumer actions. For example, it is necessary for the marketer to determine what information consumers retain with respect to his product because this will affect buying behavior. In fact, a frequent advertising objective is to increase the awareness of product features. By understanding

**FIGURE 3.1
Central Control Unit.**

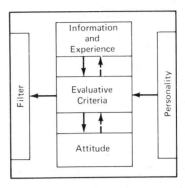

Source: J. F. Engel, D. T. Kollat, and R. D. Blackwell, *Consumer Behavior,* 2nd ed. (New York: Holt, Rinehart and Winston, Inc., 1973), p. 50. Reprinted by permission of the publisher.

the nature of this process, such agencies as the Federal Trade Commission and the Consumer Products Safety Commission could develop more effective regulatory programs.

Evaluative Criteria
Evaluative criteria are the internalized standards used by consumers to assess and compare alternative products, brands, stores, and other consumption alternatives. Consumers sometimes apply the same evaluative criteria across several products, but this is not a rule. Consumers tend to develop a set of criteria for evaluating each product type. For example, the criteria used in judging cola beverages might include taste, amount of carbonation, the presence of an aftertaste, and the price of the product. A beverage like fruit juice may be assessed on entirely different bases, such as nutritional value, texture, and aroma.

Several factors must be kept in mind when considering these evaluative criteria. They are shaped by an individual's personality, stored information, social influence, and the marketing efforts of firms. Furthermore, these criteria change over time. Consequently, the evaluative criteria relative to any product must be carefully monitored.

Because the marketing manager is committed to developing the most effective marketing program feasible, the determination of the evaluative criteria used by the prospective target market of his product is of fundamental importance. The manager should make certain that the product as perceived by the respective consumers adequately satisfies their relevant criteria. If not, consumers will not consider it as an alternative.

Attitudes

In the consumer behavior context, an attitude is interpreted as the assessment a consumer makes regarding the ability a product, brand, or store has to satisfy his or her expectations which, in turn, have been defined by his evaluative criteria. All things being equal, the alternative choice with the highest rating summed across the evaluative criteria has the greatest probability of being purchased and consumed when a corresponding need exists.

The solid lines in Figure 3.1 point out that attitudes are considered to be affected by accumulated information and experience, the evaluative criteria, and personality. In addition, the feedback effect shown by dashed lines indicates that once attitudes are formed, they tend to inhibit changes in the evaluative criteria and stored information by filtering incoming stimuli, so that contradictory inputs are screened out or modified.

Marketing decision makers now recognize that determining consumers' attitudes toward a brand, product, or store is an essential foundation for the development of effective marketing programs. Fortunately for the users of consumer behavior research, the last decade has been characterized by a number of substantial developments in the areas of attitude theory and measurement.

Personality

Every individual has a unique way of thinking, behaving, and responding. The totality of these characteristics is referred to here as *personality*. This individualized way of acting is considered to have a relatively enduring nature across time and place and has long been an important determinant of consumer behavior.

Personality directly affects the determination of which evaluative criteria will serve as the specifications an individual will use in comparing purchase alternatives. Consequently, one of marketing's responses has been to recognize distinctive personality classes as the bases for the development of advertising copy and media selection.

Filter

As mentioned earlier, the four variables of the CCU—information and experience, evaluative criteria, attitude, and personality— interact to form a filter through which all stimuli are processed. The CCU cannot process all stimuli emanating from the individual's environment. Therefore, the filter permits what appears to be the most relevant information for the consumer to be transmitted to the other variables in the CCU.

Consumer analysts agree on the purpose of the filter, but considerable confusion abounds regarding the exact nature of it. This confusion results from the fact that the filtration process can be affected by many things, such as stimuli qualities like the loudness and pitch of a radio commercial or the perceived credibility of the message itself.

CONSUMER INFORMATION PROCESSING

Using the perspective of the model, stimuli entering the filter are generally handled in four distinct phases: (1) exposure, (2) attention, (3) comprehension, and (4) retention. These four components are related in a hierarchial fashion. For example, a stimulus must be attended to (or gain attention) before comprehension can occur. However, gaining attention does not necessarily mean that the stimulus will be understood. It is important to note that the CCU influences and is also affected by all phases of the information processing function, as indicated by lines in Figure 3.2.

FIGURE 3.2
Information Processing.

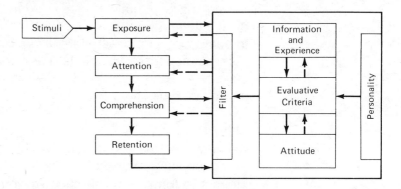

Source: J. F. Engel, D. T. Kollat, and R. D. Blackwell, *Consumer Behavior,* 2nd ed. (New York: Holt, Rinehart and Winston, Inc., 1973), p. 52. Reprinted by permission of the publisher.

Exposure

During the exposure phase of information processing a person comes in contact with external stimuli from various physical and social sources. Although there are numerous stimuli to which an individual is exposed, the following are considered to be particularly important in shaping consumer behavior: information and observable physical differences among purchase alternatives, the actions and beliefs of friends, and the influence of family members.

Attention

Attention means taking special note of something among a number of possibilities. The extent to which a particular stimulus is noted or given special consideration is affected by numerous factors. For instance, a consumer aroused by a bodily need will be more attentive to stimuli related to that need. If it is lunch time and you have skipped breakfast, you will very likely pay more attention to stimuli associated with food. Those advertisements promoting eating establishments or heat-and-serve dinners are more likely to get your attention than they would otherwise.

The preceding example focuses on the notion of *selective perception.* Marketers have become sensitive to this consumer tendency and strive to reduce its effect on the reception of their advertising in order to achieve a high level of attention. For this reason, firms use a variety of techniques to pretest the level of attention their advertising is likely to receive before it is used full-blown in the market.

Comprehension

Attention is a necessary but not a sufficient condition for comprehension, that is, attention must occur before understanding can take place, but the fact that a stimulus is noted does not ensure its comprehension. The stimuli that are attended to may be modified, possibly even distorted, by the CCU so that certain product attributes are reinforced while others are not. An individual can take note of a firm's promotional message and yet obtain ideas substantially different from those intended. That is, consumers frequently misinterpret information they are exposed to in order to make it more consistent with their established preferences and, therefore, less disruptive. This may partially explain why some consumers under certain circumstances continue to prefer a product brand proven to be inferior to others that are available at comparable prices.

Retention

The final information-processing stage included in the model is retention, which refers to those impressions from consumption-related stimuli that are stored in the consumer's conscious memory. The individual's selection process continues at this stage; consequently, the impressions stored in the memory are only a subset of those comprehended.

CONSUMER DECISION PROCESS

The Engel, Kollat, Blackwell model presents the act of purchasing as a process consisting of the following five stages: (1) problem recognition, (2) internal search and alternative evaluation, (3) external search and alternative evaluation, (4) the purchasing processes, and (5) the decision outcome. Each of these five stages is discussed in the paragraphs that follow, although not all are present in every purchase decision. The factors that determine the variation in the consumer decision stages will be discussed later in the chapter.

Problem Recognition

Problem recognition, illustrated in Figure 3.3, occurs when an individual perceives a difference between an ideal state and an actual state. This could also be called need arousal. The number of determinants of problem recognition are probably infinite. However, consumer analysts have found that a limited number of variables and/or situations can be specified as being particularly important determinants of problem recognition. One impor-

FIGURE 3.3
Problem Recognition.

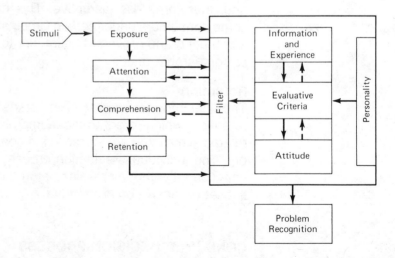

Source: J. F. Engel, D. T. Kollat, and R. D. Blackwell, *Consumer Behavior,* 2nd ed. (New York: Holt, Rinehart and Winston, Inc., 1973), p. 54. Reprinted by permission of the publisher.

tant initiating influence of problem recognition is the awareness of an external stimulus. Imagine yourself, a well-established pizza eater, walking down the street and passing a pizza parlor. The aroma of the cooking pizzas can serve to make you feel hungry and, thereby, introduce a different course of action. Such an outcome will not occur in all situations because the incoming stimulus can be screened out or distorted if it is inconsistent with one's disposition. For example, the weight watcher may distort the aroma of pizza, so that it is no longer appealing; this temptation is inconsistent with his attempts to control caloric intake.

Problem recognition can also occur through need activation which causes the individual to become alert, responsive, and vigilant because of the resulting feelings of discomfort.[5] The result is the formation of a drive that energized need-satisfying action. For example, thirst is a physiological need that arouses a state of drive, and the resulting feelings of discomfort initiate appropriate action. The ideal state, under these circumstances, of course, is the absence of thirst, and the aroused drive signifies that the actual state is short of the ideal.

However, not every perceived discrepancy between actual and ideal will result in problem recognition. There is a minimum level of perceived difference that must be surpassed before recognition occurs. The level of perceived difference that is necessary for problem recognition to result will vary among consumers and circumstances.

Even though problem recognition may occur, action can be constrained by the intervention of external influences, as represented in Figure 3.4. A consumer may recognize a problem (the perceived need for a new automobile) and make purchase plans. A change in one or more of the external influences, however, can intervene to make this action impossible. That is, an external influence such as available income can constrain or hold the decision-making process—the recognized problem of needing a new automobile remains, but the action is postponed until the constraints are removed. This is consistent with what was referred to as the deferred gratification capacity of the open-sys-

[5]D. O. Hebb, *The Organization of Behavior* (New York: John Wiley and Sons, Inc., 1949).

FIGURE 3.4
Constraints on the Decision Process.

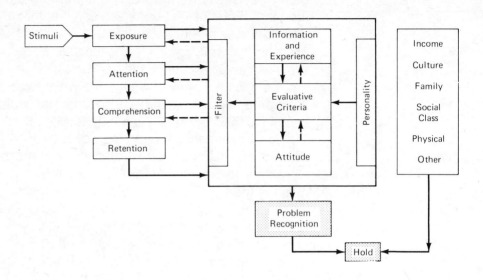

Source: J. F. Engel, D. T. Kollat, and R. D. Blackwell, *Consumer Behavior,* 2nd ed. (New York: Holt, Rinehart and Winston, Inc., 1973), p. 55. Reprinted by permission of the publisher.

tem model of man discussed in Chapter 2. These external influences can serve as constraints on the first three stages of the decision process.

Internal Search and Alternative Evaluation

Once a problem is recognized and no constraints intervene to halt the decision process, the consumer must then assess the alternatives for action. The consumer will initially search internally, although this may not be a conscious effort. Stored information and experience are examined to determine whether or not alternatives are adequately perceived and whether or not sufficient information is available to evaluate the alternatives.

If the internal search and alternative evaluation process reveals that alternatives have been well defined and a satisfactory one can be identified, the remaining stages of the decision process will be circumvented, and probably a purchase decision will be made. If a satisfactory alternative cannot be found, evaluative criteria must be defined and information obtained for the evaluative process. If the consumer is still unable to find an acceptable alternative, external search will likely be undertaken. These two stages of the decision process are illustrated in Figure 3.5. The

FIGURE 3.5
Alternative Evaluation: Internal and External Search.

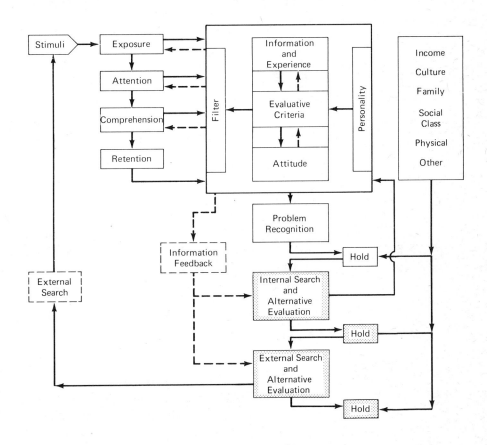

Source: J. F. Engel, D. T. Kollat, and R. D. Blackwell, *Consumer Behavior,* 2nd ed. (New York: Holt, Rinehart and Winston, Inc., 1973), p. 56. Reprinted by permission of the publisher.

figure also indicates that environmental factors can act as a constraint at either of these stages of the decision process.

External Search and Alternative Evaluation

External search is activated in nonroutine or extended problem-solving situations. A consumer may want to purchase a particular product but lack information on the alternative brands or types available, or she may not even have developed clearly defined criteria to use in evaluating the known alternatives. Consequently, she will likely search for information from a variety of sources, such as friends, relatives, and advertisements. This search generally continues until the consumer has established evaluative criteria and until she has found an acceptable choice.

There is a substantial difference among consumers in their willingness and interest to search for purchase-related information. For example, for some people apartment hunting ends when one acceptable vacancy is located; for others, a list of detailed information about five or six suitable apartments available for rent would still be inadequate.

Purchase Process

The three preceding stages of the decision process lead to the making of a purchase. The decision process does not terminate at this point, however, because the consumer must still select the store or establishment and, perhaps, engage in negotiation before the purchase transaction is completed. Actually the total purchase process refers to all aspects of the customer-store-environment interaction; even the selection of a store can be viewed as a decision process. The recognition and study of this interaction is vital to understanding consumer behavior. By referring to Figure 3.6, one can see this stage in the decision process in relation to the others.

Postpurchase Processes

The two possible outcomes of the purchase decision—postpurchase evaluation and further behavior—are also shown in Figure 3.6. A variety of circumstances may precipitate postpurchase evaluation. For instance, it is likely to occur if the purchase requires a major financial outlay and if a number of attractive alternatives are available. Here postpurchase evaluation may be

FIGURE 3.6
Complete Model of Consumer Behavior Showing Purchasing Processes and Outcomes.

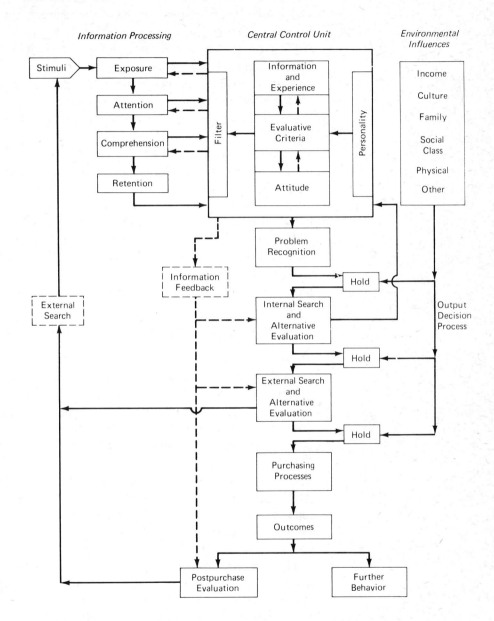

Source: J. F. Engel, D. T. Kollat, and R. D. Blackwell, *Consumer Behavior,* 2nd ed. (New York: Holt, Rinehart and Winston, Inc., 1973), p. 58. Reprinted by permission of the publisher.

engaged in to reduce uncertainty as to whether the decision made was the best one. In this case, it frequently takes on the form of additional search for product information. It is also possible that problems with the product as well as its benefits can lead to a reconsideration of the evaluative criteria. In this way the consumer learns from his experiences and is more likely to avoid mistakes of the same type in the future.

Many purchase decisions require that the consumer take further action. For example, the decision to purchase a major durable good may mean that the consumer will need to borrow money. Consequently, he or she must make a decision as to the type and source of loan to obtain. It is obvious that consumer behavior is a process, and therefore a single act can rarely be considered apart from its total consequences.

The most common outcome of a purchase is satisfaction. This serves to reinforce existing attitudes and the evaluative criteria upon which they are based. Under similar circumstances, the probability of a repeat purchase in the future is strengthened.

VARIATIONS IN CONSUMER DECISION PROCESSES

There are three variations of the consumer decision process: (1) extended decision-process behavior, (2) limited decision-process behavior, and (3) habitual decision-process behavior. The model in Figure 3.6 is a complete representation of the most comprehensive type of decision making—extended decision-process behavior. However, most consumer decision making is not this complex. Frequently, internal search will provide adequate information for the evaluation of known alternatives, that is, the consumer will not need to search for information about the feasible alternatives. Yet he lacks adequate information to select the best alternative. This is referred to as limited decision-process behavior.

The simplest and perhaps most common type of action, habitual decision-process behavior, is presented in Figure 3.7. In habitual decision-process behavior the sequence moves directly from internal search to the purchase. External constraints may still operate to halt the decision or delay its culmination, but their effect is likely to be weaker under these circumstances. Ordinarily, in routine purchasing postpurchase evaluation will not oc-

**FIGURE 3.7
Habitual Decision-Process Behavior.**

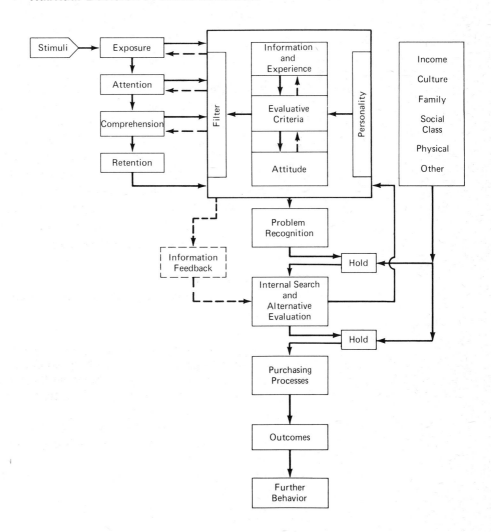

Source: J. F. Engel, D. T. Kollat, and R. D. Blackwell, *Consumer Behavior,* 2nd ed. (New York: Holt, Rinehart and Winston, Inc., 1973), p. 60. Reprinted by permission of the publisher.

cur because of existing experience with the product or service. In all other respects the process is identical to that discussed earlier. Thus, the distinction between the three variations of the decision-process is more one of degree than of kind.

DETERMINANTS OF THE TYPE OF DECISION PROCESS

There is a wide assortment of reasons for a consumer to feel apprehension or uncertainty as he or she engages in the purchase and/or use of a product. The nature and degree of his perception of this risk affect the extent of the decision-making process. Although somewhat fragmentary, research findings suggest that four types of variables determine the type of decision making the consumer is involved in: (1) situational variables, (2) product characteristics, (3) consumer characteristics, and (4) environmental variables. The following lists set forth a variety of circumstances that can occur under each.

Situational Variables

There is a higher probability of extended decision-process behavior when:

1. There has been little or no relevant experience because an individual has never purchased the product.
2. There is no past experience because the product is new.
3. Past experience is perceived as obsolete because the product is purchased infrequently.
4. Past experience with the product has been unsatisfactory.[6]
5. The purchase is considered to be discretionary rather than necessary.[7]
6. The purchase is considered to be particularly important, for example, a gift.[8]
7. The purchase is socially "visible."[9]

[6]The first four situational variables have been investigated in G. Katona, *The Mass Consumption Society* (New York: McGraw-Hill, 1964), pp. 289–290.

[7]G. Katona and E. Mueller, "A Study of Purchase Decisions," *Consumer Behavior: The Dynamics of Consumer Reaction,* L. H. Clark, ed. (New York: New York University Press, 1965), pp. 30–87, at p. 80.

[8]Katona, pp. 289–290.

[9]Dahl, Haire, and Lazarsfeld, pp. 134–135.

Product Characteristics
Extended decision-process behavior is more likely to occur when:

1. The consumer feels committed to the product for an extended period of time, so that future needs and/or product performance are difficult to forecast.
2. The consumer perceives available alternatives as having both desirable and undesirable attributes.[10]
3. The product is high priced relative to the consumer's income.[11]

Consumer Characteristics
Decision-process behavior is more likely to be extended rather than limited or habitual when:[12]

1. The consumer has a college education.
2. The consumer is in the middle-income category as opposed to high or low income.
3. The consumer is under thirty-five years old.
4. The consumer's occupation falls in the white-collar class.
5. The consumer enjoys "shopping around."
6. The consumer perceives no urgent or immediate need for the product.

Environmental Factors
Consumers have a higher probability of engaging in extended decision-process behavior when:

1. A difference is perceived between an individual's customary behavior and that of a group to which he belongs and/or an important reference group.[13]
2. There is disagreement among family members about requirements and/or the relative desirability of alternatives.
3. Strong new stimuli or precipitating circumstances exist. These may consist of general news (threat of war, inflation, and so on) or of news regarding specific products that may be transmitted by advertisers.[14]

[10]J. F. Engel, "Psychology and the Business Sciences," *Quarterly Review of Economics and Business,* I (1961), pp. 75–83.
[11]Katona, pp. 289–290.
[12]All consumer characteristics were obtained from Katona and Mueller, p. 80.
[13]Katona, pp. 289–290.
[14]Katona, pp. 289–290.

Many factors, then, are likely to evoke extended decision-process behavior. The extent of decision making varies greatly, depending on the consumer and his social environment as well as on certain product and situational characteristics.

Summary

There are essentially two ways to study consumer behavior empirically: (1) the distributive approach which focuses on behavioral outcomes and (2) the decision-process approach which describes the way consumers actually make decisions. Research done using the distributive approach is relatively simple and less expensive than are other alternatives; however, this approach can, at best, provide only a partial or incomplete explanation of consumer behavior. The decision-process approach is more advantageous than the distributive approach because it examines the processes preceding the purchase decision, the decision itself, and actions that follow the decision, and by so doing, it ordinarily provides the marketing manager with more relevant information.

The decision-process model of consumer behavior has four basic components: (1) the Central Control Unit (CCU), (2) the Consumer Information Processing Component, (3) the Consumer Decision Process, and (4) the Constraints on the Consumer Decision Process. The CCU consists of stored information and experience, evaluative criteria, attitudes, personality, and a filter and functions as the consumer's psychological command center. The Consumer Information Processing Component receives incoming stimuli and interacts with the CCU via each of its four components: exposure, attention, comprehension, and retention. The Consumer Decision Process has five stages: (1) problem recognition, (2) internal search and alternative evaluation, (3) external search and alternative evaluation, (4) the purchasing processes, and (5) the decision outcome. All stages are not necessarily included in each purchase decision. External influences such as income, the family, culture, or others can serve as constraints on the first three stages of the decision process.

Most consumer decisions are not complex enough to fully utilize the complete model (extended decision-process behavior). These decisions will follow either a limited decision-process behavior or a habitual decision-process behavior. Research suggests that the following four types of variables will determine which decision process the consumer will most likely utilize: (1) situational variables, (2) product characteristics, (3) consumer characteristics, and (4) environmental variables.

QUESTIONS AND ISSUES FOR DISCUSSION

1. "The distinction drawn between the distributive approach and the decision approach is interesting to the academician but is unimportant to the marketing strategist." Do you agree? Why?

2. How might the decision-process approach help the manufacturer of high-quality stereo equipment understand how and why consumers purchase his product?

3. The decision-process model of consumer behavior was described as multimediatory. What does this term mean?

4. Paul Smith, an enthusiastic football fan, watched three consecutive football games last New Year's Day. Two weeks later he recalls the details of every key play, yet he can only recall two of the more than one hundred commercials that were shown during that time period. Both were for a well-known beer. What explanation can you provide?

5. Comment on the following quotation: "The decision-process model can explain deliberate, well thought out consumer decision making but cannot explain impulse purchases."

6. Because attitudes have a more direct impact on behavior than do evaluative criteria, the marketing strategist is wise to restrict his attention to obtaining information on attitudes. Do you agree?

7. "Advertisers are primarily interested in getting potential consumers to understand and remember their advertisements. Therefore, the only relevant consideration in pretesting advertising is how well it is remembered." Comment.

8. The marketing research director of Gant shirts has just determined that 75 percent of the purchases of their product during the last quarter were instances of habitual decision-process behavior. What are the strategy implications of this?
9. Discuss the stages of the decision process, the variations that occur in the decision process, and the underlying determinants of these variations.
10. What type of decision making would be most likely in each of the following situations: (Assume all other things equal.)
    a. the purchase of a new tennis racket for a beginner; for a touring pro
    b. the purchase of toothpaste
    c. the purchase of a motorcycle by a student; by a bank vice-president
    d. the purchase of a gift for a "special friend."

SITUATIONAL PROBLEMS

Case 1

A manufacturer of quality dress shirts located in Iowa has recently experienced a decline in sales. The marketing director suspects that the sales decline is due to a change in consumer preferences in dress shirts. The firm decided to hire a marketing research firm to determine how consumers selected dress shirts. The Chicago-based marketing research firm they hired conducted interviews with 200 Chicago housewives. The research results suggested that consumers liked the appearance of the dress shirts but considered them to be very difficult to care for. The marketing research firm has suggested that the manufacturer modify the fabric used to reduce this problem. The marketing director is not convinced that the research firm has adequately identified the process by which consumers select dress shirts. Based on your understanding of the decision-process model of consumer behavior, what suggestions would you make to the manufacturer?

Should the manufacturer follow the marketing research firm's recommendation?

Case 2

Mr. John Sharp, the marketing director for a major manufacturer of laundry detergents, is concerned about the implications of the

Federal Trade Commission's recent position on product warranties. He has obtained the assistance of two marketing professors, W. X. Vague and D. J. Obscure. Professor Vague contends that the housewife recognizes a problem when she runs out of detergent. She solves the problem by purchasing her most preferred brand. There is typically no consideration of alternatives; consequently, postpurchase evaluation seldom occurs. He contends that there is no need for any concern for product warranties. Professor Obscure disagrees. He contends this may or may not be the case. However, it is certainly not the case when a significant new product comes on the market, for it will stimulate information search and alternative as well as postpurchase evaluations. Mr. Sharp is somewhat confused as to what position to take, particularly since his firm is clearly the leading innovator in the industry. Clarify this situation and make a recommendation to Mr. Sharp.

PART II
ANALYSIS OF GROUP INFLUENCES ON CONSUMER BEHAVIOR

OUTLINE

Cultural and Subcultural Influences

The shared values of large groups of people influence the means used to satisfy human needs. These values vary substantially among groups. For example, the people of Lincoln, Nebraska, would probably not satisfy their hunger with pickled octopus or fried snake, but some people in the world do. The French consider corn-on-the-cob as a food most appropriate for animal consumption. Whereas the color to be worn at funerals in the United States is ordinarily black, it is white in Japan and purple in Latin American countries.

This chapter deals with culture and examines the impact of the shared beliefs and values of large groups of people on the behavior of those who are its members. Specifically, these influences are observable in the products made and consumed by various groups of people. Consequently, any thorough study of consumer behavior must include an examination of the effect of large groups on individual decision making. The importance of this kind of group influence is widely accepted in marketing today and has been referred to as culturalogical to differentiate it from a psychological orientation that has essentially concentrated on the individual.

The values and influence of smaller groups within the larger culture have been less apparent and less well understood. These groups, frequently called *subcultures,* nevertheless affect consumer decision making and are particularly important in this country because the U.S. population is composed of immigrants and descendants of immigrants from throughout the world. The integrative tendency of cultures that results in similar behavioral patterns is not strong enough in America to produce uniform consuming patterns or responses to all marketers' efforts. Consequently, attention must be paid to the major groups of subcultures that comprise the main culture; therefore, an examination of the notion of subculture is included in the second half of this chapter.

Culture

THE NATURE OF CULTURE

In the simplest terms culture serves an adaptive function, that is, it is a means of helping an individual adapt or cope with the world.

A significant part of the importance of culture stems from the influence it has on peoples' perceptions, attitudes, and values. This leads to the realization that human decision making is greatly affected by the culture in which it operates.

In this book the word "culture" is used to mean the complex set of values, ideas, attitudes, and other meaningful symbols created by man to shape human behavior and the artifacts of that behavior that is transmitted from one generation to the next.[1] Three things should be noted about this definition. First, culture does not refer to the instinctive response tendencies of man, such as eating when you are hungry. Nor does it include the inventiveness that takes form as one-time solutions to problems, such as automobiles that get better gas mileage. Secondly, this definition reflects a contemporary view of culture that emphasizes the integrative and learning functions of culture. This definition also stresses the communicative aspect of culture through time, that is, the process of passing values, beliefs, and artifacts on from one generation to the next. Thus, culture can be viewed as the means and methods of coping with the environment that are shared by a large group of people and that are passed from one generation to another. This sharing and then passing on is the result of finding effective means of dealing with common problems and circumstances.

Culture includes both *abstract* and *material elements*. Abstract elements are the values, attitudes, ideas, personality types, as well as various combinations of these such as religion that can be used to characterize a large group of people. These abstract characteristics are learned over time and are transmitted to succeeding generations. Material elements refer to those objects that are employed by a large group of people in meeting their various needs. As a result, in an advanced society these take on many different forms. Examples include automobiles, buildings, computers, and advertisements as well as other items that are referred to as the artifacts of a society.

The word *society* was used in the preceding paragraphs to discuss culture, but it was not defined. "Society," as used here, refers to a collection of individuals who share a particular set of

[1] A. L. Kroeber and Talcott Parsons, "The Concepts of Culture and of Social System," *American Sociological Review,* 23 (October, 1958), p. 583.

symbols and conduct their interpersonal and collective behavior according to the prescriptions of that group of people. Hollander has summarized the relationship between society and culture accordingly: "A culture is a way of life while a society is made up of people who live by its dictates."[2]

The process of absorbing or learning the culture in which one is raised is called *enculturation* or *socialization. Acculturation* refers specifically to the learning of another culture or subculture different from the one in which the person was raised. Figure 4.1 illustrates the process by which cultural values are absorbed by an individual. The social units that an individual has the most regular and intimate contact with include the family, church, and school, and these have the greatest influence on the cultural

FIGURE 4.1.
The Process of Learning Cultural Values

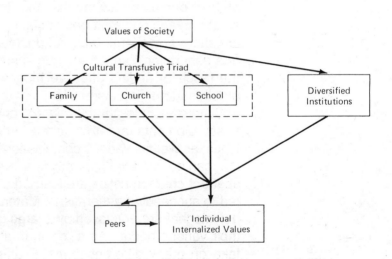

Source: J. F. Engel, D. T. Kollat, and R. D. Blackwell, *Consumer Behavior,* 2nd ed. (New York: Holt, Rinehart and Winston, Inc., 1973), p. 72. Reprinted by permission of publisher.

[2]E. P. Hollander, *Principles and Methods of Social Psychology,* 2nd ed. (New York: Oxford University Press, 1971), p. 307.

values absorbed throughout life. The influence of all other social units is "filtered" by members of the family in the early years of the typical individual. Other human groups, particularly reference groups, which are discussed in the next chapter, are also important transmitters of culture. These groups filter and modify the values of the broader culture to make them consistent with their group values.

BASIC CHARACTERISTICS OF CULTURE

To some the very essence of marketing focuses on culture and society because they perceive marketing as the delivery of a standard of living. Certainly those who characterize marketing in this way must be very interested in consumer behavior. It is only through studying the consumer's interests and decision-making process that appropriate goods and services can be delivered to him or her.

The notion that culture is an important determinant of behavior has caused consumer analysts to examine the fundamental characteristics of culture in order to discover more about its dynamics. There are five distinct characteristics or dimensions that can be identified and described to facilitate the understanding of culture and its effect on consumer behavior. These dimensions include learning, transmission, social aspects, gratification, and its adaptive characteristic. The importance of each is discussed in the following parts of this section.[3]

Culture Is Learned

Consumer behavior is learned as opposed to being instinctive. Culture provides the consumer with a framework to recognize a set of stimuli and a set of responses appropriate to those stimuli, that is, consumers are not born with the idea, for example, that a hamburger, french fries, and a Coke will satisfy their hunger.

Cultural values learned early in life tend to resist change more strongly than those learned late in life. Fundamental values refer to the ultimate reasons people have for acting as they do; these

---

[3]G. P. Murdock, "The Cross-Cultural Survey," *American Sociological Review,* 5 (June, 1940), pp. 361–370.

are intangible and deal with basic aims, aspirations, and ideals. For example, self-oriented values include the right to life and the pursuit of happiness, physical and mental well-being, self-sufficiency, and the right to endeavor to shape one's own life. Once learned and accepted, these resist change. The appropriate strategy for deeply ingrained culturally defined behavior is to modify the marketing strategy to reflect the cultural values rather than attempt to modify these culturally determined preferences. It is commonly recognized that although the family and other social groups contribute most to the socialization process, marketing can have a significant impact on this process also. For instance, there is little doubt that marketing efforts have encouraged the tendency to use whiteness as the primary indicator of the cleanliness of laundry.

Culture Is Inculcated

To say that culture is inculcated is simply to say that culture is transmitted from generation to generation. This process is performed mainly by the immediate family, but other groups and institutions contribute to it also. Ethnic, educational, and religious institutions all participate in the passing on of values, customs, and artifacts from one generation to the next. For example, some religions prohibit the consumption of certain beverages like tea, coffee, and liquor. As such, this has a direct impact on the marketing of these products. The values, norms, and behavioral patterns transmitted are generally in an ideal form. There is, however, considerable disparity between the idealized norm and the norm perceived through observation. Thus, parents as a rule instill the importance of adhering to laws, yet these same parents on occasion receive citations for speeding. Minor violations of cultural values are permitted, expected, and occasionally, encouraged whereas major violations would result in a negative reaction, such as imprisonment.

In a consumer behavior context such deviation may be less dramatic but nevertheless important to the analyst. This can be illustrated by considering the occasion when a parent stresses the importance of the performance features of a product like a stereo and then obviously buys one because it has a good-looking cabinet. Placing the emphasis on performance characteristics is ordinarily more acceptable to society generally, but these are often not the basis for making a particular purchase decision.

Culture Is a Social Phenomenon

Cultural values, habits, and patterns of behavior are shared by the people living in a particular society. The values consumers have and the consumption behavior they express are group properties; they are not distinctive to the individual consumer. Culture has an effect on all values and behavioral patterns but particularly those that are basic to social life. For example, culture transmits values such as how to get along with others, the type of food to eat, how to dress, and how to earn a living. The systematic study of culture requires that the marketing strategist focus on groups or segments. Indeed, marketing strategy must necessarily be based on assumptions about large numbers of consumers representing sizeable market segments. Thus, the planning and directing of marketing operations must be based on similarities of behavior that often result from culturally determined variables.

Culture Is Gratifying

The basic function of culture is to satisfy the needs of the people adhering to its dictates. Only those values, habits, and behavioral patterns that satisfy human needs will be continued through time. Elements within a culture that cease to gratify needs usually become extinguished, at least in the long run. For example, products such as button shoes and hoop skirts are no longer consumed because they do not satisfy consumer needs as well as do other styles of the same apparel. The notion that culture reinforces some responses serves as a basis for marketing decision making. Strategists must recognize that the advertising used and the products offered for sale must focus on satisfying needs that society approves.

Culture Is Adaptive

As indicated previously, culture is passed from generation to generation; yet this does not imply that culture is static or endowed with eternal life. Rather, culture shifts or adapts to the environment in which it operates and has contact. In the past cultural change was unbelievably slow. However, more recently the vastly accelerated technological changes and the amazing capabilities of communication are reflected in comparatively rapid cultural adaptation, particularly among the developed nations. For example, consider the speed with which the use of birth control pills and the two-child family have become accepted norms in certain segments of American society. Similarly, the gas-saving economy car, once considered acceptable as a second car, has in a brief time become one of the major product lines for automobile manufacturers.

CONTEMPORARY AMERICAN VALUES

American values were once thought of as relatively permanent sets of cultural traits transmitted from generation to generation with little alteration. Even though many American values are still relatively permanent, it is apparent that significant changes in some are occurring at an increasing pace, and the values most in transition frequently have a considerable effect on consumer purchasing decisions.

While numerous forces affect values, three institutions in the United States have had a major impact—the family, organized religion, and the schools. These institutions have changed over time, and the nature of their influence has been modified.

The relative influence of the family in transmitting American culture has declined somewhat in recent years. The most frequently mentioned reasons for a decline in the family's influence on the formation of values include the following: (1) the decrease in parent-child interaction in the formative years from birth to five, (2) the increasing divorce rate, and (3) the geographical separation of family members. Collectively, these changes have resulted in less opportunity for parents to communicate, explain, and justify their values to their children. These offer some explanation as to why the values of the youthful consumers of the seventies differ from those of their parents. There is, for example, some indication that the more youthful consumers of today are less concerned with the accumulation of material goods than were their parents.

Religious institutions in America have historically played an important role in transmitting basic values from one generation to another. However, there is some indication that church membership and attendance have declined since 1967.[4] There is also considerable evidence that young Americans question the values of institutionalized religion to a greater degree than did the previous generation. If a significant decline in the importance of religious institutions were to take place, the net effect would likely be to establish a more situational or personal set of values, that is, what feels good at a particular time is to be valued or considered appropriate.

Although the importance of the family and organized religion may have diminished somewhat in shaping values, the part played by educational institutions in this process has increased considerably in recent years. Contributing to this increased influence are (1) the growing enrollments in both preschools and universities during the 1960's and early 1970's and (2) the emergence and proliferation of new educational philosophies and techniques. The previous emphasis on description and memorization has been replaced by analytical approaches emphasizing the questioning of the old and the formation of new approaches and solutions. This inquisitiveness and the questioning of the traditional "right and wrong" has carried over into everyday life.[5] This trend is exemplified by such things as the increasing number of medical malpractice suits, the growing number of consumer-oriented organizations, and the increasing unionism of white collar workers. Thus, to an increasing extent, consumers' minds do not operate in black and white but rather in the more realistic and complicated nuances of full color.

THE RESULTS OF CHANGING AMERICAN VALUES

The modification in American values emanating from the changes in its major institutions are occurring more rapidly today

---

[4] *Yearbook of American Churches,* annual editions (New York: National Councils of the Church of Christ, 1972).

[5] J. Jameson and R. M. Hessler, "The Natives are Restless: The Ethos and Mythos of Student Power," *Human Organization,* 29 (Summer, 1970), pp. 81–94.

than in the past. Not only must these newly emerging values be identified, but the consumer analyst also has to be sensitive to what accompanies these changes. This information becomes a vital input for strategic planning. Changing American values are having an impact on American orientations. The effect of these changing values can be illustrated by considering the emphasis on youthfulness, religion in the 1970's, creative eroticism, and the increasing interest in leisure.

Youthfulness
The emphasis on youthfulness in recent years reflects a major change in American values. This youth orientation is likely to increase in importance. Individuals, groups, and organizations have and will continue to rely on the creativity of the young to deal with all types of problems. Although not their exclusive domain, the young have more opportunities than did their predecessors to acquire an education and develop creativity. Consequently, it is the young who increasingly are given the responsibilities for running corporations, government agencies, and society in general. Society has placed so much emphasis on youth that many people in all age groups want to be perceived as youthful. Marketing strategists have recognized this and have successfully used a youthful theme to promote numerous products, such as clothing, automobiles, home furnishings, and personal grooming items. For example, in attempting to attract the car buyer who is under 30 years old, a major automobile manufacturer successfully introduced a sporty, small car by emphasizing auto racing and using young attractive people in their ads. The manufacturer sold a lot of cars, but the age of the typical buyer was 46 and not 26. Thus, although the youth market in the United States is large in itself, the "youthfulness" influence on the purchase behavior of other age groups is even greater.

Religion in the Seventies
American values have long been shaped by institutionalized religion, particularly the Christian and Jewish faiths. One example of this influence is the impact of the puritan ethic. Historically, this dictated that individual and societal needs could only be satisfied through hard work and the accumulation of wealth. However, in

recent years this value has become less influential, and there has been a movement toward a theology of pleasure. This modern view emphasizes a new type of individuality and release from prohibitions. The concern for pleasure is consistent with a movement toward greater affluence, but until recently this has been constrained by the dominance of the puritan ethic.

Marketing strategists have found such changing conceptions of religious values to be important in facilitating the use of new tactics. Colors and designs can be bright and sensual; cosmetics and grooming aids can emphasize pleasure with the body; the use of credit can be stimulated with appeals to enjoy products now and pay later; even banks can throw off their stodgy, conservative images with bright red and white logos.

Creative Eroticism
Creative eroticism has emerged as the result of changing American values and has had a significant impact on marketing strategy. Creative eroticism refers to the transition from rigid prohibitions on fun with sex to the present release of such inhibitions. The response of some marketing strategists to this new freedom has become quite apparent. For example, advertising media have dropped many restrictions about what can be shown, and some ad agencies have become rather innovative in developing sensuous themes. The result of these changes are illustrated by the Noxema girl who suggests that the shaver "take it all off," the girl in the Serta mattress ad who seductively demonstrates the comfort available from that product, and Joe Namath using his not too dependable legs to model panty hose.

The Leisure Life
The increasing importance placed on leisure also reflects a change in American values and has caused some to label the hard-working, industrious person a "workaholic." The growing interest in leisure or recreation has been identified by many as the underlying factor in stimulating the demand for huge quantities of consumer goods.[6] Indeed, American consumers spend

---

[6]"83 Billion Dollars for Leisure—Now the Fastest Growing Business in America," *U.S. News and World Report* (September 15, 1969), pp. 58–60.

approximately 16 percent of their disposable personal income for leisure activities. In order to respond appropriately to this growing interest in leisure, marketing managers must answer questions like the following: How many hours of each day are allocated among work, nondiscretionary activities, such as eating and sleeping, and discretionary activities, such as playing tennis and watching television? What products are purchased for use during each type of activity? How much will consumers pay for time-saving products in order to increase the time spent in discretionary activities?

Now that some attention has been given to the effects of changes in values on American culture, it is appropriate to turn to a discussion of the variation across different cultures.

Crosscultural Analysis of Consumer Behavior

Crosscultural analysis, the comparison of similarities and differences among countries in the behavioral and material aspects of their cultures, is vital to the effective development of foreign markets. The perils of crosscultural ignorance are aptly illustrated by the Western oriented tobacco company that attempted to introduce filtered cigarettes into an Asian country. Despite warnings of impending failure, the western managers set up manufacturing and distribution facilities. Unfortunately, the management failed to consider the value placed upon sanitation in the country, the literacy rate, and the short life expectancy. The product was a dismal failure and the loss incurred by the company was considerable.[7]

Numerous experiences similar to that presented above have convinced most marketing strategists that executives with crosscultural competence or those who are foreign nationals are a necessary requirement for the successful development of international markets. This has become increasingly apparent as a greater reliance has been placed upon global markets to assure profitability. Consequently, the following conditions have been

---

[7]J. A. Lee, "Cultural Analysis in Overseas Operations," *Harvard Business Review,* 44 (March-April, 1966), pp. 106–114.

identified as essential to the successful development of foreign markets:

1. sensitivity to cultural differences
2. cultural empathy, or the ability to "understand the inner logic and coherence of other ways of life, plus the restraint not to judge them as bad because they are different from one's own ways"
3. ability to withstand the initial cultural shock or "the sum of sudden jolts that awaits the unwary American abroad"
4. ability to cope with and to adapt to foreign environments without 'going native.'[8]

Despite the dominant views listed above, in recent years some marketing strategists have become convinced that it may be possible to standardize marketing programs in a number of areas throughout the world. Although research and practice have identified numerous obstacles to such standardization, the interest in it continues to increase. The following statement represents the rationale developed by one marketing analyst to support the position that consumers are basically the same, and it also illustrates the kind of logic used to encourage this point of view.

> The desire to be beautiful is universal. Such appeals as "mother and child," "freedom from pain," "glow of health" know no boundaries.
> In a sense, the young women in Tokyo and the young women in Berlin are sisters not only "under the skin" but on their skin and on their lips and fingernails, and even their hairstyles. If they could, the girls of Moscow would follow suit; and some of them do.[9]

Thus, some contend that consumer behavior theory has universal application and that strategy developed from this theory can be used in any cultural setting. However, empirical research indicates that nearly two-thirds of multinational firms find it necessary to employ marketing strategies and programs that reflect local differences. The more emphasis put on cultural similarities, the more likely firms are to emphasize a common strategy rather than a market-to-market approach.

[8]Y. H. Furuhashi and H. F. Evarts, "Educating Men for International Marketing," *Journal of Marketing*, 31 (January, 1967), pp. 51–53.
[9]A. C. Fatt, "The Danger of 'Local' International Advertising," *Journal of Marketing*, 31 (January, 1965), pp. 60–62.

Marketing strategists sometimes are confronted with cultures that are quite similar—the United States and England for example—and sometimes with cultures that are very different—the United States and India. Far too frequently businessmen have applied a strategy that was successful in a domestic market to a foreign market without adequate consideration of the cultural differences. The likelihood of success can be enhanced by careful analyses of the cultural conditions in the existing market and the cultural conditions in the market under consideration. Where differences are observed, adjustment in the strategy employed can be undertaken. An outline for systematically analyzing the cultural determinants of success in each market is provided in Table 4.1.

Subculture

Part of the importance of the goods and services made available to the consumer lies in their ability to provide an individual with a symbolic expression of uniqueness—a representation of self through product characteristics. This opportunity becomes more of a frustration as the offerings in the marketplace continue to grow and the consumer faces a selection dilemma among the multiplicity of possibilities.

It is at this point that the consumer analyst sees the role of subcultures within a society as that of assisting the individual who is identifying with a small group and its preferences. Such an identification provides a consumer with one means of differentiating between what will satisfy and what will not.

THE NATURE OF SUBCULTURE

A culture represents a loose agreement in the values, behavioral patterns, and symbols it upholds. Yet there are smaller groups of people within the larger society who have modified these ways of dealing with the environment and with persons enough to be at variance with the general living patterns. These smaller groups are referred to as subcultures.

Some products may be favored specifically by the people in a particular subculture. The purchase of squid is usually made by

TABLE 4.1
Outline of Crosscultural Analysis of Consumer Behavior

1. *Determine relevant motivations in the culture*
   What needs are fulfilled with this product in the minds of members of the culture? How are these needs presently fulfilled? Do members of this culture readily recognize these needs?

2. *Determine characteristic behavior patterns*
   What patterns are characteristic of purchasing behavior? What forms of division of labor exist within the family structure? How frequently are products of this type purchased? What size packages are normally purchased? Do any of these characteristic behaviors conflict with the behavior expected for this product? How strongly ingrained are the behavior patterns that conflict with those needed for distribution of this product?

3. *Determine what broad cultural values are relevant to this product*
   Are there strong values concerning work, morality, religions, family relations, and so on, that relate to this product? Does this product connote attributes that are in conflict with these cultural values? Can conflicts with values be avoided by changing the product? Are there positive values in this culture with which the product might be identified?

4. *Determine characteristic forms of decision making*
   Do members of the culture display a studied approach to decisions concerning innovations or an impulsive approach? What is the form of the decision process? Upon what information sources do members of the culture rely? Do members of the culture tend to be rigid or flexible in the acceptance of new ideas? What criteria do they use in evaluating alternatives?

5. *Evaluate promotion methods appropriate to the culture*
   What role does advertising occupy in the culture? What themes, words, or illustrations are taboo? What language problems exist in present markets that cannot be translated into this culture? What types of salesmen are accepted by members of the culture? Are such salesmen available?

6. *Determine appropriate institutions for this product in the minds of consumers*
   What types of retailers and intermediary institutions are available? What services do these institutions offer that are expected by the consumer? What alternatives are available for obtaining services needed for the product but not offered by existing institutions? How are various types of retailers regarded by consumers? Will changes in the distribution structure be readily accepted?

Source: J. F. Engel, D. T. Kollat and R. D. Blackwell, *Consumer Behavior,* 2nd ed. (New York: Holt, Rinehart and Winston, Inc., 1973), pp. 95–96. Reprinted by permission of the publisher.

those who enjoy the finer points of Italian cuisine, while the appeal of sauna equipment is most likely to be found among those of Scandinavian descent. However, because sufficient similarities exist among various subcultures, there is a common acceptance of many products. The appeals of quick-serve eating establishments and motel facilities demonstrate this kind of general acceptance.

TYPES OF SUBCULTURES

Among subcultures there are a number of points of commonness that permit grouping of identifiable characteristics. Four types of subcultures are described below: nationality, religious, geographic, and ethnic. Ethnic subcultures, particularly the black subculture, is given a somewhat more extended analysis in this section because of its importance in contemporary America.

Nationality Subcultures

Nearly every metropolitan area has within its boundaries groups that are relatively homogeneous with respect to nationality. These areas frequently become known as Little Italy, Little Poland, or Chinatown, and often distinctive products and/or consumption patterns become associated with the residents. Many times the media, primarily newspapers and radio, cater to these markets. Marketing efforts focused on ethnic groups are essential for the success of many firms in metropolitan areas. For example, General Motors is reported to be more successful than its competitors in New York City because of its strong penetration into ethnic markets through a dealer organization built upon subculture realities.

Religious Subcultures

Religious subcultures may exert considerable influence on those whose members choose to conform closely to group norms. Mormons, for example, refrain from consuming tobacco, liquor, and certain other stimulants; Christian Scientists restrict their search for information and use of medicines; Seventh Day Adventists abstain from eating meat; many Jews purchase Kosher foods on a regular basis; Christians from some fundamental denominations avoid ostentatious displays of wealth; and the Amish avoid mechanized life-styles and individualized personal appearance. Some groups identified with the Jesus movement are creating a subculture based upon emulation of first-century Christianity in contrast to the contemporary practice of conspicuous consumption. It is obvious from these few examples that certain subcultural beliefs and values actually restrict the market for a number of products.

Many conditions can cause the influence of the subculture to decline. Increased mobility, education, and income provide challenges to the traditional activities and affect behavior. However, the basic values of a subculture may continue to have an influence on decision making for some time.

Geographic Subcultures

Differences among people of separate geographic areas often have an impact on decision making and, thus, affect consumption patterns. Consumption patterns of some goods and services even vary across the United States. Several years ago Tucker observed the following geographical variations:

> The West Coast drinks more gin and vodka, the East more Scotch and the South more bourbon. Birch beer and cream soda are soft drink favorites of some importance in New England. They do not exist in Birmingham or Shreveport. . . . Maxwell House Coffee has a special blend for its western customers, stronger roast than is popular in the East. Beef supplied to northern and eastern markets is heavier and hung longer than is available in the South and West, where baby beef is popular.[10]

The Southwest appears to have a characteristic style of life that emphasizes casual dress, outdoor entertaining, and unique forms of recreation. Furthermore, people in this area are considered to be more receptive to new products and services than are those in the Midwest. It is generally maintained that even though these geographic differences are currently important, the increasing mobility of society is contributing to their decline.

[10]W. T. Tucker, *The Social Context of Economic Behavior* (New York: Holt, Rinehart and Winston, Inc., 1964), pp. 38–39.

Ethnic Subcultural Influences

The fourth type of subculture is based on ethnic or racial differences and, as mentioned earlier, is given a more extended analysis because of the importance it has in contemporary America. Ethnic subcultures, particularly the black subculture, have been the focus of numerous research efforts in recent years. The black subculture is not synonymous with black skin color. Rather, the black subculture refers to the common heritage of slavery, a history of income deprivation, a shared history of discrimination and suffering, limited housing opportunities, and denial of participation in many aspects of the predominant culture. Consequently, blacks raised as part of the dominant white society may have no more appreciation of the black subculture than any other member of the dominant group.

Although research suggests that there is greater similarity in the purchase patterns of black consumers than there is among whites, black consumption patterns appear to be heterogeneous enough to justify the use of segmentation strategies similar to those used in white markets. For example, there is a growing black middle class, many of whom are well educated professionals earning sizeable incomes and live in quiet suburban neighborhoods. However, the number and purchasing power of black consumers limit the feasibility of using extensive segmentation strategies. Moreover, the processes of acculturation and assimilation are likely to reduce the distinctiveness of the black subculture in future years. This is particularly true if black consumers continue their move toward the acceptance of white middle class values. Even though blacks remain at a disadvantage in their striving toward the goals dictated by these white values, they nevertheless could continue to aspire to achieve them.[11]

Distinctive Characteristics of the Black Subculture.   The black subculture has a number of distinctive characteristics that influence the behavior of its members. The major ones are: (1) low income, (2) differential family characteristics, and (3) being subject to racial discrimination.

[11]R. A. Bauer and S. M. Cunningham, "The Negro Market," *Journal of Advertising Research,* 10 (April, 1970), pp. 3–10.

Low Income.   Members of the black subculture are frequently perceived to have, and justly so, low incomes. In fact, while 10 percent of white households have incomes below the poverty level, more than 30 percent of black households have this unfortunate distinction. Particularly discouraging is the fact that the relative deprivation of blacks has continued to increase in recent years. Such extensive relative deprivation has a direct effect on the values transmitted to all members of the subculture. The consumer analyst has an extremely difficult time distinguishing between the effects of income and ethnic background. That is, suppose that research indicates that whites consume more Scotch than do blacks. (Actually, one research effort suggests that blacks consume three times as much Scotch per capita as do whites.) The crucial question is: "To what extent is the observed variation attributable to differences in income, education, reference-group orientation, and/or other such factors rather than ethnic background?"

Family Characteristics.   Systematic comparisons of black and white families have indicated that black families are considerably less stable. The traditional indicators of family stability are the proportion living with their spouse, the proportion of illegitimate births, premarital conceptions, and children living with both parents. As would be expected, family stability affects occupational success. A study by the U.S. Department of Labor concluded:

> At the heart of the deterioration of the fabric of Negro society is the deterioration of the Negro family. . . .
> There is probably no single fact of Negro American life so little understood by whites. . . . It is more difficult, however, for whites to perceive the affect that three centuries of exploitation have had on the fabric of Negro society itself. Here the consequences of the historic injustices done to Negro Americans are silent and hidden from view. But here is where the true injury has occurred; unless this damage is repaired, all the effort to end discrimination and poverty and injustice will come to little.[12]

[12]Office of Planning and Research of U.S. Department of Labor, *The Negro Family: The Case for National Action* (Washington, D.C.: U.S. Government Printing Office, 1965), p. 5.

The diverseness of some family characteristics of the black subculture can influence their selection and use of products. Conditions such as the high proportion of female-headed households or the large extended network of familial interactions can have a great impact on family consumption. Of course, it must be remembered that some segments of black consumers have family characteristics comparable to society generally. This is particularly true of the growing black middle class referred to earlier.

Racial Discrimination. Racial discrimination directed toward the black subculture has been so massive and enduring that it must be considered in the analysis of consumer behavior. Consider, for example, the substantial impact that forced housing conditions has had on the consumption of other goods and services. In some cities the containment of blacks in a limited number of neighborhoods has had a direct effect on the stores they shop in and the variety of goods purchased.

Of course, discrimination has taken on other forms that shape consumer behavior. For example, because of the location of most public golf courses and the restrictive membership policies of many private clubs, most blacks never have become interested in golf. Consequently, black consumers have not represented an important market segment for golf equipment.

Black Subcultural Consumption Patterns. A number of marketing researchers have attempted to determine whether or not there are distinct black consumption patterns. Research to date suggests that the similarities between black and white purchase patterns are much greater than the differences, but there are some differences. For example, research indicates that:

1. Blacks save more out of a given income than do whites with the same income.[13] However, blacks use fewer savings and insurance services, tend to use less advantageous types of

[13]M. Alexis, "Some Negro-White Differences in Consumption," *American Journal of Economics and Sociology,* 21 (January, 1962).

financial services, and end up with less total financial resources than do whites. The savings approach of blacks tends to widen the gap of well-being between black and white households.[14]

2. Blacks spend more for clothing and nonautomobile transportation; less for food, housing, medical care, and automobile transportation; and equivalent amounts for recreation and leisure, home furnishings, and equipment than do whites with comparable incomes.[15]

3. Blacks tend to own higher priced class automobiles, higher priced models regardless of make, and automobiles with more cylinders than do white families with comparable incomes. In this same study, race was more closely related to automobile characteristics than income, education, sex, age, family size, or miles driven per week.[16]

4. Blacks appear to be more brand loyal than whites with the same characteristics.[17]

Mass Media and Interpersonal Communications in the Black Subculture.   Marketing researchers have expended considerable effort to discern distinctive media exposure patterns and interpersonal communication processes. Some major research findings are presented below.

1. Blacks respond more favorably to advertisements with all black models or to integrated ads than to advertisements with all white models. Black consumers under the age of 30 appear to react unfavorably to advertisements with integrated settings. Whites appear to react to black models as favorably or

[14]S. R. Hiltz, "Black and White in the Consumer Financial System," *American Journal of Sociology,* 76 (1971), pp. 987–999.

[15]J. Stafford, K. Cox, and J. Higginbotham, "Some Consumption Pattern Differences Between Urban Whites and Negroes," *Social Science Quarterly* (December, 1968), pp. 619–630.

[16]F. C. Akers, "Negro and White Automobile Buying: New Evidence," *Journal of Marketing Research,* 5 (August, 1968), pp. 283–290.

[17]F. G. Davis, "Differential Factors in the Negro Market" (Chicago: National Association of Market Developers, 1959), p. 6; privately published report based on data collected by *Ebony* magazine.

more so than to white models, although this varies by product category.[18]

2. Black consumers appear to respond more positively to advertisements than do white consumers.[19]

3. Black television viewers have a less favorable opinion of white-oriented programs and watch more television than do whites. They also watch more on the weekend in contrast to whites' higher viewing through the week.[20]

LOW INCOME MARKET

Any discussion of subculture would be incomplete without some discussion of the low income market. Although there is a tendency for some researchers to perceive the black subculture to be synonymous with low income consumers, this is clearly inappropriate. Systematic analysis of the low income market must carefully eliminate the effects of race. Research focusing on the low income market was stimulated considerably by Caplovitz's assertion that the poor pay more for goods and services than do the more affluent. There is a growing body of literature on this question, and some studies have produced contradictory results. The conclusion that has generally been accepted is that retailers ordinarily do not discriminate among buyers on the basis of income or ethnic characteristics. That is, merchants do not charge higher prices in the ghetto but, in fact, may charge lower prices about as often as higher ones. There is even some evidence that automobile salesmen charge higher prices to higher income people. However, the poor may pay more because of the unavailability of efficient retailers in their neighborhood, differences in the quality and variety of service offered to them, differences in credit costs, and their pattern of purchasing in smaller quantities and package sizes.

[18]A. M. Barban, "The Dilemma of 'Integrated' Advertising," *Journal of Business,* 42 (October, 1969), pp. 477–496; J. W. Gould, N. B. Sigband, and C. E. Zoerner, "Black Consumer Reactions to 'Integrated' Advertising: An Exploratory Study," *Journal of Marketing,* 34 (July, 1970), pp. 20–26.

[19]B. S. Tolley and J. J. Goett, "Reactions to Blacks in Newspapers," *Journal of Advertising Research,* 11 (April, 1971), pp. 11–17.

[20]J. W. Carey, "Variations in Negro-White Television Preference," *Journal of Broadcasting,* 10 (1966), pp. 199–211.

Summary

Culture can be defined as the complex set of values, ideas, attitudes, and other meaningful symbols created by man to shape human behavior and the artifacts of that behavior, all of which are transmitted from one generation to the next. It includes abstract elements such as values and attitudes as well as material elements such as automobiles, buildings, or other artifacts of a society. Culture has five distinct dimensions. It is learned and not instinctive. It is transmitted from generation to generation. Cultural values, habits, and patterns of behavior are shared by the people in a society. Its basic function is to satisfy the needs of the people. Culture adapts to the environment in which it operates.

American values have changed significantly over time, and the effect on consumer behavior has been substantial. Changes in three major institutions—the family, organized religion, and the schools—have caused these value changes. Four areas illustrate the result of changing American values: Americans of all ages desire to be perceived as youthful; the impact of puritanical religious beliefs is decreasing significantly; creative eroticism is being met with less and less resistance; and living the leisure life is growing in popularity. The modern marketer is effectively utilizing these changes in promoting his products.

The analysis of crosscultural differences is vital to the successful development of foreign markets. Executives competent in this area are needed by firms developing the international field. This chapter presents an outline to assist the marketer in analyzing crosscultural consumer behavior.

Subcultures are small groups of people within the larger society who have adopted ways of dealing with the environment and with people that are at variance with the general living pattern. Major types of subcultures are nationality, religious, geographic, and ethnic. The black subculture is particularly important in contemporary America. It is characterized by low income, differential family characteristics, and vulnerability to racial discrimination. Extensive research in the area of black subculture has produced findings valuable to the marketer. Differences in black and white consumption, mass media, and interpersonal communications patterns are noted.

The low income market has come to light recently as a result of the recently raised question of whether or not the poor pay more for goods and services than do the affluent. Arguments exist on both sides of the question.

QUESTIONS AND ISSUES FOR DISCUSSION

1. Culture is something over which marketers have no control; therefore, the marketing manager's task is to identify basic cultural values and consumption patterns in light of the products his firm distributes. Evaluate this statement.
2. Some consumer analysts believe that culturally unacceptable products can be made acceptable. What are some products that are culturally unacceptable in the United States? What marketing strategies might be used to make cigars for women and purses for men culturally acceptable products in this country?
3. What are the essential elements that you would include in the definition of culture?
4. Although there are culturally distinctive consumption preferences, how do you explain the success of many products in very different cultures. For example: Coca Cola in the United States and India and the Fiat in the United States and Italy.
5. There are numerous changes occurring in American values. How will changes such as (1) ecological consciousness and (2) the equality of women effect consumption generally?
6. What effect might the changing emphasis on leisure time have on the consumption of the following product types: (1) professional sports, (2) fishing equipment, (3) single family homes, and (4) food.
7. How might information on the culturally based differences between blacks and whites help the distributor of Dr. Pepper or the Commission on Product Safety?
8. A deodorant producer that has been very successful in the United States should experience considerable success in England because the cultures are very similar. Discuss.
9. A family planning agency has determined that it has been less effective in the low income subculture than in any other.

What should they understand about the characteristics of this group to improve their effectiveness?

SITUATIONAL PROBLEMS

Case 1

Health Foods Incorporated, a small producer and distributor of a limited line of health foods, e.g., organic foods such as soy flour, wheat germ, and goat's milk, has experienced considerable success since its inception 10 years ago. In his quest for continued growth, Bob Brown, President, has commissioned an extensive marketing study to aid in strategy development. One of the particularly interesting findings reported in the study was that Health Foods had a very low penetration in the black subculture. This low penetration could not be attributed to age, income, or occupation.

What may be the primary reason for the low penetration experienced by Health Foods Incorporated?

What stragegy would you suggest to achieve a higher level of success among black consumers?

Case 2

The Wow Company produces and distributes movies for general consumer viewing throughout the United States and Canada. The increasingly competitive nature of the movie industry in these countries has caused Wow to look to new markets. The markets currently being considered are the Arab countries, South America, and Scandinavia. Being uncertain as to which market holds the greatest potential, the Wow management has hired the services of a well-known marketing research company. The research company has requested that the Wow management develop a statement to serve as a basis for the research. They have asked that the statement contain a list of questions about movie attendance that would enable them to compare these three markets.

What information about the three markets should the Wow management request the research company to obtain?

OUTLINE

Social Class and Group Influences

The preceding chapter focused on the effects that culture and select subcultural influences have on consumer behavior. The present chapter adopts a somewhat smaller unit of analysis and focuses on social class and social groups. Reference groups, a concept long of interest to consumer analysts, are also discussed.

Social Class

People generally tend to associate with those whom they consider to be like themselves. Frequently they have similar occupations, levels of formal education, and are likely to live in comparable circumstances. Under such arrangements, fundamental values and viewpoints about life are shared. There is a particular social consciousness associated with these shared characteristics and a social status attached to them. A hierarchy among status groups has developed because some are regarded as having more social prestige and are, therefore, superior to the others.

Historically, sociologists have been particularly interested in the phenomenon of social structure for its own sake. Consumer analysts, on the other hand, have become attentive to social stratification as it can have a significant influence on consumer behavior. This section of the chapter pays specific attention to social class as one form of social stratification. Social class will first be defined briefly, with its dimensions identified and discussed. This will include a representation of the social class structure in the United States. The final part of this section will draw attention to the issue of the relative importance of social class and income in explaining and predicting consumer behavior.

SOCIAL CLASS DEFINED

Social classes are relatively permanent and homogeneous divisions in a society into which individuals or families sharing similar values, life-styles, interests, and behavior can be categorized.[1]

[1]J. F. Engel, D. T. Kollat, and R. D. Blackwell, *Consumer Behavior,* 2nd ed. (New York: Holt, Rinehart and Winston, Inc., 1973), p. 112.

Of course, it is much easier to provide such a definition then to operationalize it. There are no absolute boundaries separating social classes, and there has been considerable disagreement as to where one social class ends and another begins.

CLASS DISTRIBUTION IN THE UNITED STATES

The exact distribution of individuals into separate class categories depends upon the definitions used. The mainstream of social research has commonly used Warner's six-class system. One representation of the distribution of the U.S. population by these six classes is shown in Figure 5.1 with the upper upper and lower upper classes combined.

FIGURE 5.1.
Social Classes in the United States.

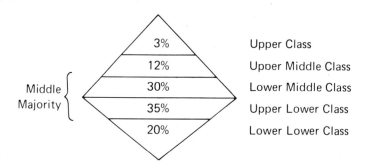

Source: Charles B. McCann, *Women and Department Store Newspaper Advertising* (Chicago: Social Research, 1957), p. 94. Reprinted by permission of publisher.

The lower middle and upper lower classes are the largest groups of consumers in America. This is the so-called "mass market" or "middle majority" to which most business organizations and political parties, among others, direct their attention.

To illustrate the differences that exist among social classes, it is useful to consider the characteristics of the three most important groupings from a marketing perspective. As shown in Figure

5.1, these groups include the upper middle class, the lower middle class, and the upper lower class, or what is frequently referred to as the working class.[2]

The *upper middle class* is primarily made up of people in managerial or professional occupations who live in urban areas. Typically they have an above average education, sophistication, cultural interests, and are community minded. They tend to value individuality and self-expression and emphasize quality and good taste in their purchasing practices. As can be noted above, this group comprises about 12 percent of the population.

The *lower middle class* is essentially composed of white collar workers, small businessmen, and highly skilled blue collar workers. These people are generally quite practical in their orientation and have strong convictions about what is right and wrong. Being respectable citizens and maintaining middle class status are important to them. The lower middle class includes approximately 30 percent of the population.

The *upper lower class or working class* is made up of people who are in various service occupations requiring few skills as well as in many blue collar occupations. Those who comprise this group have values and behavioral patterns similar to the lower middle class. However, they are generally less well educated, less aware and less involved in activities beyond the immediate family, and they tend to emphasize more short-range goals. More than a third of the population are working class people.

Such differences among social classes continually affect consumer behavior, not only in shaping interests in various products and brands, but also in influencing where people shop and the level of service they expect to receive.

SOCIAL CLASS DETERMINANTS

Social classes take shape through what have been called determinants—those characteristics that differentiate the members of one social class from another. Although there are a number of ways that can be used to determine a person's social class, there is considerable similarity among the various approaches. One of

[2]H. W. Boyd, Jr. and S. J. Levy, *Promotion: A Behavioral View* (Englewood Cliffs, New Jersey: Prentice-Hall, Inc., 1967), p. 44.

the more helpful approaches follows. It concentrates on five dimensions of social class. These five include occupation, personal interactions, possessions, and value orientation. Each of these is discussed in the following paragraphs.

Occupation

Many believe that an individual's occupation is the best single clue to his or her social class membership. This appears to be true because one's life's work has a substantial influence on the way he or she lives. For instance, in many cases the wardrobe that an individual begins to assemble upon taking his or her first job reflects the expectations associated with this new position. This can be illustrated by considering what would likely be among the clothing items purchased by the new accountant working for a public accounting firm as compared to those bought by a young commercial artist. A man who is a young accountant would probably begin by purchasing conservative suits, while the artist may buy distinctive sport shirts and slacks.

Occupations may also be ranked according to the prestige, honor, and respect associated with them by members of society.- Surprisingly to some, the resulting rankings are quite stable over time.

Personal Performance

Individual achievement is also related to social class status. Ordinarily this is concerned with occupational accomplishments, but it may involve nonjob performance as well. These latter accomplishments include service to various community groups or even superior family role performance.

Such community participation includes functioning as a successful United Fund chairperson, member of the local board of education, member of the chamber of commerce, or serving on the city council. These organizations demand a great deal of time and usually pay no salary to their members, but each position offers considerable public visibility and attention. Consequently, such people develop the behavioral pattern expected of them by the public. These influences are of interest to the consumer analyst because they may affect purchasing patterns—first among the individuals who hold these positions and then more importantly among those who use public figures as references.

For example, it is reasonable to expect a leading member of the local chamber of commerce of a community that is very economically dependent on the automobile industry to drive an American-made car. Furthermore, the very visibility of people holding such community service positions puts their taste in clothing on open display.

Personal Interactions

Personal interactions are particularly important in determining social class status. Whom one relates to on a regular basis, how one is treated, and how one treats those with whom he interacts, serve to identify the social class to which he belongs.

There are rather rigid barriers to social interaction among members of different social strata. In the United States these rarely take the form of explicit restrictions, but they are nevertheless effective. For example, a lodge or club may require that a new member be sponsored by a current member, or it may be that the initiation fee is sufficiently high so as to limit membership to the desired group.

Such memberships result in interaction that directly affects consumer decision making. For instance, whom one uses as a source of information about product brands or stores often comes from the ranks of those individuals with whom one associates on a day-to-day basis.

Possession

Personal possessions are often used as indicators of social status. The old idea of keeping up with the Joneses implies a social consciousness of quantity and quality of consumption. Also, Veblen's theory of conspicuous consumption draws specific attention to the practice of some people who engage in buying to publicly verify their newly acquired wealth.

Historically a number of products have held particular attractiveness as symbols of status for members of the mass market. The automobile has been one of the most visible, although its importance in this respect has faded in recent years. Other products have replaced it. For example, the ownership of a vacation home, a third car, a pleasure home, or a backyard swimming pool have special connotations for some middle class Americans.

This does not mean that these items are not purchased for their functional features, but it suggests that in promoting them special attention should be given to their capacity to offer a status appeal.

The way an individual selects and uses possessions is sometimes referred to as his life-style. Decisions about possessions and their relation to social class are questions of extreme importance to the consumer analyst.

Value Orientation

Fundamental beliefs and personal orientations vary across social classes. For example, there are identifiable differences in beliefs among members of different social classes about family formation, child rearing, the home, and work. Such variations affect market behavior and may even provide a basis for market segmentation. Several of these differences and their impact on marketing strategy development are discussed in the next chapter.

MEASUREMENT OF SOCIAL CLASS

A number of methods have been developed for measuring social class. However, most consumer researchers use what has been called the objective method for placing respondents into classes. The most frequently used variables in this classification process are occupation, income, education, size and type of residence, ownership of personal possessions, and organizational affiliations.

Even though some of the application procedures are rather technically detailed and intellectually intriguing, the resulting classifications are only approximations. However, these groupings of individuals generally are sufficiently different from each other as to be helpful to the analyst and manager.

For example, the manager of a public agency responsible for state employment services may find it helpful to vary his agency's efforts in matching applicants and job opportunities when dealing with people from different social classes because of the variation in their values and interests.

A NOTE OF DISCONTENT WITH SOCIAL CLASS

Although social class remains a helpful basis for market segmentation and for planning marketing strategy, there is some dissatisfaction with the use of social class as a means of explaining consumer behavior over and above the effect of income. For example, Segal and Felson state:

> Since material consumption is a component of life-style, and since life-style has been regarded by sociologists largely as a function of placement in the social stratification system, we as sociologists anticipated that social stratification would indeed make a contribution to the explanation of economic behavior.
>
> Our major finding is that stratification does not in fact make such a contribution. . . . In the middle of the occupation distribution . . . where the bulk of the labor force is concentrated, the distinction between blue-collar and white-collar life-styles as manifested through money spent on durable goods, housing, and automobiles, seems not to exist. . . . Other research dealing with a wider range of consumer behavior is consistent with our findings on the primacy of income.[3]

Some of this "other research" referred to in the above quotation has been reported in several recent articles. For instance, Myers and Mount found a general superiority of income over social class in segmenting the consumer market for a wide variety of goods and selected services. Their findings were based on the analysis of data collected via 6000 interviews with people from households in the greater Los Angeles area.[4]

Before social class is discarded as a tool for analysis by consumer analysts, it should be kept in mind that the studies of social class and behavior have not been exhaustive. Furthermore, the most recent research has found a relationship between social class and buying behavior even though income was determined

[3]D. R. Segal and M. Felson, "Social Stratification and Family Economic Behavior," in *Family Economic Behavior: Problems and Prospects,* E. B. Sheldon, ed. (Philadelphia: J. B. Lippincott Company, 1973), p. 159.
[4]J. H. Myers and J. F. Mount, "More on Social Class vs. Income as Correlated of Buyer Behavior," *Journal of Marketing,* 37 (April, 1973), pp. 71–73.

to be more closely related. Also, for some marketing problems the social class distinctions offer a richer differentiation among the segments. For example, the deliberation that takes place in the decision making process and the fundamental value considerations may be better understood through social class analysis.

Social Groups

Social groups have a massive impact on all human thought and action. Groups serve as the mechanism by which we learn the values, norms, and behavior patterns that are required by the society in which we live. Therefore, a meaningful analysis of consumer behavior must take into account the functioning of groups as a factor affecting consumption decisions. Furthermore, it is sometimes appropriate to focus on a group as a consuming unit rather than simply on individuals as consumers. For instance, many industrial purchasing decisions are made by groups rather than by individuals. Similarly, it is frequently necessary to consider the family as the consuming unit.

Social groups are formed and maintained in three basic ways.[5] The first is that of a collection of people occupying the same approximate space. Membership in this type of group does not include personal interaction; the people involved are largely unaffected by the presence of the others in this group environment. Examples of this type of group are the riders on a bus or the shoppers in a store. In most instances shoppers have no personal interaction and relatively little effect on each other. The second form is a collection of people who are basically different from one another but have some commonality. The shared characteristic may be demographic, psychological, or socioeconomic. For instance, a purchaser of a Rolls Royce and the purchaser of a Pinto would be considered to be members of the same group (automobile owners), and yet they may have little else in common. The third form that a group can take is a collection of people who interact regularly and communicate among

[5]S. Asch, *Social Psychology* (Englewood Cliffs, New Jersey: Prentice-Hall, Inc., 1957), Chapter 6.

themselves in such a manner that the group itself takes on a unique character. The notion of a group character suggests that the group is something more than the sum of its parts; it becomes an entity by itself. Fraternities, basketball teams, and bridge clubs are examples of this third type of group.

The first two forms are appropriately termed *social aggregates* because they do not possess the vital element of member interaction which is the distinguishing factor of a true group. This is not to say that aggregates should not be the object of study by consumer analysts. Members of aggregates may have common attitudes and behavioral patterns even though they do not purposefully meet and exchange information. However, the group that is characterized by regular contact and exchange of information is believed to have a greater impact on behavior than is the other type of group. Fortunately for consumer analysts, social psychologists have done extensive analyses of social groups that provide insight into why groups are formed, how they function, and how they influence member behavior.

TYPES OF SOCIAL GROUPS

Most people are members of several groups. Some of these groups have a greater effect on values and behavior than do others. For instance, church membership may have a greater impact on an individual's values and behavior than membership in a flying club. In order to permit some generalization about the relative influence of various groups, attempts have been made to distinguish among them. Such differentiation follows.

Primary groups are aggregates of individuals small enough and intimate enough so that all members can communicate regularly with each other on a face-to-face basis. These generally include the family, friendship groups, and small work groups. *Secondary groups* are all the other groups to which people belong and have significantly less face-to-face exchange, such as professional associations, university classes, and many community service organizations. Increased mobility and modern communications systems have somewhat blurred the distinction between primary and secondary groups. However, marketers maintain a strong interest in those primary groups characterized by considerable interaction among members because they tend to have a more pronounced and lasting effect on consumer behavior than do most secondary groups.

A second fundamental distinction frequently made among groups is based on structure and membership requirements. *Formal groups* are those characterized by an explicit structure, specified membership requirements, and typically, a specified goal. The membership requirements may be minimal, such as the payment of dues, and the structure limited, but the requirements exist. A ski club, for instance, may require the payment of dues and student status and may have only a president. Yet, such a group can have a considerable impact on the type of equipment that members purchase and the locations at which they ski. *Informal groups* that usually develop on the basis of proximity, common interests, or similar circumstances have no explicit structure or membership requirements. The groups exist solely for the satisfaction of the members. Both formal and informal groups affect consumer decision making; however, formal groups have been the object of more research because they are easier to identify.

Recognizing the fact that it is often more meaningful to study consumers as members of groups rather than as isolated individuals has strengthened the analyst's understanding of consumer behavior. The task is usually complex, though, because each consumer is a member of several groups and all may influence a person's behavior.

FUNCTIONS OF GROUPS

From a consumer behavior perspective groups perform three functions that are worth noting. First, groups have a substantial influence on the awareness and preference for behavioral alternatives and the resulting life-styles. Second, groups serve society as conformity-enforcing mechanisms. Third, groups are important forces in the establishment and maintenance of an individual's self-concept. Each of these functions will be developed in the following paragraphs.

Developing Behaviors, Life-styles, and Attitudes

Groups develop member awareness and preference for certain consumption behavior through the socialization process. The *socialization process* refers to the manner in which a new member learns the value system, the norms, and the required behavior patterns of the groups and organizations into which he or she is entering.[6] The socialization of children occurs through the influence of family and playmates in the neighborhood as well as through institutional groups such as the schools. For instance, the family influences the child in such diverse areas as what to eat for breakfast, how much television to watch, and whether drinking alcoholic beverages is to be restrained or not.

At one time it was thought that the childhood socialization experiences were the only really important ones, but in recent years it has been recognized that adult socialization can also occur and markedly influence decision making. Such learning and adaptation frequently occurs when adults change jobs, marry, or move to a new location.

Groups serve an important function in attitude formation and change. Individuals are not born with certain attitudes, nor are they developed in a vacuum.[7] Most attitudes are acquired by relating oneself to a variety of groups. Consumer analysts have established the existence of a relationship between an individual's attitudes and the attitudes of groups of which he is a member, but the precise nature or strength of the relationship has not been fully explored. The task of studying the nature of this relationship is complicated by the fact that consumers are members of many groups and differentially accept influences of each.

Compliance to Group Norms

Groups serve a normative function in that they cause members to comply with certain norms, that is, to behave in similar pat-

[6]E. H. Schein, "Organization Socialization and the Profession of Management," in *Organizational Psychology,* D. A. Kolb, I. M. Rubin, and J. M. McIntyre, eds., (Englewood Cliffs, New Jersey: Prentice-Hall, Inc., 1971), p. 3.

[7]T. M. Newcomb, "Attitude Development as a Function of Reference Groups: The Bennington Study," in *Readings in Social Psychology,* E. E. Maccoby, T. M. Newcomb, and E. L. Hartley, eds., (New York: Holt, Rinehart and Winston, Inc., 1958), pp. 265–275.

terns. Marketing analysts are particularly interested in the normative function of groups because it is of assistance in determining whether or not a product will be accepted by a large enough group to make it a successful venture.

Norms Defined. Norms are statements or beliefs of the majority of group members that define what the activities of group members should be. These may be said to exist when the individuals involved agree, either explicitly or implicitly, that all members will regularly behave in a certain manner. The behavior prescribed may be consequential, such as renouncing material wealth as in the case of some religious groups, or insignificant, such as not wearing a necktie.

When a new member wishes to join a group, that person receives pressure to conform to the group's standards. Although a group member may deviate from some norms while accepting others, he or she will find that conforming is often rewarded by the rest of the group, while nonconformity results in a withholding of the rewards or even in sanctions. Thus, norms become stable expectations held by a consensus of the group concerning the behavioral rules for individual members.

Why People Conform to Norms. Once it has been established that members do conform to the norms of groups, it is necessary to consider why such conformity occurs. Homans' theory of social exchange is based on the premise that the behavior of one individual responding to another is more or less reinforcing or punishing to the behavior of that individual.[8] If, for example, you were invited to join another person on a shopping trip, there will be *rewards* (companionship, esteem accorded by the invitation, etc.), but there may also be *costs* (time lost, giving up association with others, etc.). The nature of interactions with another individual or group will be determined by a person's perception of the profit derived from the interaction. Homans defines this in familiar economic terms:

Profit = Rewards – Costs

[8]G. Homans, *Social Behavior: Its Elementary Forms* (New York: Harcourt, Brace, Jovanovich Inc., 1961), Chapters 3 and 4.

Based on this premise, individuals can be seen as arranging their social relations so as to maximize total profit. Thus, the groups an individual chooses to belong to and the degree to which there is adherence to the norms of that group are both based upon the net profit figure and not on rewards or costs alone. This view of conforming to norms provides the consumer analyst with a set of tools (concepts) to understand the formation of the group, the formation of group norms, and the extent of influence that results.

Conformity to Group Norms.   A group dimension of particular interest to marketing analysts is the tendency of individuals to conform to group norms. Asch demonstrated the group pressure phenomenon in a situation where two sets of individuals were asked if there was a difference in the length of two lines. In a normal setting there was no difficulty in correctly getting the answer that the lines were of equal length. But when wrong answers were deliberately given by three cooperating students, 37 percent of the other respondents also gave the wrong answer.[9]

The extent to which an individual conforms to a group's standards is a function of several variables. For instance, the study described above suggests that the pressure to conform increased as the number of agreeing individuals increased, but only up to a point. That is, increasing the number of agreeing individuals does not create a progressively greater impact.

The stability and cohesiveness of a group also affects the extent to which individuals accomodate the requirements. For instance, Festinger demonstrated that the more stable and cohesive a group is, the more likely it is to have conformity power over deviant members.[10]

In an experimental setting, Venkatesan demonstrated the effect of group pressure on the decision making process of its

[9]S. E. Asch, "Effects of Group Pressure Upon the Modification and Distortion of Judgments," in *Consumer Behavior,* H. H. Kassarjian and T. S. Robertson, eds., (Glenview, Illinois: Scott, Foresman and Company, 1973), pp. 215–324.

[10]L. Festinger, "Informal Social Communication," *Psychological Review,* 57, (1950), pp. 271–292.

members.[11] It was shown that when the superiority of one product among alternatives was not obvious, individuals tended to choose the preference of the majority.

Groups and the Self-Concept

The way individuals perceive themselves has great relevance for marketing managers. People will attempt to purchase items that fit the interpretation they have of themselves or that will improve their self-concept.

This notion of self-concept involves the attitudes and perceptions one uses to define his or her personhood. Comb and Snygg enlarge on this: "By concepts of self we mean those more or less discrete perceptions of self which the individual regards as part, or characteristic of his being. They include all perceptions the individual has differentiated as descriptive of the self he calls I or me."[12]

The symbols that people use to form and express their self-concept include the goods and services they buy and the way they use them. It is helpful at times to see these consumption patterns as being consistent with some internalized view that may be a combination of what one actually perceives him or herself to be and what he or she is striving to be.

The self-concept of an individual is also related to how that person believes others see him. The life-style adopted by a man or woman includes the selection and use of items in a manner that will reflect his or her perceived status among others.

The importance of the self-concept to marketing analysts is illustrated in Figure 5.2. Assume that an individual *A* perceives himself as being thrifty, economical, and practical. He may purchase a Volkswagen as a symbol of these qualities, thereby achieving internal self-enhancement. The audience *B* may include peers, family, and significant others. The doubleheaded arrows b and c in Figure 5.2 indicate that the Volkswagen is attributed meaning by *A* and that the audience *B* is also attribut-

[11]M. Venkatesan, "Experimental Study of Consumer Behavior Conformity and Independence," *Journal of Marketing Research,* 3 (November, 1966), pp. 384–387.

[12]A. W. Combs and D. Snygg, *Individual Behavior: A Perceptual Approach to Behavior,* rev. ed. (New York: Harper & Row, 1959), p. 10.

FIGURE 5.2.
Relationship of the Consumption of Goods as
Symbols to Self Concept.

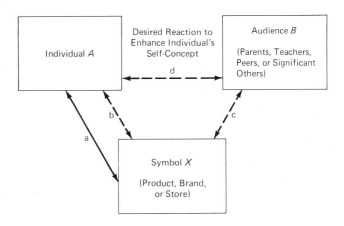

Source: E. L. Grubb and H. L. Grathwohl, "Consumer Self-Concept, Symbolism and Market Behavior: A Theoretical Approach," *Journal of Marketing,* 31 (October, 1967), p. 25. Reprinted from the *Journal of Marketing* published by the American Marketing Association.

ing meaning to it. If the Volkswagen *X* has a meaning common to *A* and *B,* communication of self has occurred, and the reaction of *B* will provide self-enhancement to individual *A.* Empirical support for the process of establishing congruence of self-concept and brand/store choice now permits marketing analysts to be concerned with the development of marketing strategies from such a base. The clothing store that wants to focus on the avante-garde type customer must offer a product line and store design that enhances that self-concept for customers.

REFERENCE GROUP

Although the impact of the group has long been recognized, confidence in the ability of group theory to explain consumer attitudes and behavior has been shaken by the reporting of contradictory evidence. For instance, members of a particular group may have similar preferences for automobiles but not for clothing. Confidence in the basic force, however, has been renewed by the development of reference-group theory. Reference-group theory developed as a result of the recognition that not all groups to which an individual belongs exert the same influence or hold the same relevance for him. In fact, some groups of which the person is not even a member may be of considerable influence.

Functions of Reference Groups

Reference groups perform a normative and a comparative function.[13] The *normative function* refers to a group having a consensus of opinion with which the individual agrees and in which the person seeks to gain or maintain acceptance. That is, such reference groups serve as a source of individual norms, attitudes, and values. The *comparative function* refers to the means by which the individual uses a group to establish his or her frame of reference for value formation and decision making. In this sense, the group itself serves as an actual standard. These two forms of influence, that is, the normative function and the use of the group as a frame of reference for the individual are the most meaningful for consumer analysts. These reference groups may differ greatly in size, composition, structure, and purpose, but their most important characteristic is the degree of influence they have over the consumer.

A particularly appealing dimension of reference group theory is the fact that it incorporates both membership and nonmembership groups. Consumers may select as a reference group a nonmembership group to which they aspire to belong and begin to conform to the perceived norms. For instance, if one wishes to join a tennis club there may be certain kinds of equipment that are considered appropriate and, therefore, necessary. Consumers may even use as a reference a group to which they can never belong. That is, even when there is no possibility of attaining membership, a consumer may adopt those attitudes and behaviors of a group that are reasonably consonant with the realities

[13]H. H. Kelly, "Two Functions of Reference Groups," in *Readings in Social Psychology*, G. E. Swanson, T. M. Newcomb, and E. L. Hartley, eds., (New York: Holt, Rinehart & Winston, 1952), pp. 410–414.

of his own personal world. The fact that this does occur is one basis for having Bob Griese advertise men's clothing or Billie Jean King endorse tennis rackets.

MARKETING ANALYSIS OF REFERENCE GROUP INFLUENCE

Various marketing analysts have described the importance of reference group influences on consumer behavior, but researchers have given only limited empirical attention to the area. The research that has been done can be placed into two categories: (1) studies establishing that reference groups do influence consumption decisions and (2) studies to determine the consumption situations affected by reference groups.

The fact that reference groups influence consumption decisions has been demonstrated in a number of studies. One of these studies was an experiment that simulated the purchase of bread. Housewives were required to choose a loaf of bread from four alternatives identified only by a letter on the wrapper. The study demonstrated that the preferences formed for each "brand" as represented by a different letter of the alphabet as well as the identifiable variation in preferences could be attributed to the influence of the consumer's reference group.[14]

The amount and nature of reference group influence on individual consumption decisions appears to be affected by the product category involved and the characteristics of the group. The following two sections discuss the nature of these two dimensions.

Product Categories.   Several studies have shown that the amount of reference group influence upon consumption is related to the type of product involved. Using this perspective, Bourne differentiated among products subject to strong and weak group influences. The results of Bourne's analysis are summarized in Table 5.1. The Product +, Brand + category refers to those products that have significant specifications among friend-

[14]J. E. Stafford, "Effects of Group Influence on Consumer Brand Preferences," *Journal of Marketing,* 3 (February, 1966), pp. 68–75.

TABLE 5.1
Reference Group Influence on Product Decisions

	Weak⁻	Strong⁺	
Strong⁺	Clothing Furniture Magazines Refrigerator (type) Toilet soap	Cars Cigarettes Beer (prem. vs. reg.) Drugs	+
Weak⁻	Soap Canned peaches Laundry soap Refrigerator (brand) Radios	Air conditioners Instant coffee TV (black and white)	−

Brand or Type

−   Product   +

Source: Foundation for Research on Human Behavior, *Group Influence in Marketing and Public Relations* (Ann Arbor, Michigan: The Foundation, 1956), p. 8. Reprinted by permission of the publisher.

ship groups. Products such as automobiles, cigarettes, beer, and drugs are subject to strong norms that affect specific brands selected as well as the product purchased. Conversely, the Product–, Brand – category includes items such as soap, canned fruit, and radios which are not subject to the influence of reference groups with respect to either the product or the brand purchased.

Bourne's analysis established four categories dealing with the varying effects of reference groups on consumer behavior:

1. Product + , Brand + . Reference groups influence whether or not the product itself is purchased and, if it is purchased, what brand is selected (automobiles, cigarettes).
2. Product + , Brand – . Reference groups influence whether or not the product is purchased but not which brand is selected (instant coffee, air conditioners).

3. Product − , Brand + . Reference groups do not influence the purchase of the product but do influence the brand selected if a purchase is to be made (clothing, furniture).
4. Product − , Brand − . Reference groups generally have no influence on either the purchase of the product or the brand selected (soap, canned fruit).

The research by Bourne and others suggests that reference group influence is strong when a product is a conspicious expression of personal tastes, that is, the ability of a product to attract attention significantly contributes to whether or not it is susceptible to reference group influence. Products are conspicuous when they are noticed and identified by others.[15] Reference groups also tend to have a particularly pronounced influence when the consumer has little knowledge about a product.

Group Characteristics.   The amount of reference group influence is determined partially by the characteristics of the group. Specifically, some studies have demonstrated that the more cohesive the group is, the greater the group influence is likely to be on individual choices. Cohesiveness appears to have its most important function in providing an agreeable environment in which informal leaders can effectively operate.[16] More importantly, it has been concluded that the higher the degree of brand loyalty exhibited by the group leader, the more likely the other members are to prefer the same brand and the more likely they are to become brand loyal.

When the marketing strategist attempts to apply the reference group concept, two problems must be overcome. First, it must be determined if the purchase of the product and its brand is influenced by reference groups. Second, if the reference group concept is relevant, it must be determined which reference groups will have an influence. The concept of reference groups is of obvious significance in understanding consumer behavior. However, the attempts so far to apply the concept to marketing problems have been less than totally productive.

[15]Foundation for Research on Human Behavior, *Group Influence in Marketing and Public Relations* (Ann Arbor, Michigan: The Foundation, 1956), p. 10.
[16]J. E. Stafford, pp. 68–75.

Summary

Social classes are relatively permanent and homogeneous divisions in a society into which individuals or families sharing similar values, life-styles, interests, and behavior can be categorized. The most common class distribution in the United States is Warner's six-class system which ranges from an upper upper class to a lower lower class. From a marketing perspective, the following three classes are the most important: upper middle class, lower middle class, and the upper lower class. A helpful method for differentiating social classes makes use of a member's occupation, personal performance, personal interactions, possessions, and value orientation. An objective method for measuring social class most frequently uses the following variables: occupation, income, education, size and type of residence, ownership of personal possessions, and organizational affiliations. Although the research into social class and consumer behavior has not been exhaustive, in general, social class has not been an effective means of explaining consumer behavior over and above the effect of income.

Social groups can be classified as primary or secondary and formal or informal. Primary groups have more relative influence over its members than do secondary groups. Formal groups have explicit structures, membership requirements, and specified goals, while informal groups do not. Groups perform three significant consumer behavior functions. First, they have a substantial influence on the awareness and preference for behavioral alternatives and their resulting life-styles. Second, groups serve a normative function by causing members to comply with certain norms. Third, groups are important forces in the establishment and maintenance of an individual's self-concept.

Reference groups perform normative functions by serving as a source of individual norms, attitudes, and values. They also perform comparative functions when individuals use a group to establish their frame of reference for value formation and decision making.

The amount and nature of the influence that reference groups have on consumer behavior is determined by product category and group characteristics. Product categories that have a strong influence are those products that are readily noticed and identified by others and those about which the consumer has little knowledge. Group characteristics tend to have significant influence on consumer behavior when the group is a cohesive one and when the group leader exhibits a high degree of brand loyalty.

QUESTIONS AND ISSUES FOR DISCUSSION

1. What is the relationship between social class and income? Is income a better indicator of a person's potential to consume than is social class?
2. Some would contend that although a social class structure was present in the United States a hundred years ago, it hardly exists in the 1970's and is certainly of little importance. Do you agree?
3. A large manufacturer of recreational equipment is interested in increasing his penetration in existing markets and expanding to new markets. Why would information on social class be of assistance to this firm?
4. The owner of a retail clothing store that has an upper middle class clientele has requested your assistance in the development of a new promotional campaign. What type of campaign would you recommend?
5. "Formal groups have a good deal of influence on my parents' values and behavior but not on mine. I'm still in college and I only belong to a couple of formal groups. Besides, people of my generation are less influenced by groups of any kind." Discuss.
6. Distinguish between primary groups, formal groups, and reference groups. Which is of greatest interest to the marketing analyst?
7. What is a group norm and why do members comply with these norms? Identify a group you belong to and name at least three norms of that group.
8. Identify three reference groups that are important to you. Are these the same three you would have named five years ago? Are the three reference groups of equal influence on your values and behavior?

9. Consider the following three decisions: (1) the purchase of a bicycle, (2) the purchase of a major clothing item, and (3) the purchase of a gift to be presented to a former teacher at her retirement dinner. What reference groups would be important in making these decisions? Were the same reference groups considered in all three instances?

10. "The self-concept is interesting and, perhaps, relevant to certain types of purchases (automobiles, clothes), but the concept is of no value to the producers of soft drinks, television sets, motorcycles, and in fact, most product purchases." Discuss. Do your comments also hold true for the purchase of services?

SITUATIONAL PROBLEMS

Case 1

The Vandale Furniture Company has produced fine quality furniture and distributed it throughout the Midwest since 1909. The furniture is sold through a limited number of carefully selected furniture and department stores. Mr. Bob Vandale, son of the founder, personally inspects each retail outlet twice a year to make certain they are providing the type of service commensurate with Vandale's quality image. The Vandale executives, somewhat concerned about the growth potential in their market, are currently considering two alternative growth strategies.

ALTERNATIVE 1: Expand the number of quality-oriented retail outlets that sell Vandale furniture.

ALTERNATIVE 2: Produce a lower quality product line and distribute it through discount type outlets.

What assistance can the consumer analyst offer as a result of studying the variation in consumption patterns among the different social classes?

If the Vandale management selects Alternative 2, should the Vandale name be used and should the existing distribution outlets be used?

Case 2

Hammond-Lee Corporation produces a complete line of women's clothing which is sold throughout the eastern states. The company has traditionally focused on producing quality clothing for the "mature woman." Eighteen months ago the company introduced a collection of leisure outfits, pantsuits, and dresses designed for the youthful woman. This line was distributed through the same retail outlets, and Hammond-Lee's high quality and tasteful fashion were stressed in promotional efforts. The success of this line has been disappointing, and management feels that a significant increase in sales must occur in the next 12 months or the line should be discontinued.

What suggestions can be made to the Hammond-Lee Corporation that would increase their current sales of the new product line?

OUTLINE

The Family in Consumer Behavior

There has been a good deal of talk regarding the diminishing importance of the American family and speculation as to what social forms will replace it. Despite these conjectures, there is substantial evidence that the traditional family unit will continue to be the favored living arrangement in the future.[1]

In studying the family as it relates to consumer behavior at least two perspectives may be used. First, the family may be viewed as an agent that influences the behavior of its individual members. This involves an awareness of the effect that various beliefs, life-styles, socioeconomic status, and patterns of interaction among members have on an individual member's market behavior. The family is, therefore, seen as a reference group.

Because of the nature of man, a young person must be cared for and nurtured both physically and psychologically; most often this is handled in a family environment. Parsons and Bales contend that no society has found an effective substitute arrangement for the family.[2] Even in the kibbutz where a community-oriented structure exists, the basic socialization responsibilities remain with the parents, that is, the family continues to exist as a distinct unit. Because the socialization process begins at birth, the family's influence on the behavior of the individual member can be substantial.

The second perspective focuses on the family as a unique entity. The family is viewed as a unit that has specific identifiable characteristics and an existence beyond a simple summation of the behavior or outlook of its individual members. The uniqueness of the consumption patterns of the family entity is often a product of the intimacy of shared concerns and priorities, and these result in behavioral patterns worthy of special study.

These two perspectives—the family as an influencing agent and the family as a unique consuming unit—will form the basis for the discussion found in this chapter. The importance of each of these two perspectives with respect to their impact on con-

[1]B. J. Wattenberg, "The Forming-Families: The Spark in the Tinder, 1975–1985," in *1974 Combined Proceedings: New Marketing for Social and Economic Progress and Marketing's Contributions to the Firm and to the Society,* R. C. Curhan, ed., (Chicago: American Marketing Association, 1975), p. 53.
[2]T. Parsons and R. F. Bales, *Family: Socialization and Interaction Process* (New York: The Free Press, 1955).

sumer behavior can be illustrated with the following two brief situations.

SITUATION 1: The effect of family influence on individual consumer behavior involving product purchased.

Bill Scott never buys retreaded tires. He remembers a very serious accident that occurred in the family car when he was a youngster because the tread separated from the tire while driving on the highway. Not only was this situation still clear in his mind, but his father discussed it with him several times after it happened.

SITUATION 2: The family functioning as a consuming unit involving brand preferences.

Several members of the Howard family prefer Coke and Pepsi over private brands. However, the family as a whole has decided that purchasing private brands will permit them to continue to enjoy soft drinks at a lower price.

Before proceeding further, it is essential that several alternative configurations of the family be identified and defined. These include the nuclear family, extended family, family of orientation, family of procreation, and the household.

Family Forms

There are important variations in what have been called families or family groups that must be differentiated for increased clarity and understood as offering overlapping circles of influence. What follows is not an attempt to be exhaustive, but to deal with the more common forms that the family takes.

First, the term *family* generally refers to a group of people who are related by blood, marriage, or legal adoption. Individuals who simply live together in an apartment or dormitory as roommates are not considered a family in the customary use of the term. This general definition does not sufficiently delineate the family entity so as to permit identification of the influences and interactions that are important to the consumer analyst. Considerable clarification can be achieved by distinguishing among the following: the nuclear family, the extended family, the family of orientation, and the family of procreation. It will also be helpful to differentiate between a family and a household.

Nuclear family refers to the immediate kin group of father and/or mother and their offspring or adopted children who ordinarily live together. A temporary separation of a member does not dissolve this kinship. For example, a son or daughter away at college is still part of the nuclear family. The members of a nuclear family have considerable face-to-face contact on a regular basis. This living together and the intimate sharing that takes place over time are major characteristics of the nuclear family. It is also the family grouping that has been studied the most.

The *extended family* includes the nuclear family plus other relatives, such as grandparents, uncles, aunts, cousins, and in-laws. As a focus of attention in terms of their possible influence on the family members' behaviors or the behavior of the family unit, there is a practical limit as to who is included for study. The extent to which a relative is considered a part of the extended family is essentially determined by the regularity and intimacy of the interaction with the family members.

The family that one is born into or adopted into is called the *family of orientation.* This family group typically initiates the enculturation process that continues throughout life. The interpretation of family roles, various help patterns (exchange of money, advice, gifts, and services), and fundamental values are identified and passed on to offspring by this family. The family of orientation essentially begins with the nuclear family but ordinarily is expanded over time and becomes the extended family.

The *family of procreation* is established when one marries, that is, this represents the formation of a new family unit capable of existence as a separate entity.

All families are households; however, not all households are families. The term *household* refers to a living unit or entity for consumption purposes, and in the United States about 80 percent of these units are families. A person living alone represents a separate, fully functioning living unit and is also considered a household. Nevertheless, a single person does not constitute a family because the term *family* is used to refer to at least two related people. Nor would two single girls living together in an apartment be referred to as a family although they do constitute a household.

The purpose of this chapter is to concentrate on families. Generally, they are more permanent, demonstrate greater interdependency among members, and have historically assumed more significant roles in society than have nonfamily households. Furthermore, the nuclear family in particular is the optimum unit of study because of the following reasons:[3]

1. The family is the accumulating unit, the inventory of acquisitions over time being a nuclear family inventory. The items accumulated include various possessions such as cooking utensils, furniture, books, an automobile, and usually some form of real estate.
2. The nuclear family is typically the decision-making unit in asset accumulation and consumption.
3. The nuclear family is more accessible for study than are its competitors and more easily definable for purposes of study than is the household, for example, which may include lodgers who have little part in family acquisition.

Although these points essentially draw attention to the family as a consuming unit, it is also important to recognize the impact of the family as a socializing influence on its members. Even though these two dimensions of the family are interrelated, it is helpful to separate them for discussion. Therefore, the next section will give specific attention to family influences on its members.

Family Influences on Individual Members

The family shapes its members' personality characteristics, attitudes, and evaluative criteria, that is, the way its members look at the world and how they relate to it. To a large extent this influence is informal and exerted on the individual over an extended period of time. Part of this influence includes the acquiring

[3]R. Hill and D. M. Klein, "Understanding Family Consumption: Common Ground for Integrating Uncommon Disciplinary Perspective," in *Family Economic Behavior: Problems and Prospects,* E. B. Sheldon, ed., (Philadelphia: J. B. Lippincott Company, 1973), p. 4.

of a consumer outlook. As Boyd and Levy have contended, "... people are born with apparently insatiable needs and desires. From their first moments they are learning what specific things to consume and the ways to consume them, and, quite as important, what not to consume."[4]

In describing similar circumstances, Riesman and Roseborough stated that what children learn from their parents is a kind of basic set of domestic arrangements, for instance, a view of furniture as specific functional items to acquire rather than as a stylistic concept and, consequently, the need for home furnishings such as ranges, refrigerators, and television sets. The same individuals are likely to learn styles and moods of consumption from their peers.[5]

The amount of influence the family has will vary at different periods of its members' lives. For example, a very young child may have relatively little contact outside its immediate family environment until the age of four or five years. Typically, the number of socializing agents increases substantially upon entering school with the regular nonfamily contact with teachers and schoolmates.

Figure 6.1 illustrates the relations among larger social systems, the family, and the individual. It can be noted that the nuclear family plays two important roles. First, the interaction among family members helps shape individual personalities, evaluative criteria, and attitudes. Second, the nuclear family often performs a mediating or interpretation function in exchanges among members, particularly as these relate to resolving differences concerning the needs of the family as a whole. These two functions are stimuli or inputs into the individual's central control unit and are subject to the complex processes of exposure, attention, comprehension, and retention. As such, they have varying degrees of influence on an individual's psychological make-up.

[4]H. W. Boyd, Jr. and S. J. Levy, *Promotion: A Behavioral View* (Englewood Cliffs, New Jersey: Prentice-Hall, Inc., 1967), pp. 48–49.

[5]D. Riesman and H. Roseborough, "Careers and Consumer Behavior," in *Consumer Behavior: The Life Cycle and Consumer Behavior, Vol. II*, L. Clark, ed. (New York: New York University Press, 1955), p. 3.

FIGURE 6.1.
**Family Influences on Individual Personality Characteristics,
Attitudes, and Evaluative Criteria.**

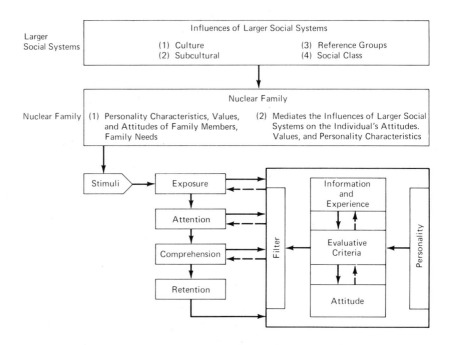

Source: J. F. Engel, D. T. Kollat, and R. D. Blackwell, *Consumer Behavior,* 2nd ed. (New York: Holt, Rinehart and Winston, Inc., 1973), p. 192. Prprinted by permission of the publisher.

One example of these family influences in action is the impact that a family's social class can have on its life-style and subsequently on its members' buying behaviors. The differences that arise from social class membership basically are reflected in variations in values, interpersonal attitudes, self-perceptions and daily life routines.[6] A brief reference to each of these four factors

[6]T. S. Robertson, *Consumer Behavior* (Glenview, Illinois: Scott, Foresman and Company, 1970), p. 122.

will illustrate their possible effect on individual family member behavior and some marketing implications.

VALUES

Values are fundamental principles to which individuals subscribe; these can vary across social classes. For example, some research suggests that people from low socioeconomic classes value personal advancement and self-sufficiency less than do middle class people. This difference can have a significant impact on an individual family member's personal desire for education, his motivation while in an educational environment, and even his attitude toward providing financial support for education as a taxpayer. Furthermore, any such influence on educational attainment may have a life-long effect on an individual's market behavior. For example, the better educated are generally more astute shoppers. They are also more likely to show an interest in the arts, the public park system, and sports like golf and pleasure boating.

The value placed on time as a scarce resource also varies from one social class to another. The middle class has generally placed the most value on the careful planning and budgeting of their time. This is consistent with their high achievement orientation. The high valuation of time also affects consumer behavior. For instance, the willingness to engage in prepurchase search for information, the specific sources used, as well as one's interest in labor-saving products are influenced by the perceived value of a person's time.

INTERPERSONAL ATTITUDES

Interpersonal attitudes refer to the predisposition of family members toward interactions among themselves as well as toward those outside the family. Differences in interpersonal attitudes do exist across social classes and shape individual family member behavior. For instance, middle class husbands and wives are more likely to jointly pursue various family functions such as decision making in child rearing, family budgeting, and in expenditures for major purchases than those in lower class families. As a result, a middle class woman may be more apt to postpone a purchase decision until she has obtained her husband's views than is a woman from a lower socieconomic class.

Also, middle class families generally relate socially to more people than do lower class families. This includes having more nonfamily members into the home for meals, entertainment, and socializing. This kind of interpersonal interaction has a long-term effect on children and a more immediate impact on other members' market activities. Middle class individuals are more likely to seek information from others when making a major purchase decision than are individuals from lower social classes.[7] This latter behavioral pattern may substantially alter the information base from which one operates in his prepurchase deliberation.

SELF-PERCEPTION

Levy found that the way one thinks of or perceives himself also varies by social class.[8] For instance, lower class women understand their own bodies less well and have more taboos about them than do middle class women. Lower class women were also found to have more traditional views toward interpersonal relations. One's masculinity and physical strength were found to be of more concern to the lower class male then they were to middle class males.

Lower class people generally have less self-confidence and feel less in control of their own destiny.[9] Consequently, they are more likely to believe that if they get ahead, it is the result of chance or luck rather than the result of personal effort. These views are shared among family members and are passed on from one generation to the next. Their influence on family members' market behavior can take on many forms. For example, such a

[7]C. E. Block, "Prepurchase Search Behavior of Low-Income Households," *Journal of Retailing,* 48 (Spring, 1972), pp. 3–15.

[8]S. J. Levy, "Social Class and Consumer Behavior" in *On Knowing the Consumer,* J. W. Newman, ed. (New York: John Wiley and Sons, Inc., 1966), pp. 150–152.

[9]E. Herzog, *About the Poor: Some Facts and Some Fictions* (Washington, D.C.: U.S. Department of Health, Education, and Welfare, Social and Rehabilitation Service, 1967), pp. 40–43.

prevailing family view may lead to a discouragement of a member's efforts for individual self-improvement through technical training or enrollment in a self-development course such as that offered through adult education programs. It may also encourage a greater interest in gambling such as that which is available through state-sponsored lotteries.

DAILY LIFE ROUTINE

Each family develops its own routine to cope with the daily demands placed upon it. In fact, an interesting exercise for each of us is to attempt to set down in some detail the way our family handles the responsibilities of a typical day.

In most families this routine varies between weekdays and the weekend and, to some extent, by season. The record of such a routine would at least include the time when family members arise; how meals are prepared and eaten (e.g., in some families the meals are prepared jointly while more typically this responsibility falls upon one member—the wife); when members leave for work, school, other regular activities; how much time is spent apart, together, and in what activities; and how the family closes the day.

The word "routine" is used to imply a regular pattern. The awareness of this regular pattern continues over time and, coupled with what is known about learning theory, strongly suggests that the daily family life routine can have an important impact on the individual family member's behavior. The strong interest of other family members in particular sports, for example, may shape one's interests also. Furthermore, what food is served at home and how it is served affects younger members' eating patterns outside the home and their meal preparation and entertainment style when they establish their own family later in life.

CONCLUDING COMMENT

As an individual interacts with other family members he simultaneously influences these individuals as he is being influenced by them. Furthermore, no other single group or individual ordinarily has as many opportunities for shaping a person's behavior as does his or her family. As mentioned earlier, the nuclear family is a primary group with frequent face-to-face contact among its members. It also shares a common pool of financial resources as well as consumption needs. Therefore, family members tend to be more alike in their thinking and behavioral patterns than they would be if they were not in the same family.

The Family as a Buying and Consuming Entity

As pointed out in the introduction to this chapter, the family, particularly the nuclear family, is a very significant economic and social unit in most societies. Personal goals and expectations are brought together, shared, and shaped by family members in such a way that the family itself takes on a set of characteristics that reflect those of its members but which, nevertheless, are unique to it. Decisions regarding the purchase and use of goods and services are made by families through the interaction of its members. Consequently, it can be said that family decision making, similar to that of individuals who act on their own behalf, can be characterized by a decision-process model.

Families and family behavior have been studied extensively by social scientists in a number of disciplines including sociology, social psychology, anthropology, home economics, consumer psychology, economics, and marketing. However, as Ferber pointed out at a recent symposium focusing on the family, relatively little attention has been given to bringing together the various dimensions of consumer behavior within the framework of the family to provide a more realistic explanation of economic behavior.[10]

ALTERNATIVE MODELS

Ferber has developed what he calls a simplified decision-making framework with specific attention given to family saving and spending.[11] This is shown in Figure 6.2. The basis for the frame-

[10]R. Ferber, "Family Decision Making and Economic Behavior" in *Family Economic Behavior: Problems and Prospects,* E. B. Sheldon, ed. (Philadelphia: J. B. Lippincott Company, 1973), p. 29.
[11]R. Ferber, pp. 30–38.

FIGURE 6.2.
Interrelation of Saving and Spending Decisions.

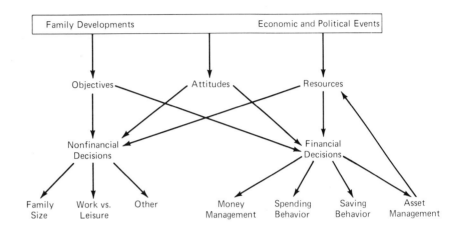

Source: R. Ferber, "Family Decision Making and Economic Behavior" in *Family Economic Behavior: Problems and Prospects*, E. B. Sheldon, ed., (Philadelphia: J. B. Lippincott Company, 1973), p. 31. Reprinted by permission of the publisher.

work is the division of family economic decisions into two types —financial and nonfinancial. Those decisions in the financial grouping include decisions dealing with money management, savings, spending, and asset management. Because this framework was used primarily to discuss financial decisions, all other decisions that a family may make are grouped together under what is called nonfinancial.

One can quickly note in Ferber's framework that both financial and nonfinancial decisions are affected by the available financial resources of the family, by the objectives or goals of the family, and by the attitudes of the family members. The family's objectives and attitudes relate to a wide variety of topics and, therefore, encompass both the material and the nonmaterial goals of the family in both the short and long run. Attitudes include expectations and outlooks of the different family members on economic and related issues as well as their system of preferences and value judgements concerning alternative types of economic behavior.

This framework takes note of the fact that family decisions in some instances are dominated by influences that are external and not under the family's control. In particular, these include economic and political events in the community in which the family lives and personal experiences of the individual family members such as births, deaths, marriages, and accidents.

A number of more detailed models of family decision making have been developed. One of the most recent contributions has been made by Sheth. He offers a comprehensive model of family decision making in consumer behavior. The model presented in Figure 6.3 is a representation of his attempt to specify the nature of family decision making in consumer behavior and to bring together the findings of various social scientists in a comprehensive representation. An overview of Sheth's theory is presented here, but the details may be found in *Models of Buyer Behavior: Conceptual, Quantitative, and Empirical.*[12]

In viewing the Sheth model, it can be noted at the far right that the consumption of a family is classified as that of (1) the individual members, (2) the family as a whole, and, (3) the household unit. Examples of individual member's consumption include their use of shaving cream, which may just be used by the father (husband), nail polish by the mother (wife), and comic books or toys by the child (children). However, various food items and hand soap, for example, are consumed by everyone in the family. Furthermore, certain goods and services (e.g., utilities such as water, electricity, and natural gas) as well as such items as paint, wallpaper, and the living room furniture are used by the family indirectly in the process of living together in the same residence. The latter fit into Sheth's third category of consumption. This approach to classifying family consumption points out that the demand for goods and services may be collective and direct, collective and indirect, or individual.

In Sheth's theory, as represented by the model shown, family consumption is considered to follow family buying decisions. This

---

[12]J. N. Sheth, *Models of Buyer Behavior: Conceptual, Quantitative, and Empirical* (New York: Harper & Row, Publishers, 1974), pp. 18–33.

FIGURE 6.3.
A Theory of Family Buying Decisions.

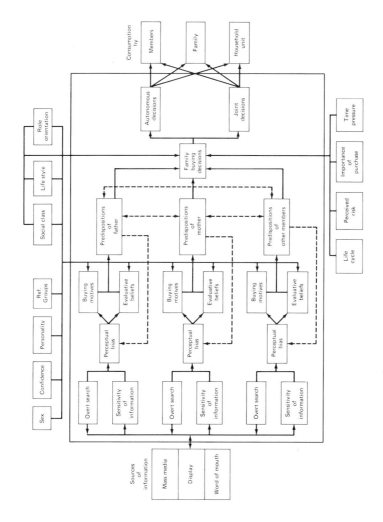

Source: J. N. Sheth, *Models of Buyer Behavior: Conceptual, Quantitative, and Empirical* (New York: Harper & Row, Publishers, 1974), pp. 22–23. Reprinted by permission of publisher.

137

indicates that generally gifts, rentals, and acquisitions by means other than buying are not explicitly taken into account. This seems appropriate because these latter forms represent a small proportion of the goods and services consumed by most families.

Family buying decisions are identified as either autonomous—made by a single member—or joint—made by at least two members of the family. The theory as a whole has four major subsections that can be observed in the model. These are listed below without detailed explanations.

1. Individual members of the family, their predispositions, and the underlying buying motives and evaluative beliefs about products and brands
2. Determinants of the motives and beliefs of the individual members that are both external and internal
3. Determinants of autonomous versus joint family decision making
4. The process of joint decision making, with consequent inter-member conflict and its resolution.

Although the Ferber and Sheth models differ substantially, they nevertheless each draw attention to the importance of focusing on the family as a unique consuming unit. The next section specifically takes note of the fact that families change over time, that is, that the family is a dynamic entity.

THE FAMILY AS A DYNAMIC ENTITY

For many reasons family composition changes over time, and this may substantially alter the family needs, its decision-making process, and its market behavior (where it shops and what it buys). One way of viewing these changes that has proven helpful is through what has been called the *family life cycle.* A common representation of this follows below. It should be noted, however, that in this categorization there are three listings that are included here as a representation of the usual format although they are not families but nonfamily households. Furthermore, these three nonfamily households represent pre- and postfamily entities.

1. Bachelor State: young single people not living at home (nonfamily household)

2. Newly Married Couples: young with no children
3. Full Nest I: young married couples with youngest child under six
4. Full Nest II: young married couples with youngest child six or over
5. Full Nest III: older married couples with dependent children
6. Empty Nest I: older married couples, no children living with them, household head in labor force
7. Empty Nest II: older married couples, no children living at home, household head retired
8. Solitary survivor in labor force (nonfamily household)
9. Solitary survivor, retired (nonfamily household)

This scheme takes note of the fact that changes in family composition are likely to be more important in terms of market behavior than one's age or simply the aging process of the family members. To illustrate the importance of family composition to consumer behavior, a brief summary is presented of the major dimensions of four of the above listed stages in the life cycle and some of their marketing implications.

Bachelor Stage
Although earnings are low in relation to what they will be later in one's career, this income is subject to few rigid demands; so consumers in this stage have substantial discretion over how they spend their money. Part of this income is typically used to purchase a car and basic household equipment. Those at this stage also tend to be more fashion- and recreation-oriented, spending a substantial proportion of their income on clothing, entertainment, food away from home, vacations, leisure time pursuits, and other products and services involved in the mating game.

Newly Married Couples
Newly married couples without children are usually better off financially than they have been in the past or will be in the near future because both husband and wife are frequently employed. To illustrate the economic importance of changes in the family life cycle, attention may be given to the results of establishing this new family, that is, the movement from stage one, Bachelorhood, to stage two, Newly Married—no children.

As Wattenberg observed, " . . . it is . . . no secret that when a young man and young woman decide to get married they trigger a vast chain of intense economic activity unmatched in the human life cycle."[13] He illustrated this point by referring to a 1972 study by Trendex that dealt with the brief six-month period surrounding a marriage. This included the three months before a couple's wedding and the first three months after it. Couples at this stage in the family life cycle comprised only 2.5 percent of all U.S. households; however, they represented substantial sales to a number of industries. The following are examples:

58% of the total for sterling flatware
41% of stereo and hi-fi equipment
27% of sewing machines
25% of total bedroom furniture
16% of vacuum cleaners
13% of clothes dryers
13% of refrigerators
11% of hard-surface floor coverings

For marketing managers in these industries this segment of the population represents one that deserves considerable attention.

Full Nest II
At this stage the youngest child is six or over and in school; the husband's income has ordinarily improved; and if the wife has not been employed, she often returns to work outside the home. As a result, the family's financial position improves. Consumption patterns during this time continue to be heavily influenced by the children's needs. Consequently, a number of different products and services are purchased in relatively large quantities, including doctors' services and medicines, tennis shoes, laundry detergent, snack foods, bicycles, music lessons, and school supplies.

Empty Nest II
By this time the family head has retired and so the couple usually suffers a substantial reduction in income. Although it is increasingly popular for a retired person to take on some part-time work, it ordinarily does not make up for the difference between pre-

[13]B. Wattenberg, p. 52.

retirement income and retirement income. Expenditures on the home and related items are scaled down, and apartment living may begin. Unfortunately a sizable number of the couples in this group will be forced to live at a level approaching subsistence. Furthermore, health concerns receive more attention, and some even move to more agreeable climates or retirement centers in their area.

Concluding Comment and Marketing Implications

The words "typically" and "ordinarily" have been used throughout this last section on the family life cycle. This does not mean that all families fit neatly into one of these developmental stages. In fact, everyone knows of other configurations of family life; we may even have grown up in one. One of these other family groupings is the single parent family with young children. To a large extent these families' needs and behavioral patterns follow those in the Full Nest I stage. However, to meet these needs the remaining parent will likely be employed and probably make more extensive use of day care facilities and baby sitters than would be the case if both parents were in the family. Also, in many such families the expenditures for child care are substantial and, therefore, force the family to live at a somewhat lower level than would be necessary if it had two adults present.

The special needs and desires of families at each stage of the family life cycle offer unique market opportunities, that is, these needs and desires offer opportunities for governmental agencies, nonprofit organizations and businesses to be of service. Specifically, the life cycle concept can be used to:

1. **Identify Target Markets.** Studies of consumer expenditures reveal that the consumption of many products and services varies significantly by stage in the family life cycle. This provides a means of identifying specific groups of consumers within the broader consumer market that have the greatest interest in certain products or services. As a result, marketing efforts to provide for these needs and desires can be more effective and efficient. For instance, with a target market clearly identified products can be tailored to the consumers' requirements, distribution provided in convenient outlets, and advertising undertaken in media that reach the target market with a minimum of wasted coverage.

2. **Forecast Demand.** The Census Bureau publishes estimates of the future size and age structure of U. S. families. In addition, it is possible to obtain consumption rates of products and services broken down by life cycle, age, and other demographic data. By identifying the consumption patterns of those segments of the life cycle that are predicted to expand significantly, it is possible to single out product and service groupings that are likely to enjoy above average growth rates in the future.

FAMILY ROLE STRUCTURES

This section is concerned with the role and influence of family members in the decision-making process. Family role structure refers to the behavior of nuclear family members at each stage in the decision-making process. One means of gaining an understanding of family role structure is by studying the various forms of role specialization that occur in families.

Role specialization within the family can affect both the decision-making process and the decisions made. This specialization takes a number of forms; two are used here to illustrate the importance of role specialization and the nature of its influence. First, role dominance will be discussed, followed by the gatekeeper concept.

Role dominance refers to the extent to which one member of a family has greater influence in the family decision-making process than do other members. Typically husband-dominant or wife-dominant decision making has been the focus of attention. These are decisions involving both spouses but where the ideas of one have greater impact. There have been a number of studies conducted to identify patterns of dominance and the circumstances that foster such dominance. Marketing and advertising managers are particularly interested in determining which spouse has the most influence in various types of decisions so that promotional strategy can be oriented accordingly.

A person's background can contribute to role dominance. There is evidence to indicate that the degree of dominance by one member can vary among groups with differing cultural backgrounds. Also, several researchers have found evidence to suggest that husband dominance appears to be more likely when the husband is successful in his occupation. The wife's influence increases with age and is generally greater if she is employed.[14] It is important to note, too, that existing evidence also shows that dominance by one family member depends upon the particular type of decision being made, that is, a family cannot ordinarily be classified as being wife-dominant or husband-dominant, because when confronted with certain decisions the wife will have the greatest influence, and in other situations it will be the husband who is dominant. For example, Davis found that the husband is more influential in the decision to purchase the family car, while the wife has considerably greater relative influence in furniture purchasing decisions.[15]

To many families the fact that the husband or the wife dominates, that is, has the greater influence, in certain decisions is simply the result of conscious role specialization. The wife, because of her formal and informal training as well as her interests, is more knowledgeable in particular decision areas. Her dominance is the recognition of this expertise. In other decision areas, it is the husband who is the recognized family authority who dominates for similar reasons. However, this role specialization may also be the result of the acceptance of the traditional masculine/feminine roles. When most family decisions of a particular type are made by both husband and wife exerting equal influence, these have been called *syncratic.*

Using a sample of 73 Belgian household, Davis and Rigaux studied the average relative influence of husbands and wives, the extent of role specialization for each decision, and the similarity among decisions in terms of marital roles.[16] Figure 6.4 positions 25 decisions in terms of two axes. The first is a scale of the relative influence between husband and wife. Average relative influence for a decision when aggregated over families

[14]L. E. Ostlund, "Role Theory and Group Dynamics," in *Consumer Behavior Theoretical Sources,* S. Ward and T. S. Robertson, eds. (Englewood Cliffs, New Jersey: Prentice-Hall, Inc., 1973), p. 263.

[15]H. L. Davis, "Dimensions of Marital Roles in Consumer Decision Making," *Journal of Marketing Research,* 7 (May, 1970), pp. 168–177.

[16]H. L. Davis and B. P. Rigaux, "Perceptions of Marital Roles in Decision Processes," *Journal of Consumer Research,* 1 (June, 1974), pp. 51–61.

FIGURE 6.4.
Extent of Role Specialization: Marital Roles in 25 Decisions.

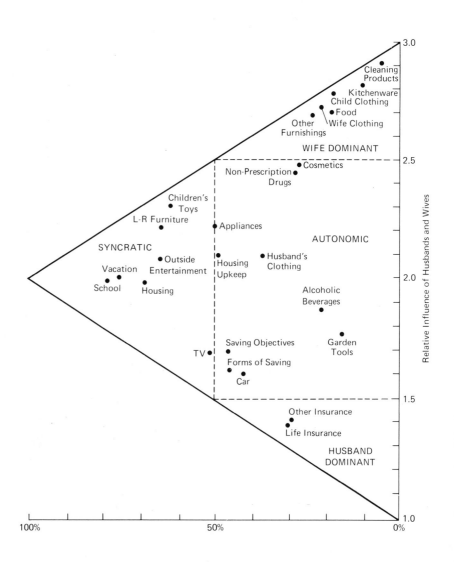

Source: H. L. Davis and B. P. Rigaux, "Perceptions of Marital Roles in Decision Processes," *Journal of Consumer Research,* 1 (June, 1974), p. 54. Reprinted from the *Journal of Consumer Research* published by The Policy Board, *Journal of Consumer Research.*

can range along a continuum from 1 (all respondents reporting husband-dominance) to 3 (all respondents reporting wife-dominance). The second axis is a scale of the extent of role specialization as measured by the percentage of families reporting that a decision is jointly made.

This type of analysis has practical implications for managers. For example, the classification of a decision into one of the four types of influences—wife dominant, husband dominant, autonomic, or syncratic—suggests the need for unique communication strategies. When a decision is either husband or wife dominant, messages must be designed in reference to the designated spouse. A syncratic decision pattern calls for messages developed to appeal to the couple as an entity. Decisions that are generally autonomic—family decisions made most often by either the wife or husband—require yet another approach. In this latter case there are really two separate audiences—one consisting of wives and the other of husbands.

The Davis and Rigaux study also focused on the changing "decision unit" during the decision-making process. The family decision-making process was divided into three phases, including problem recognition, search for information, and final decision. Using this format it was possible to show that some changes in husband and wife influence do occur from the time a problem is recognized until a final decision is made. This, too, has implications for managers in their strategy development. It may be necessary, for example, to initiate problem recognition by directing one's message to the husband and wife (syncratic), while at a later point the decision is essentially wife dominant.

Another form of role specialization is what a number of consumer analysts have called the *gatekeeper concept.* The "gatekeeper" refers to an individual who acts as a valve and filter affecting the flow of information coming into the family. In a number of families the homemaker still illustrates this concept at work. The fact that she is at home more than other members as well as her concern for the general well-being of the family puts her in a position to receive, screen, and sort incoming messages. For instance, as the mail arrives she may sort out and at times discard "junk mail" that was addressed to the "occupant" or even to other specific members of the family. Salesmen who call during the day are also subjected to her gatekeeping action. In a business setting a manager's secretary or assistant may function in a similar capacity.

To the consumer analyst such role specialization must be identified and understood because it can have a substantial impact on consumer behavior. For example, when a homemaker functioning as a family gatekeeper discards a mailer intended to motivate the family member most responsible for lawn weed killer, and if that member be the husband, the message never reached its destination. Obviously it has no impact on him. Under these circumstances the firm marketing the new weed killer probably should have used another medium to deliver its message or substantially modified the mailer so as to increase its chances of reaching the desired destination.

Summary

Generally speaking, the family is a group of persons who are related by blood, marriage, or legal adoption. The nuclear family—the immediate kin group of father and/or mother and their offspring or adopted children who ordinarily live together—is the optimum consuming unit to study. A household is different from a family in that the former is merely a living unit or entity for consumption purposes. It can contain a single person.

The family's social class gives rise to variations in values, interpersonal attitudes, self-perceptions, and daily-life routines. The interaction among family members results in similarities in thinking and behavioral patterns that would not exist if the individuals were not in the same family.

The family decision-making models of Ferber and Sheth provide insight into the family as a buying and consuming entity. Ferber's model displays the interrelation of financial and nonfinancial decisions with key influential variables. The more detailed Sheth model is a comprehensive representation of the findings of various social scientists. The theory depicts in four major subparts family buying decisions made either jointly or by single members.

The family life cycle is used to view how the family's consumption patterns change over time as family composition changes. For example, the bachelor stage is characterized by significant spending on entertainment, food away from home, vacations, etc., while the newly married couple either spends or causes to be spent (by their friends and family) substantial amounts on sterling flatware, stereo equipment, etc. The family life cycle can be used by the marketer to identify target markets and to forecast demand.

Family role specialization via role dominance and the gatekeeper concept can affect the decision-making process. Research has shown that buying decisions can be scaled as to wife dominance, husband dominance, or joint decisions, and that these roles can change during different phases of the decision process. The gatekeeper concept is important because the person in this role can prevent marketing information directed at another family member from reaching them.

QUESTIONS AND ISSUES FOR DISCUSSION

1. During the next 10 years the increasing divorce rate will probably make the United States essentially a country dominated by single people. Furthermore, this trend will substantially alter the interest in such items as cooking utensils, lawn and garden tools, and family restaurants. Is there evidence to support such forecasts? Discuss.

2. Is it reasonable to conclude that once a woman marries her family of orientation generally has little or no effect on her buying behavior? Discuss.

3. How can firms selling the following products and services make use of the family life cycle concept in identifying their target market and planning appropriate advertising strategy?

(a) home movie cameras
(b) airline travel
(c) life insurance
(d) mobile homes.

4. Do fundamental values change with the times so that what families hold to be important today will probably not last through this generation? How are changing values likely to alter family purchasing patterns?

5. What effect will the increasing number of women in full-time employment likely have upon the usefulness of the gate-keeper concept in studying family decision making?

6. To what extent does the family influence its members' individual buying behaviors with respect to each of the following?

    (a) the brand of notebook paper purchased by a high-school student for use in school
    (b) preferences for various snack foods
    (c) movies attended by students away at college
    (d) the first car that a young woman buys.

7. How does the role of the child in family decision making ordinarily change over time? Can this change effect family buying patterns? If so, give some examples.

8. Assume that the information given in the chart that follows has just been obtained from a major consumer research study. It lists several types of purchases and indicates that they were found to be syncratic, wife dominant, or husband dominant. How could this information be used by a marketing manager in the development of marketing strategy?

Product/Service Purchased	*Dominant Influence in Purchase Decision*
(a) Household cleaning products	Wife-dominant
(b) Family vacations	Syncratic
(c) Stereo equipment	Syncratic
(d) Ready-to-eat cereal	Wife-dominant
(e) Over-the-counter sleep aids	Husband-dominant
(f) Bank credit cards	Syncratic

9. The style of living that a family chooses has a greater influence on its purchase patterns than does its social class status. For example, some families are very casual in their style of living; consequently, the products and services they buy reflect these interests. Furthermore, such a family can take on this casual style while being a member of any social class. Is this a true statement? Discuss.

10. Studying the American family in the detail presented in this chapter and then using this information to develop better marketing plans is an invasion of privacy beyond a reasonable point. It can only lead to the manipulation of family decision making. Is this a real concern? If so, what can be done about it?

SITUATIONAL PROBLEMS

Case 1

Camptown Corporation has a series of 30 campsites located on major interstate highways across the Midwest through which it serves campers. Each facility is corporate owned and represents a substantial investment. All camp sites are modern and provide nearly any service the overnight camper would want. Success has been modest and management feels that to significantly increase profit, more campers will have to be attracted during the spring and early fall—just before and after the primary vacation season. Families with children have been Camptown's major customer group (families with children constitute about 80 percent of their present customers).

What suggestions can be made to the Camptown management that would be helpful in their effort to realize greater utilization of their campsites during the spring and fall?

Case 2

The lack of proper child immunization is beginning to present a major health threat in this country. Unfortunately, many parents seem to believe that because they personally hear of few, if any, cases of diseases like polio and measles, their children no longer need to be immunized against these diseases. This is not true, and public health officials at all levels are very concerned about such an attitude.

What assistance can the consumer analyst offer as a result of studying family decision making that would help change this public view?

What organization(s) should be involved in dealing with this problem, and what specific strategy would you suggest?

PART III

ANALYSIS OF INDIVIDUAL INFLUENCING FORCES ON CONSUMER BEHAVIOR

Information Processing and the Affect of Personality

The consumer's psychological command center, the central control unit (CCU), is the fundamental mechanism of the consumer's decision processes. The components of the CCU function to shape the consumer's decision process in two crucial ways: (1) by controlling and interpreting information received through the senses, and (2) by directing the consumer's actions. The four primary components of the CCU, depicted in Figure 7.1, fall into two main categories: personality and attitudinal group. The attitudinal group includes information and prior experience, evaluative criteria, and attitude.

This chapter focuses on two major aspects of the consumer decision process: information processing and personality. More specifically, attention is given to the manner in which the CCU controls and interprets the information the consumer receives through his senses. This chapter also examines personality—one of the basic components making up the CCU. The next three chapters focus on the attitudinal group, including learning (information and prior experience), evaluative criteria and attitudes.

FIGURE 7.1.
Central Control Unit.

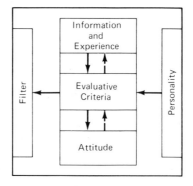

Source: J. F. Engel, D. T. Kollat, and R. D. Blackwell, *Consumer Behavior,* 2nd edition (New York: Holt, Rinehart and Winston, Inc., 1973), p. 209. Reprinted by permission of the publisher.

Information Processing

Consumers are constantly exposed to a variety of stimuli from many sources. In fact, the number of stimuli (i.e., sensory inputs) confronting a consumer is so great that the processing of them is one of man's most significant activities. The consumer's psychological command center (CCU) includes a complex mechanism that interprets these stimuli and assigns them meaning.

Information processing refers to all the means by which a sensory input is transformed, reduced, elaborated, stored, recovered, and used by a consumer in decision-making situations. These processes are generally conceptualized as four distinct phases: (1) exposure, (2) attention, (3) comprehension, and (4) retention.[1] As represented in Figure 7.2, these four phases interact with the filter component of the CCU to determine which stimuli will be carefully evaluated and stored in the consumer's memory. The filter temporarily stores incoming information until

FIGURE 7.2
Information Processing within Central Control Unit

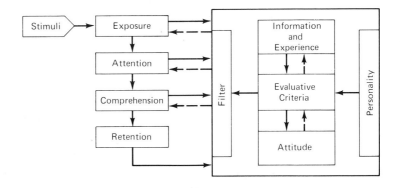

[1]W. J. McGuire, "Personality and Susceptibility to Social Influence," *Handbook of Personality Theory and Research,* E. F. Borgatta and W. W. Lambert, eds. (Chicago: Rand McNally & Co., 1968), pp. 1130–1187.

a preliminary evaluation is completed. Researchers have estimated that this temporary storage is less than a second for most incoming information and that most stimuli that receive this preattentive processing are not attended to by the consumer. Thus, although advertising folklore suggests that the average consumer is exposed to about 1600 advertisements each day, consumer analysts now indicate that consumers consciously attend to only about 0.5 percent of these stimuli and only a few of these stimuli are retained for any period of time.[2] A consumer's attention might be attracted by the use of color or music or some other device. However, whether or not the stimulus is processed further depends on the preattentive processing that occurs in the filter.

Those stimuli that pass the critical initial screening process undergo further processing.[3] The four components within the CCU interact within the filter to determine which stimuli are most pertinent and, thus, should undergo further processing. As indicated in Figure 7.2, the filter directs and interprets the consumer's information processing activities throughout all four phases. Because these four phases are related in a hierarchical fashion, a stimulus must be attended to before comprehension can occur. Similarly, a stimulus must be comprehended before it can be retained. Achieving a certain stage in the consumer's information processing activities is a necessary but not sufficient condition for achieving the following stage. In other words, the fact that a marketer's efforts are attended to does not necessarily mean that the efforts (stimulus) will be comprehended by the consumer.

The implications of consumer information processing are worth noting. Gaining message exposure is not the marketer's greatest problem, for exposure primarily requires careful media selection. The marketer's real difficulty is to design messages that do not activate the filter in such a way so as to prevent further processing or to distort the input. Generally this will re-

---

[2]R. A. Bauer and S. A. Greyser, *Advertising in America: The Consumer View* (Cambridge, Mass.: Graduate School of Business Administration, Harvard University, 1968).

[3]D. A. Norman, "Toward a Theory of Memory and Attention," *Psychological Review,* 75 (November, 1968), pp. 522–536.

quire that the messages be compatible with the consumer's personality and attitudinal components. Thus, even though a 25-year-old bachelor is not likely to attend to messages encouraging saving for retirement, he might very well acknowledge, comprehend, and retain messages urging saving for a new car or a trip to Europe.

EXPOSURE

Exposure, the initial phase of information processing, occurs when an individual is confronted with a stimulus that activates his senses. The senses transport the stimulus energy to the brain which generates the sensations of sight, hearing, smell, touch, or taste. This phenomenon seems simple enough and the application for the marketing manager straightforward. Unfortunately, this is not the case. The major difficulty confounding exposure is that people selectively expose themselves to stimuli; that is, consumers do not indiscriminately expose themselves to stimuli, rather they are selective about the information to which they permit themselves to be exposed. The marketer's efforts to disseminate information to consumers is further complicated by the fact that selective exposure is particularly pronounced in the case of persuasive communications. For example, research has indicated that there is a relationship between whether or not a person smokes and the readership of articles alleging a relationship between smoking and cancer. In one study in particular, 67 percent of the nonsmokers claimed high readership of the articles, versus only 44 percent of smokers.[4]

Consumer analysts are not in agreement as to the reason consumers selectively expose themselves to communications. Some consumer analysts contend that selective exposure results from the consumer's desire to avoid information that is inconsistent with existing beliefs and dispositions,[5] whereas other analysts contend that factors such as education and back-

[4]C. Cannell and J. C. MacDonald, "The Impact of Health News on Attitudes and Behavior," *Journalism Quarterly,* 33 (Summer, 1956), pp. 315–323.

[5]J. Mills, "Interest in Supporting and Discrepant Information," *Theories of Cognitive Consistency: A Sourcebook,* R. P. Abelson, E. Aronson, W. J. McGuire, T. M. Newcomb, M. J. Rosenberg and P. H. Tannenbaum, eds. (Chicago: Rand McNally & Co., 1968), pp. 771–776.

ground cause people to process information selectively.[6] In any event, selective exposure is a problem the marketing strategist must contend with, because the actual audience almost always is smaller than the desired audience. Thus, the marketing strategist must carefully evaluate the media exposure patterns of his target market to achieve the greatest possible exposure for the firm's communications.

ATTENTION

Certain stimuli that consumers are exposed to are temporarily stored within the CCU to permit further processing. In order for a stimulus to be comprehended, it must pass through two more processing stages: (1) preattentive processing and (2) analysis for pertinence.

Preattentive Processing

Preattentive processing refers to the triggering of an initial response when a consumer is presented with a new stimulus.[7] This triggering may take the form of a turning direction, a growing sense of alertness, and so on. Preattentive processing prepares the consumer for contending with a new stimulus and mobilizes him for action. Essentially, then, preattentive processing refers to the process by which stimuli are analyzed for meaning largely on such physical properties as loudness, pitch, and so on. This preliminary analysis is assisted by learned tendencies to organize and categorize stimuli based on physical properties.

Figure 7.3 is an illustration of the tendency consumers have to organize stimuli. Does the illustration contain rows of dots or columns of dots? Because the dots are closer together in the horizontal direction, most people report seeing rows; that is, the horizontal dots are recognized as being in closer proximity. There is a widespread tendency to organize objects in proximity to interpret them in this manner.

[6]D. O. Sears, "The Paradox of DeFacto Selective Exposure Without Preferences for Supportive Information," Abelson, et al., pp. 777–787.

[7]R. Lynn, *Attention Arousal and the Orientation Reaction* (Oxford: Pergamon, 1966).

FIGURE 7.3.
An Illustration of Proximity

An understanding of preattentive processing can substantially benefit the marketing strategist. For example, the marketer must realize that consumers tend to assign similar quality evaluations to products in proximity. Thus, if a low-quality product is stocked by a retailer to offer a low-price alternative to the consumer, that product may affect the evaluations of other merchandise in the store's product line. Indeed, if maintaining a high-quality evaluation is desired, it may benefit the merchant to not handle the low-quality product or perhaps to physically separate or, in some manner other than just price, distinguish the low-quality product from the high-quality product line.

Analysis for Pertinence
After a stimulus has been considered in a preliminary manner, it is further processed to determine its pertinence for the consumer. Whereas preattentive processing is an almost automatic and undirected screening, the evaluation of a stimulus' relevance to a consumer is internally directed and more complex. Those stimuli that emerge from this analysis are those perceived pertinent to the consumer given the present circumstances. Consumer analysts have identified numerous factors that affect the determination of pertinence; the following are, however, particularly important.

1. **The Influence of Need States.**   The consumer's predominant needs, both physical and psychological, substantially affect the stimuli perceived to be important and, consequently, to require further processing. For example, hungry people are most likely to give food-related responses when ambiguous stimuli are seen or heard. Furthermore, the hungry consumer will more readily attend to food advertisements than will his nonhungry counterpart. Similarly, an appeal to social acceptance through avoidance of body odor will be more readily noticed by those who fear social rejection.

Thus, the marketing strategist should, to the extent possible, identify market segments that are experiencing a high need state for his generic product or perhaps conditions that are associated with a high state. A household with a new baby typically experiences a high need for the many products required to provide proper care. Marketing communications relative to such products that are directed at this consuming unit will have a better chance of being attended to and, thus, the possibility of being comprehended.

2. **The Influence of Values.**   The consumer's values have a substantial effect on whether or not a stimulus is passed on for further information processing. Researchers have demonstrated that stimuli consistent with a consumer's values are more quickly recognized and more likely to be attended to than are stimuli inconsistent with a consumer's values.[8] Thus, the marketing strategist might reasonably conclude that preferred brand names will be recognized more quickly than nonpreferred brands. This explains why certain advertisements are noticed more quickly than others. The key appears to lie in the extent to which the brand name is featured. Whereas a stimulus that is consistent with an individual's values is likely to be evaluated as pertinent and, consequently, attended to, a stimulus that reflects something with low value is likely to be avoided.[9] In other words, consumers establish barriers to prevent or inhibit their attending

[8]D. E. Broadbent, "Word-Frequency Effect and Response Bias," *Psychological Review,* 74 (January, 1967), pp. 1–15.

[9]D. P. Spence, "Subliminal Perception and Perceptual Defense: Two Sides of a Single Problem," *Behavioral Science,* 12 (May, 1967), pp. 183–193.

to stimuli that have little or no value for them. Thus, if a consumer has a low regard for foreign-made automobiles, he will be less likely to notice advertisements featuring foreign automobiles than those featuring domestically produced automobiles. The marketing strategist must carefully direct communications to focus, to the extent possible, on segments that have assigned a favorable value to the brand.

3. **The Influence of Cognitive Consistency.** The components within the CCU interact to provide an individual's cognitive structure. This cognitive structure functions to enable the individual to cope with his environment by attending to stimuli that are consistent with the consumer's CCU. For example, assume that a consumer opposed to the consumption of alcoholic beverages is exposed to an advertisement urging him to consume Budweiser beer. Even though such an advertisement may receive preattentive processing, the consumer is fully capable of screening out this stimulus. This stimulus would probably be screened out on the grounds of no pertinence. Attending to this ad could produce a state of inconsistency that would be psychologically uncomfortable and thus contrary to the consumer's tendency to maintain consistency with the components of the CCU.[10]

In summary, then, the marketing strategist must recognize that consumers selectively attend to marketing stimuli. The consumer may observe an advertisement out of the "corner of his eye," engage in preattentive processing, and then redirect attention accordingly. The consumer may be committed to a brand or store and, hence, resist a challenge to his preference. Consequently, the effective allocation of marketing effort necessitates an understanding of the needs, values, and attitudes of the consumers for whom the effort is intended.

COMPREHENSION

The fact that a stimulus has received focal attention and has been determined to be pertinent to the consumer does not as-

[10]M. J. Rosenberg, "Inconsistency Arousal and Reduction in Attitude Change," *Current Studies in Social Psychology*, I. O. Steiner and M. Fishbein, eds. (New York: Holt, Rinehart and Winston, Inc., 1965), pp. 123–124.

sure correct comprehension of the information. The CCU's filter assigns meaning to the stimulus in a way that can deviate from objective reality; that is, a consumer can attend to a marketer's communication and yet obtain ideas substantially different from those intended to be conveyed. There are many ways in which this takes place, but two of the ways particularly important to marketing strategists are: (1) distortion of physical stimuli properties and (2) miscomprehension of communication message content.

Distortion of Physical Stimulus Properties

Several studies in the past 25 years have indicated that consumers cannot distinguish between the physical properties of cola beverages (Coca Cola, Pepsi Cola, and R. C. Cola) when the brand name is not identified.[11] Even when lesser known brands were included, consumers were unable to correctly identify the well-known brands. However, when the brand name of a cola beverage is identified, consumers contend that they can detect taste differences and frequently express strong brand preferences. Similar results have been obtained with respect to numerous products such as beer[12] and turkey.[13] This research indicates that consumers can attend to a marketer's communication or even consume a product and yet comprehend information consistent with their CCU. In other words, consumers modify or distort information they attend to in order to make it more consistent with their personal preferences and, therefore, less disruptive.

This type of distortion frequently occurs in consumer decision making. For example, when the soft drink Twink was introduced, the company experienced sales well below the estimated potential.[14] A taste test was conducted in which labeled and unlabeled samples of this brand and competitive brands were compared.

[11]F. J. Thumin, "Identification of Cola Beverages," *Journal of Applied Psychology,* 46 (November, 1962), pp. 358–360.

[12]R. I. Allison and K. P. Uhl, "Brand Identification and Perception," *Journal of Marketing Research,* 1 (August, 1964), pp. 80–85.

[13]J. C. Makens, "Effect of Brand Preference Upon Consumers' Perceived Taste of Turkey Meat," *Journal of Applied Psychology,* 49 (August, 1965), pp. 261–263.

[14]"Twink: Perception of Taste," *Cases in Consumer Behavior,* R. D. Blackwell, J. F. Engel, and D. T. Kollat (New York: Holt, Rinehart and Winston, Inc., 1969), pp. 38–43.

The findings indicated that Twink received excellent ratings in comparison with others when it was unlabeled. The ratings were completely reversed, however, when the brands were identified. It thus appears that the product image, name, or some other consideration affected taste ratings. As a result, the promotional program was totally revamped while the product formulation was left unchanged. The marketing strategist must be aware of the distortions that are likely to take place with respect to his product and develop the product name, image, and promotional program accordingly.

Distortion of Message Content

We all have expectations about the content of the stimuli confronting us, and frequently our reaction to a stimulus reflects the expectation rather than the stimulus itself. For example, a liquid cold remedy was introduced in a test market in an attempt to make inroads into the market share of Vick's Nyquil. The advertisements used in the promotional campaign were very similar to those employed by Nyquil, and there was considerable evidence that consumers thought that they were viewing Nyquil ads. Their familiarity with Nyquil produced certain expectations, and as a result, they miscomprehended the competitor's promotional efforts. The miscomprehension of message content frequently occurs to prevent disturbance of existing preferences and dispositions, particularly if consumers are reasonably satisfied with the brand they are now using. The numerous mechanisms that produce this distortion require that the marketer identify the market segment for which the message is intended and then pretest the message to determine if the target market has a tendency to miscomprehend the message being used.

RETENTION

Information comprehended by consumers is processed further to determine whether or not it should be stored in long-term memory. As was true with the three previous stages of information processing, consumers continue to be highly selective about the information to be retained. Only a limited amount of information that is attended to and comprehended is retained in the consumer's CCU. Consumer analysts have determined that the factors influencing the consumer's decision to retain information are basically the same as those affecting the decision to attend to information. Perhaps the key factor affecting the decision to retain information is the pertinence the information has for the consumer. Only information that is judged to be pertinent to the consumer's needs and existing dispositions is retained, and even such information will be forgotten without some reinforcement. As a result, information the consumer judges to be threatening to his cognitive consistency can easily be kept from permanent memory. Thus, the marketing strategist who seeks to get consumers to retain a message about a brand other than their preferred brand faces a very imposing task.

There is no question that marketing stimuli are rapidly forgotten after the initial exposure. For example, only 24 percent could name at least one advertised product on a television show; fewer than one third could identify a commercial appearing within less than two minutes prior to an interview, and residual recall of commercial content after a longer period levels off at 12 percent or less.[15] Of course, this is not surprising because advertising stimuli, by and large, are only marginally pertinent to the consumer in most viewing or listening situations. It is also possible that existing brand or product preferences are protected through failure to recall contradictory stimuli, in which case prevention of cognitive inconsistency could be another explanation, but it is likely to function in only a minority of situations.

Effect of Personality on Consumer Behavior

The preceding section focused on the manner in which the consumer's CCU functions to control and interpret information received from the senses. As indicated previously, the information processed by a consumer is directly affected by two categories of components comprising the CCU: (1) personality and (2) attitudinal group. Marketing strategists have long sought to under-

---

[15]L. Bogart, *Strategy in Advertising* (New York: Harcourt Brace Jovanovich, 1967), chapter 5.

stand the process by which these variables affect information processing, for a considerable amount of marketing effort has the goal of affecting the information processed by consumers as well as the behavior manifested. The personality component has fascinated marketing analysts partially because of the concept's inherent intellectual appeal and partially because of the seemingly valid belief that personality directly affects not only information processing but product and brand choice as well. The remainder of this chapter focuses on the personality component of the CCU.

PERSONALITY THEORIES IN CONSUMER BEHAVIOR

Personality is a frequently used and reasonably familiar term. Most people have at various times characterized someone as having a pleasant personality or occasionally, perhaps, an obnoxious personality. While this use of the word "personality" typically conveys meaning, it lacks the precision necessary for managerial application. Actually, there is little agreement on what the components of personality are and how these components become organized into a meaningful whole. Thus, an examination of the major personality theories is essential to acquiring an appreciation of the potential contribution of this concept.

Most definitions of personality are quite general, and the term is frequently used in different ways. The common element of all definitions of personality is the notion that personality is a consistent pattern of responses to environmental stimuli. This consistent pattern of responses permits the categorization of people in a number of ways, such as stuffy, methodical, or egotistical. A consumer's reaction to a need, a routine situation, or new stimulus is determined by his normal mode of coping with his environment. Marketing strategists' fascination with personality stems from the belief that this consistent mode of behaving will enable marketers to understand consumer behavior. The assumption is that if they really understand a consumer's personality, they will understand why a person consumes the way he does and, then, perhaps they can effectively influence that consumption behavior.

Psychoanalytic Theory

Psychoanalytical or Freudian theory posits that personality is composed of three systems of interdependent psychological forces or constructs: the id, ego, and superego.[16] The interaction of these three systems determine the person's behavior. The *id,* the original source of all psychic energy, seeks to achieve immediate gratification of all biological or instinctual needs. Thus, all a consumer's instinctive cravings, needs, and desires originate in the id. If all the pleasure-seeking impulses emanating from the id were openly expressed, the consumer would quickly violate society's norms, rules, and regulations. Indeed, proponents of the psychoanalytic theory would contend that uncontrolled behavior that directly satisfies all instinctive needs and desires is inherently bad. The *superego,* the internal representative of society's norms and values, acts to inhibit the impulses emanating from the id that would be contrary to society's norms and values. Thus, the superego can be thought of as the consumer's conscience or moral arm that serves to direct behavior. The *ego* functions to control and direct the id's impulses so that gratification can be achieved in a socially acceptable manner. The ego controls behavior by selecting the instincts that will be satisfied as well as the manner in which they will be satisfied. This is accomplished by integrating the often conflicting demands of the id and superego. According to psychoanalytic theory, the id is entirely unconscious and the ego and superego partially unconscious, resulting in an unconscious determination of behavior. Consequently, only the highly trained professional psychologist by means of projective techniques and in-depth interviews is capable of identifying the consumer's true personality.

Psychoanalytic theory provided the conceptual basis for motivational research. Consumer behavior, according to motivational researchers, is the result of unconscious consumer motives that can only be determined through the use of indirect assessment methods that include a wide assortment of projective techniques.

[16]W. D. Wells and A. D. Beard, "Personality and Consumer Behavior," *Consumer Behavior: Theoretical Sources,* S. Ward and T. S. Robertson, eds. (Englewood Cliffs, N.J.: Prentice-Hall, Inc., 1973), pp. 141–199.

The following are some motivational research explanations of consumer behavior:[17]

1. A man buys a convertible as a substitute mistress.
2. A women is very serious when she bakes a cake because unconsciously she is going through the symbolic act of birth.
3. Men want their cigars to be odiferous in order to prove that they (the men) are masculine.

These subjective interpretations of consumer motivations, although perhaps atypical, highlight the danger of using a personality model developed in and for a clinical setting to explain consumer behavior. The individual focus characterizing psychoanalytic theory is inappropriate to the marketing analyst whose interest is in groups or segments of consumers. Indeed, even if individual information could be obtained, its application by the marketing strategist is not readily apparent. While psychoanalytic theory has been extensively and justly criticized, few would deny that it had a tremendous impact on marketing in the 1950's and 1960's and, to a lesser extent, in the 1970's.

Social Psychological Theory
Social psychological theory developed as a reaction to the psychoanalytics' rigid adherence to the biological determinants of personality. Social psychological theorists contend that social variables, not biological ones, are the most important determinants of personality. Man is conscious of his needs and wants; consequently, his behavior is directed toward satisfying them. The following are representative needs considered to be basic determinants of personality by proponents of the social psychological orientation: the striving for superiority, freedom from loneliness, security, satisfying human relationships, and coping with anxiety.

One paradigm reflecting this orientation suggests that consumer behavior results from three predominant interpersonal orientations—compliant, aggressive, and detached. A psycho-

[17]P. Kotler, *Marketing Management* (Englewood Cliffs, N.J.: Prentice-Hall, Inc., 1972), p. 107.

logical instrument—the CAD scale—has been developed to measure these three basic orientations.[18] The *compliant* person wants to be appreciated, wanted, loved, and included in the activities of others. The compliant person is so other-oriented that he becomes overgenerous, overgrateful, and overconsiderate. For example, the compliant person seeking reassurance of his acceptance by others is likely to seek the security afforded by personal grooming products. The *aggressive* person seeks success, prestige, and the admiration of others. The aggressive person values other people only if they are useful to achieving a goal. The aggressive person considers everyone to be motivated by self-interest, and concern for others is manifested only to cover up the person's real goals. For example, the aggressive person seeking a separate identity will be more concerned with distinctive brands of personal grooming products. The *detached* person seeks freedom from obligations, independence, and self-sufficiency. The detached person does not want to be influenced or to share experiences with others; rather he or she seeks to put emotional distance between themselves and others. For example, the detached person will probably not be concerned with products (such as personal grooming products) or brands that ensure interpersonal acceptance.

The marketer of personal grooming products can reach two conclusions from the research on the CAD personalities. First, the interpersonal goals and values of consumers will result in different levels of acceptance of personal grooming products. Second, a consistent, focused marketing program emphasizing a particular set of interpersonal values can attract a large number of consumers of a particular personality type.

Trait-Factor Theory

According to trait-factor theory, an individual's personality is composed of a set of traits or factors. The relatively enduring and distinctive ways in which consumers differ from one another are referred to as *traits.* Therefore, traits can be considered consumer difference variables. Proponents of trait-factor theory con-

---

[18]J. B. Cohen, "An Interpersonal Orientation to the Study of Consumer Behavior," *Journal of Marketing Research,* 4 (August, 1967), pp. 270–278.

tend that consumers have relatively stable traits that produce similar effects on behavior, regardless of the situation. Furthermore, although a trait is common to many individuals, there is considerable variation in the degree to which one consumer expresses that particular trait.

The consumer analyst who adheres to this orientation typically selects one of the many personality inventories (e.g., California Personality Inventory, Edwards Personal Preference Schedule, Gordon Personal Profile) and attempts to find a statistical relationship between a set of personality variables and some type of consumer behavior. The use of such an inventory is particularly appealing to the more quantitatively oriented marketing analysts because it permits the use of relatively sophisticated statistical techniques. In the past decade and a half trait-factor theories have been used almost exclusively as the conceptual basis for personality research in marketing. The following section discusses the results of some of this research and the implications for marketing managers.

PERSONALITY AND PRODUCT CHOICE

The consumer analyst's fascination with personality stems from the belief that a consumer's personality substantially influences consumer behavior. Many consumer analysts would contend that consumption patterns are an expression of a consumer's personality and, consequently, knowledge of a consumer's personality is strategic to the marketing decision maker. The personality's central role in the CCU attests to the believed importance of this component. The rich literature on personality in psychology and the inherent intellectual appeal of the concept has, however, produced unrealistic expectations regarding its capacity to explain consumer behavior.

Consumer analysts have made numerous attempts to demonstrate the relationship between personality and product or brand choice. For example, an attempt to demonstrate the relationship between brand of automobile purchased and personality proved rather unsuccessful.[19] There is, however, some indication that

[19]F. B. Evans, "Psychological and Objective Factors in the Prediction of Brand Choice," *Journal of Business,* 32 (October, 1959), pp. 340–369.

personality is related to the type of automobile owned; that is, the convertible owner appeared to be more aggressive, impulsive, sociable, and somewhat less stable and reflective than the standard or compact owner. A number of marketing analysts also have found a relationship between personality and product use. For example, there appears to be a tendency for women who are enthusiastic, sensitive, and submissive to be more prone to purchase private brands than their counterparts.

In general, when marketing analysts have employed more sophisticated analytical techniques they have found that a relationship exists between personality and certain types of products (e.g., convenience products).[20] Thus, even though the unsuccessful attempts to relate personality and consumer behavior outnumber the successful ones, the consumer analyst's interest in personality continues to be strong.

IMPLICATIONS FOR MARKETING STRATEGY

In order to effectively market a product, the marketing manager must frequently segment the market; that is, the marketing manager must adapt his marketing effort to the demands of relatively homogeneous groups that make up the market. Traditionally, marketers have segmented along such demographic dimensions as age, income, occupation, and social class. Many marketing managers, however, contend that demographic variables lack the richness needed to accurately focus marketing efforts. The speculation is that personality captures much of the richness not present in demographic variables.

The marketing strategist must address the issue of whether personality variables provide an effective basis for allocating marketing effort. Most attempts to base marketing strategy on personality have not been unequivocally successful. In order for personality information to substantially aid the marketing strategist, a few basic conditions must prevail. First, consumers with common personality dimensions must be homogeneous with respect to such demographic factors as age, income, and location so that they can be communicated with economically through the

[20]D. L. Sparks and W. T. Tucker, "A Multivariate Analysis of Personality and Product Use," *Journal of Marketing Research,* 8 (February, 1971), pp. 66–70.

mass market. This is necessary because data on media patterns are typically available in terms of demographic characteristics. In the absence of identifiable common characteristics, there is no practical means of focusing on a specific market segment. Second, personality differences must reflect clearcut variations in consumer preferences that can be focused on through modifications in marketing effort. In other words, consumers may have different personalities and still prefer the same products. If this is the case, personality information contributes little if at all to effective marketing decision making. Third, the market segments identified by personality measures must be of sufficient size to be reached economically. Thus, even though personality may enable successful identification of a segment of consumers, the segment must be of sufficient size to be profitable.

Most marketing strategists would contend that these criteria have not been sufficiently met and, consequently, personality has not been demonstrated to be a significant input to marketing decision making. The usefulness of personality information has not yet been unequivocally determined. The next section, however, focuses on select recent developments that provide considerable cause for optimism.

MARKETING APPLICATIONS OF PERSONALITY

Several recent marketing research efforts have produced useful results for marketing strategists. In particular, four major modifications in the use of personality have been made, and this has contributed substantially to the usefulness of personality information to marketing decision makers. These modifications are: (1) consumption-related personality inventories, (2) psychographic (AIO) inventories, (3) use of personality as a moderator variable, and (4) use of personality as an intervening variable.

Consumption-Related Personality Inventories
Consumer analysts now believe that much of the disappointment with personality information resulted from the use of standardized inventories designed for use in the psychological clinic and, consequently, the improper application of these standardized inventories may have obscured the value of personality informa-

tion. It seems obvious that better results should be expected when personality measures related to the process of buying and consumption are used.

The construction of consumption-related personality inventories is difficult and tedious but offers considerable benefits. Consider five dichotomous orientations of housewives toward housework that served as the basis for a personality inventory developed specifically to distinguish views toward household cleaning.[21]

1. *Flexible versus rigid.* This dimension focused on the need to maintain a flexible or strict cleaning schedule and organization of time to this end.
2. *Evaluative versus nonevaluative.* To what extent is cleaning central to a housewife's evaluation of herself and others in the role of wife and mother?
3. *Objective versus family role.* This dealt with the degree to which cleaning is seen as essential to family nature as opposed to being a necessary utilitarian task—in other words, is cleaning an 'act of love?'
4. *Emancipated versus limited.* The emancipated housewife was defined as that woman holding the point of view that she can participate in a larger social context outside the home.
5. *Appreciated versus unappreciated.* This dimension showed the housewife's perception of the extent of appreciation by husband and children of her efforts in their behalf.

When the personality inventory based on these five dimensions was administered to 300 housewives, it suggested the following results: The emancipated, nonevaluative, objective, and flexible housewife does not consider cleaning to be a measure of her worth nor is cleaning an expression of her love, whereas the traditional, restricted, evaluative housewife views cleaning as a measure of her worth and an expression of love.

The results of this research effort suggest that the strategist who wants to focus on these segments must develop different products, different packages and designs and communicate differently with these two segments. The differences observed in these housewives suggest that the marketing strategists must

[21]I. S. White, "The Perception of Value in Products," *On Knowing the Consumer*, J. W. Newman, ed. (New York: John Wiley & Sons, Inc., 1966), pp. 90–106.

develop totally different marketing strategies for each segment; the failure to do so might result in the loss of both segments.

Psychographic (AIO) Inventories

Psychographic inventories attempt to describe the life-styles of select segments through the use of activity, interest, and opinion statements. The marketing analyst must have consumers respond to a number of activity, interest, and opinion (AIO) statements and then use statistical techniques to group the AIO statements into similar categories. This grouping permits the marketing analyst to develop a psychographic portrait of users and nonusers for the product under study. For example, one such marketing study portrayed the user of eye makeup to be younger, better educated, and more likely to be employed outside the home.[22] The users of eye makeup were more fashion conscious, cosmopolitan, and future oriented than nonusers. Thus, the marketing strategist has established that the use of eye makeup is but a part of a consistent behavioral pattern that provides valuable information input for media selection and advertising content decisions. Furthermore, the market strategist can use such information to identify likely users of related products, that is, other products that are consistent with that life-style.

Personality as a Moderator Variable

Consumer analysts now realize that personality interacts with other variables, particularly the environment, to determine behavior; that is, personality may permit accurate predictions of behavior in some situations but not in others. Because certain groups are differentially affected by certain personality traits, these personality traits are said to moderate the situation. Predictions that specify the situation should be more accurate.

Suppose that the distributor of a name brand of bourbon attempts to determine the relationship between the purchase of his bourbon and personality. This distributor would very likely determine that the socially concerned person would purchase name brand bourbon to serve to guests but purchase inexpensive house brands for his personal use. Thus, if the marketing strate-

---

[22]W. D. Wells and D. J. Tigert, "Activities, Interests and Opinions," *Journal of Advertising Research,* 11 (August, 1971), pp. 27–35.

gist can identify the key situations, personality information can be a valuable informational input to strategy development.

Personality as an Intervening Variable

Consider the case of the Flavorfest Company to demonstrate the use of personality as an intervening variable.[23] The Flavorfest Company manufactures and distributes a well-known bottled condiment product. The firm has long dominated the market for this product line which includes other spices and seasoning items. Flavorfest could base a marketing program on the assumption that all potential customers are equally valuable prospects, but such an assumption should be verified by research. Actually, it is more likely that substantial consumer differences exist. The research summarized below disclosed the existence of three distinct market segments.

1. Heavy Users (39 percent of the market)
   a. Demographic attributes: housewives aged 20–45, well educated, higher income categories, small families with most children under five, concentration in northeast and midwest regions and in suburban and farm areas.
   b. Motivational attributes
      i. Strong motivation not to be old-fashioned and a desire to express individuality through creative action and use of exciting new things.
      ii. The traditional role of housewife is viewed with displeasure, and experimentation with new foods is done to express her individuality—not to please her family.
      iii. The image of Flavorfest suggests exciting and exotic taste, and the product is reacted to favorably in terms of taste, appearance, and food value. It is highly prized in experimental cooking; hence, there is substantial compatibility between user's values and product image.
2. Light to Moderate Users (20 percent of the market)
   a. Demographic attributes: housewives aged 35–54, large families with children under 12, middle-income groups, location primarily in Southeast, Pacific states, and Southwest.
   b. Motivational attributes
      i. A strong desire to express individuality through creative cookery, but this desire is constrained somewhat by a conflict-

[23]J. F. Engel, H. G. Wales, and M. R. Warshaw, *Promotional Strategy* (Homewood, Illinois: Richard D. Irwin, Inc., 1971), pp. 160–162.

ing desire to maintain tradition and subvert herself to her family's desires.

ii. The desire to experiment with new foods is also constrained by a lack of confidence in the results of her experimental cooking.

iii. The image of Flavorfest is favorable. The product is liked in all respects, but it is confined largely to use with one type of food. It is viewed as unacceptable in other uses; hence, her vision is limited regarding new uses of Flavorfest.

3. Nonusers (41 percent of the market)

a. Demographic attributes: older housewives, large families, lower income brackets, location primarily in the Eastern states and some parts of the South.

b. Motivational attributes

i. A strong motive to maintain tradition and emotional ties with the past; identification with her mother and her role in the home.

ii. A conservative nonventuresome personality.

iii. Her role as mother and housewife discourages experimental cookery, and Flavorfest is thus looked on unfavorably. The image of Flavorfest connotes exotic flavors and a degree of modernity that is unacceptable.

iv. No interest is expressed in new uses and experimentation with Flavorfest, for the product does not represent the values embraced by these housewives.

This research clearly indicates that there are important demographic and motivational differences between users and nonusers of Flavorfest. The findings summarized above indicate that the heavy-user segment is relatively large, and Flavorfest products are well regarded by the housewives in this segment. Furthermore, the potential exists for stimulating greater use in this segment because of the product's use in experimental cookery.

The nonuser segment, on the other hand, requires a different marketing strategy. This segment is large but is made up of people with relatively low purchasing power living in areas where population growth is stagnant. The negative values expressed toward Flavorfest suggest that there is little opportunity for stimulating the sale of Flavorfest in this market segment.

The light-to-moderate user segment represents the greatest opportunity for increased sales. The desire for creative cookery is present but is constrained by a desire to maintain tradition and by a lack of confidence in the results of experimental efforts.

However, the favorable opinion of Flavorfest suggests that sales could be stimulated by demonstrating the compatibility between pleasing the family and creative cookery.

Summary

Consumer information processing is the means by which a sensory input is transformed, reduced, elaborated, stored, recovered, and used in consumer decision making. The process can be broken down into four phases that interact with the filter of the central control unit to determine which stimuli will be carefully evaluated and stored in the consumer's memory. The first phase of information processing is *exposure*—the confronting of an individual with a stimulus that activates his senses. This is not an easy task for the marketer because consumers selectively expose themselves to stimuli. The second phase, *attention,* consists of preattentive processing and analysis for pertinence. Preattentive processing is the triggering of an initial response when a consumer is presented with a new stimulus. A determination of its pertinence for the consumer must follow. This chapter addresses the following three important factors affecting determination: (1) the consumer's predominant needs, both physical and psychological, (2) the consumer's values, and (3) the consistency of the consumer's cognitive structure. During the third phase of information processing, *comprehension,* the central control unit's filter assigns meaning to the stimulus. Two ways in which consumers can obtain ideas different from those conveyed by the marketer are through distorting the properties of physical stimuli to make them more consistent with their own personal preferences and distorting the content of a message and reacting to the expected and not the actual stimulus. After selected information has been comprehended in the third phase, the process enters the fourth phase—*retention* in long-term memory. The key factor affecting the retention of information is the pertinence that it has for the consumer.

Personality—an important component of the central control unit—can be thought of as a consistent pattern of responses to environmental stimuli. Three major personality theories are examined. The psychoanalytic or Freudian theory determines a person's behavior through the interaction of three systems of interdependent psychological forces—the id, ego, and superego. Social psychological theory considers social variables, not biological ones, to be the important determinants of personality and contends that man consciously directs his behavior toward need satisfaction. According to trait-factor theory, one's personality is composed of a set of traits or difference variables, the implication being that types of consumer behavior can be statistically related to a set of personality variables. The consumer analyst's attempts to show that personality substantially influences consumer behavior have resulted in more unsuccessful trials than successful ones.

On the basis of difficulties with market segmentation and related problems, most marketing strategists would contend that personality has not been demonstrated to be a significant input to marketing decision making. However, recent research efforts have produced four major modifications in the use of personality theory that may make it useful. First, consumption-related personality inventories have been constructed to replace standardized inventories specifically designed for use in the psychological clinic. Second, psychographic inventories have been developed that describe the life-styles of select segments through the use of activity, interest, and opinion statements. Third, personality has been found to interact with other variables as a moderator to determine behavior. Fourth, and finally, personality has become meaningful as an intervening variable.

QUESTIONS AND ISSUES FOR DISCUSSION

1. Comment on the following statement: "Because exposure is the initial stage of consumer information processing, the marketing strategist should focus most of his efforts on it to achieve maximum exposure."

2. The marketing director of a major amusement park in St. Louis is developing a new promotional campaign. What fac-

tors are likely to affect the attention-getting potential of marketing communications about this park? What can be done to increase the attention-getting potential of this firm's promotional efforts?

3. Pancake Syrup Incorporated has recently developed and introduced a totally new pancake syrup called "Sweet-n-Thick." The laboratory taste tests indicated that the product would be well received by consumers. Unfortunately, this has not been the case. What possible explanations are there for the disappointing performance of this new product? How might an understanding of consumer information processing help explain this situation?

4. Charlie Johnson, advertising director for a small savings and loan company in Chicago, has recently introduced an advertising campaign modeled after the campaign of a very large and successful Chicago bank. Based on your understanding of consumer information processing, is the campaign likely to be successful? Why or why not?

5. How does the consumer's psychological command center (CCU) affect the information processed?

6. Of what importance is the personality component in the consumer's CCU? Does a consumer's personality affect the information that the consumer processes? How does personality relate to the product features considered to be important by a consumer?

7. What are the basic differences between the three major personality theories? How might the marketing strategies developed by proponents of each of these theories differ from one another? Which of the theories is likely to provide the greatest contribution to the marketing strategist?

8. Why do consumer analysts continue to consider personality a central concept despite the many disappointing experiences marketing strategists have had with it?

9. How might information on the personality differences between consumers of Coca Cola and 7-Up help a 7-Up distributor?

10. How might the marketing director of Flavorfest Company use the information on the distinct market segments for his products?

Case 1

The Second National Bank has recently introduced a new service called the 24-hour teller. This service enables Second National's customers to make deposits and withdrawals 24 hours a day, seven days a week at four locations in town. The bank's management, extremely proud of being the first in this area to provide this innovative service, has provided the marketing director with a generous budget to promote this service. The marketing director has decided to stress the innovative and progressive nature of the service. Radio and television commercials will feature the bank president explaining how this service is just another indication of why Second National is the best bank in the area. When the proposed program was presented to the board of directors they had reservations about the appropriateness of the promotional program.

What possible reasons might the board of directors have for suggesting that the proposed program would not be successful?

How might an understanding of consumer information processing have aided the director of marketing in the development of this promotional program?

Case 2

The Lone Star Company, a manufacturer of quality motorcycles, has for some time attempted to identify a viable basis for segmenting its market. Its product line consisted of two basic types of bikes: (1) the power bike, designed for racing and climbing, and (2) the pleasure bike, designed for leisure and economy. After numerous unsuccessful attempts to segment the market on the basis of income, age, education, and social class, the marketing research director has observed some personality differences between the purchasers of the two types of bikes. In particular, the purchaser of the power bike appears to be more aggressive, more rigid, more objective, and more self-centered than the purchaser of the pleasure bike.

How might the observed personality differences help the marketing director to more effectively market Lone Star's bikes?

What reservations, if any, do you have about the value of personality information as a basis for segmenting this market?

Outline

The Role of Learning

The learning process is fundamental to most aspects of consumer behavior; consequently, it is an extremely important topic to understand.

Historically, much of the research that focused on learning as a formal process concentrated on simple mechanical types. These typically included what has been called *classical conditioning* and *instrumental conditioning.*[1] Classical conditioning theory had its origin in the work of Pavlov and is often exemplified by referring to the salivation of a dog at the sound of a dinner bell. In a learning situation such as this, the relevant action follows some triggering event. In instrumental conditioning the reverse is true. The sought response or action precedes what is called the *conditioning stimulus.*

In a consumer behavior context instrumental conditioning has been called trial-and-error learning;[2] that is, a consumer recognizes a personal desire for a particular product or service and proceeds to determine the most preferred one by trying in turn what appear to be reasonable alternatives. It is not unusual to find consumers using this method of selection when buying such products as cough medicine, cake mixes, dog food, and hand lotion.

Most of the work in both classical conditioning and instrumental conditioning has involved experimental psychologists using various animals, particularly rats. The assumption made by these researchers is that the learning process in its simplest form occurs in all species, including man. Stated more simply, it is basically the same wherever it is found. However, the more complex process of symbolic learning—the involvement of what has been called thinking or ideation—is unique to man.[3] It is this complex form that is of greatest interest to the consumer analyst and that

[1]M. L. Ray, *Psychological Theories and Interpretations of Learning: Technical Report* (Cambridge, Massachusetts: Marketing Science Institute, 1973), pp. 2–3.

[2]F. Hansen, *Consumer Choice Behavior: A Cognitive Theory* (New York: The Free Press, 1972), p. 126.

[3]B. R. Bereleson and G. A. Steiner, *Human Behavior* (New York: Harcourt Brace Jovanovich, 1964), pp. 133–134.

which the analyst has been examining. But, this symbolic learning is also the most difficult to study.

Learning in Consumer Behavior

As a way of introducing the subject of learning and of illustrating the variety of circumstances where it is involved in consumer behavior, the hypothetical situations included in Table 8.1 are offered as instances of consumer learning. Each of the topics identified is important to the consumer analyst because it relates specifically to market behavior and subsequently to the success of a firm's marketing strategy. Nevertheless, the situations have been substantially condensed to facilitate their usage here.

Actually, each situation described in Table 8.1 represents a rather complex phenomenon, such as brand loyalty as portrayed by the consistent buying of Kodak film. There are a number of factors that were influential in shaping the observed behavior. The following descriptions identify some of these missing details:

Some basic interest in photography is involved, and this was learned. The interest was probably developed over an extended period of time, with the nuclear family probably having had some impact on nurturing it.

The depth of one's interest also develops over time and contributes to formulating the criteria used to evaluate the picture-taking process.

Attention has been given to determining when it is appropriate to take pictures as well as the kind of equipment and supplies to use for obtaining acceptable results. In most cases, these decisions were made over time by gathering information using a number of means including: observing others; discussions with various people; reading, listening, and/or viewing advertisements; and personal trial and error.

Experience in shopping may also influence the brand of film purchased. The relative importance of patronage factors varies among consumer groups but usually includes convenience, product line, service, and price level.

TABLE 8.1
Instance in Consumer Learning

Consumer Behavior Topical Issue	Situation Observed Among Some Consumer Group	What Was Learned
1. Brand loyalty	Consistent buying of Kodak film	Among brands of film considered, this brand has proven to be most satisfactory in terms of price, quality, and availability.
2. Brand switching	Changing brands of toothpaste	The brand previously used has been found to be less desirable in terms of taste and texture than the new brand now being purchased.
3. Promotional message retention	Recall of the slogan of a well-known company, e.g., "Have it your way."	The advertising theme was associated with a particular fast food restaurant and the service feature of the firm.
4. Store or establishment loyalty	Visiting the same service station regularly for auto-related products	Over time, alternatives were considered, and this station was found to be the most preferred in terms of the evaluative criteria used.
5. Changing evaluative criteria	Starting to shop at a discount supermarket where prices are consistently lower on selected items	Shopping at this store is helpful in holding down family food expenditures.

As time passes and an individual accumulates experience in purchasing and using a product such as photographic film, that person ordinarily will attempt to simplify the decision process and the actual act of buying. What this typically leads to is the learning of a behavioral set through the integration of several basic elements of behavior into a meaningful group. In a nontechnical sense, three major components make up this behavioral set. These are shown in Figure 8.1.

FIGURE 8.1.
Elements of Behavioral Set

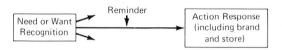

When a personal need or want is recognized (frequently this involves an external reminder such as an advertisement or someone saying, "Let's go on a picnic and don't forget to bring your camera"), a pattern of action quickly comes to mind. This often includes the brand of film to buy as well as where to make the purchase. What has been learned over time has greatly simplified the purchase process and shortened the amount of time that is needed to complete the act of buying. Some analysts have called this "routinized buying behavior."

Actually nothing is quite as important in predicting what choice will be made by a consumer as knowledge of past behavior in similar situations. This fundamental role of learning in economic behavior is described by Katona:[4]

> Learning, in the broadest sense of the term, is a basic feature of any organism. The human organism acquires forms of behavior, it acquires forms of action, of knowledge, or emotions. What has been done does not necessarily belong only to the past and is not necessarily lost. It may or may not exert influence on present behavior. Under what conditions and in what ways past experience affects later behavior is one of the most important problems of psychology.

Most of what is stored in the central control unit (CCU) is learned. This is shown in Figure 8.2.

Before proceeding further, a formal definition of learning must be set forth. It is also important to identify the key components of the learning process.

[4]G. Katona, *Psychological Analysis of Economic Behavior* (New York: McGraw-Hill Book Company, 1951), p. 30.

FIGURE 8.2.
Learning Process and the Central Control Unit

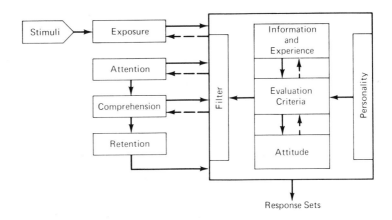

Source: J. F. Engel, D. T. Kollat, and R. D. Blackwell, *Consumer Behavior,* 2nd ed. (New York: Holt, Rinehart and Winston, Inc., 1973), p. 228. Reprinted by permission of the publisher.

The Learning Process and Its Components

LEARNING DEFINED

There are a number of definitions of learning, but one in particular is most appropriate to the subject of this book. As used throughout the text, *learning* is defined as those changes in responses and response tendencies due to the effects of experience. This definition acknowledges that learned behavior must include changes in attitudes, emotions, evaluative criteria, and personality as well as the more easily observed variations in physical behavior that have taken place over time due to individual experience. It should also be noted, however, that this definition excludes changes in these variables resulting from physiological factors such as natural growth, deterioration due to the aging process, fatigue, or drugs.[5] Of course, it is quite appropriate to

[5]B. R. Bereleson and G. A. Steiner, p. 135.

take these physiological factors. into consideration when attempting to affect the learning process. For example, observable changes in the motor capacity of young boys aged nine or ten from one summer to the next may greatly alter their ability to learn to catch and throw a baseball. This change due to the natural physical maturing process can increase their self-confidence and, as a result, make them more interested in the game of baseball and the equipment that goes along with it.

As pointed out in Chapter 2, the models of man of most help to the consumer analyst have consolidated considerable work done in a number of areas and have moved toward more comprehensive theory. In the learning area, this is exemplified by the declining interest in simple, mechanistic, S-R (stimulus-response) type explanations to recent efforts which pay more attention to the internal processes of individuals such as thinking and problem solving. These latter processes are recognized as an intricate part of the S-O-R relationship, where the (O) represents the internal state of the individual.[6]

THE COMPONENTS OF THE LEARNING PROCESS

As indicated earlier, the learning process can be broken down into several key components. These include drive, cue, response, reinforcement, and retention. The nature of each of these will be discussed in this section.

Drive

Drive refers to any strong internal stimulus that impels action. It is a force that arouses an individual and keeps him ready to respond and is thus the basis of motivation. A motive is also an internal stimulus. However, it is directed toward a specific goal, whereas a drive is a more general state of being aroused.

Traditionally, drives have been classified as either *primary* or *secondary.* Primary drives are essentially based on innate physiological needs such as thirst, hunger, pain avoidance, and sex. However, more recently these drives have been recognized to

[6]M. L. Ray, p. 18.

reflect the need for curiosity, exploration, or novelty.[7] Secondary drives are learned; that is, they are acquired over time through experience.

An individual is subject to many drives of both types, the intensity of which will vary from time to time. In some cases this changing intensity is rather easy to explain, while in others it is not. For instance, it is relatively easy to understand that one's thirst will generally heighten with physical activity or with the heat of the day. Observation of this change in drive intensity has definite market implications. When the thirst drive is strong, consumers are more receptive to a suggestion to have a cold drink. Furthermore, if this thirst is satisfied with a cold glass of Nestea iced tea, for example, this may provide sufficient impetus to try this brand again when similar circumstances arise.

At times it may be possible for a firm to simulate an experience such as that just described in an advertisement and realize some of the same impact on the consumer as the actual experience would have had. If the consumer can "see himself in the staged episode," learning can take place. This is consistent with human learning generally: Individuals often benefit from the experiences of others with whom they can identify. Using this idea in advertising reduces the need for the firm to attempt to time the placement of their ads to correspond with the greatest intensity of a particular consumer drive.

Nevertheless, it is still a reasonably common practice for some retailers to attempt to retain sufficient flexibility to be able to insert ads for selected special purpose products on short notice. The intention is to chose times that are likely to correspond to the highest level of drive intensity among consumers in their target market. For example, rain coats, ice-and snow-melting products, snow shovels, and umbrellas are frequently shown in advertisements that are prepared under pressure of last minute deadlines imposed to take advantage of changing weather conditions. Some department stores have felt these kinds of opportunities to be sufficiently important for them to employ private weather-forecasting services.

[7]M. L. Ray, p. 28.

Cue

Cues, as the term is used here, are stimuli that occur externally to the individual and can emanate from any environmental source. To be relevant in consumer behavior, they must affect individual market actions or response tendencies. This effect can arise through visual perception or through any of the other human senses. It is frequently the marketing manager's desire to create cue stimuli that trigger a move to action that culminates in the buying of some specific good or service as well as in the visiting of a particular store.

Although it is necessary to focus attention on the cue in consumer behavior, it should not be forgotten that in most situations the object of primary concern to the manager is the desired response. For instance, it may take considerable time and creative talent to develop an interesting as well as an attractive advertisement. Furthermore, this may be extremely important in gaining attention, but if the ad does not contribute to moving the members of the target market toward purchasing the product or service involved, more than likely it has failed. This perspective is also consistent with consumer interests. As the results of the American Association of Advertising Agencies' 1974 study—*The Consumer View of Advertising*—shows, the most important issue to consumers in their perception of advertising is the communication of product benefits; that is, consumers perceive advertising as cue stimuli that provide them with information including product features, availability, and price.[8]

Most firms make use of a concept called *generalization* in their use of cue stimuli. Generalization refers to the process that enables the individual to respond to a new stimulus as he has learned to respond to a similar but somewhat different one in the past.[9] The use of a variety of ads with a common theme in a promotional campaign has been an attempt by advertisers to employ the generalization concept and to reduce consumer boredom. In some cases, for example, this can be facilitated by simply shortening the 60-second television commercials to 30

[8]R. Bartos, *The Consumer View of Advertising—1974* (New York: American Association of Advertising Agencies, 1975), pp. 38–41.

[9]F. Hansen, p. 124.

seconds. The appeal of this approach is enhanced because of its economy.

Response

Response refers to the outcome or what occurs as the result of the interaction among drive, cue, the variables of the CCU, and environmental forces. The definition of learning referred to earlier stated that the outcome can take several forms that are of interest to the consumer analyst. These include consumer attitude change. This objective may be illustrated by an example from the public sector. A school board that has experienced a series of defeats of its request for additional operating funds may believe that public attitudes toward the local schools need to be altered before voter approval can be obtained. Such an evaluation of the situation by the board could lead them to initiate an informational campaign. This effort may be directed toward supplying influential citizen groups with critical data on the current state of the schools and program plans for the coming year. In this situation, the desired outcome of the action undertaken—the informational effort—is positive attitude change, the assumption being that more favorable public attitudes will lead to subsequent success in passage of the operating levy.

Many other responses can be used to illustrate what is relevant to those interested in consumer behavior. Some examples include the modification of consumer perception of a hardware store's image, the gaining of consumer awareness of Kellogg's new Corny Snaps, the addition of a previously excluded brand of hand soap to the list of those considered when purchasing this generic product, the association of a new logo with its sponsor by an important customer group, the trial of a new brand of nonpetroleum-based lubricant by a significant number of race car drivers, and the increase of voter registration in an area by a specified amount.

In a scientific sense, it is easier to study simple responses such as eye movement or changes in an individual's pulse rate following some stimulus than to focus on more complex market situations. However, most business managers and public administrators are only interested in changes in eye movement patterns or pulse rates if the observed results can be linked to relevant market behavior. Unfortunately, progress in most disciplines is usually slow in moving from laboratory experimentation to field application; although some success can be claimed, consumer behavior has been no exception.

Reinforcement

Reinforcement involves the matching of the consequences or outcomes of a response with the anticipated benefits; that is, it is the extent to which the actual benefits of a response coincide with what is considered acceptable, given the reason for action. Generally, the better the match between expectation and outcome, the greater the probability that the same response will be made under similar circumstances in the future. For example, assume that upon getting the urge to consume a candy bar you try a bar that you have never eaten before. If this is a satisfying experience, it increases the likelihood that under similar conditions at some future time you will buy this same candy, or stated more formally by Bayton, "When consumption or utilization of the goal-object leads to gratification of the initiating needs there is reinforcement."[10]

It is necessary to keep in mind that the phrase "under similar circumstances" was used above. Sufficient variation can occur to cause the consumer to deviate from what was learned previously. This variation can be effected by any of the variables. For instance, the consumer may simply feel differently, his or her drive state having been modified, or it may be that the cue was different. Still another source of variation in the circumstances is the response alternatives open to the consumer. For instance, the unavailability of the consumer's favorite brand of golf balls because it is out of stock could lead to the unplanned purchase of a competitive brand. The out-of-stock condition is an inhibitor to carrying out the planned buying action. It is important to consider what possible effects this condition can have on future purchases of this product.

[10]J. A. Bayton, "Motivation, Cognition, Learning—Basic Factors in Consumer Behavior," *Journal of Marketing,* 22 (January, 1958), p. 288.

Retention

The remembering of learned material and experiences over time is called *retention.* That which is not retained is considered forgotten. The human ability to remember is of considerable importance to those interested in consumer behavior.

Although there is substantial disagreement about the nature of the forgetting process, most analysts agree that some forgetting does take place and, all other things being equal, the more time that has passed since learning something, the less likely it is going to be remembered. For example, assume that two different yet rather similar promotional letters were sent to you, a non-savings and loan saver. Each was from a different savings and loan association in your community urging you to open a savings account at their institution. Also assume that you received one of these letters on January 1 and the other on January 15. On February 1 it is more likely that you will remember more details from the second letter, all other things being equal.

Having read the previous paragraph, one is quickly tempted to respond that "all other things" are ordinarily not equal. For instance, one of the two savings and loans referred to above may be located more conveniently to your home. Because convenience of location has consistently emerged as a major determinant in consumer selection of a savings and loan association for a new savings account, this alone may have substantially affected your retention of the two messages.

A number of other factors can also affect retention. Some of these include the clarity of the message, the similarity of competing messages, the individual's interest in the subject, the extent to which what was learned was consistent with one's values and previous experience.

Despite the multiplicity of influences on retention, once something is learned, it appears that it is never completely forgotten. Therefore, to say that a response tendency has been extinguished merely means that the response in question has been repressed (generally through nonreinforcement), or it may have essentially been displaced by the learning of an alternative that is incompatible with the original response.[11] An example of this latter situation is the successful effort of convincing consumers to purchase a new product in place of that which they have used satisfactorily before. There are a number of these situations in the men's shaving product area. Just think for a moment of all the alternative shaving systems now on the market. The male consumer has not been asked to forget his current method of shaving but to realize the added benefits by using the "new" shaving system offered. To some extent, the same approach has been used in amateur photography. Both Kodak and Polaroid have been very innovative in making new, improved means of picture taking available to the amateur.

The interrelationship of the five key components of the learning process is shown in Figure 8.3.

What follows in the next section are examples of some more notions from learning theory that are applicable to consumer behavior.

Further Notions from Learning Theory as Applied to Consumer Behavior

This section is not meant to be an exhaustive treatment, but simply a way of illustrating that there is a wide variety of possible applications of learning theory to the consumer in the market. The concepts discussed include semantic generation, semantic satiation, covert involvement and vicarious practice, aha experiences, and mental completing.

SEMANTIC GENERATION

Semantic Generation refers to the process of establishing meaning for words that essentially have no meaning. Some firms have intentionally sought to develop brand names or corporate names that have had no previous meaning. This enables the firm to create an appropriate meaning. Standard Oil of New Jersey, for example, went to considerable expense and took three years to create the name EXXON. J. Kenneth Jamieson, Chairman, said to the employees, "EXXON is unique, distinctive, and it's all

[11]B. R. Bereleson and G. A. Steiner, pp. 137–138.

FIGURE 8.3
Learning Process

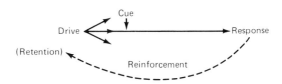

ours."[12] Several years ago Pontiac coined the word "pizazz" as a product feature. It had no meaning apart from that which consumers associated with it via their encounter with the advertising for Pontiac automobiles, dealers, and the car itself.

The employment of semantic generation can be very useful in the communication process in that it enables an organization to exercise greater control over what is associated with its corporate name, brand, or advertising campaign. Of course, some firms take an entirely different strategy and attempt to capitalize on what they perceive to be well-established words, that is, words that elicit strong, deeply seated meaning. These include such brands as Mr. Clean household cleaner, Ultra Brite toothpaste, Prime dog food, Love cosmetics, and Sweetheart dishwashing liquid.

SEMANTIC SATIATION

Semantic satiation refers to the fact that continued use of a meaningful word can make it less meaningful. It means the general weakening and increase in ambiguity of what is associated with the word.

The meaning of the word "discount" to many people has become weak through overuse in referring to a wide variety of marketing practices. The usage pattern of the term "cut rate"

[12]"Name Change Brings Excedrin Headaches and Costs Approximately $100 Million," *Wall Street Journal* (January 9, 1973), p. 34.

had a similar history and consequently became rather meaning-less.

With the extensive use of the broadcast media, particularly television, by some consumer goods' manufacturers, semantic satiation can occur more quickly. Part of what has been expressed as consumer boredom may be a symptom of semantic satiation.

COVERT INVOLVEMENT AND VICARIOUS PRACTICE

Covert Involvement encompasses the internal responses to stimuli, in other words, mental or emotional feelings. By this means a consumer may experience some of the benefits from a product or service by simply thinking about it.[13] This might be as exciting as the thrill of a ride on a fast moving snowmobile in northern Minnesota or just the feeling one gets from a refreshing drink of iced tea on a hot day.

Dichter called this phenomenon a mental rehearsal of the anticipated experience.[14] In this way the individual can learn about the results of his or her action before actually engaging in it. Some firms have been particularly skillful in facilitating covert involvement through their commercials. For example, television commercials for Nestea show various people taking a cooling plunge into a pool upon drinking a glass of Nestea. Coca-Cola and Pepsi have also been shown in pleasure-filled settings that can be easily identified with and mentally rehearsed. Furthermore, the benefits of purchasing certain products are more of an emotional nature than they are of a physical one, and these may never be experienced in a real-life setting. Consequently, the benefits are part of a mental fantasy.

Vicarious practice is closely associated with the concept of covert involvement. Learning is generally strengthened by seeing the object of attention in use. This permits an individual to visualize its use and is therefore sometimes referred to as observational learning or modeling.

[13]S. H. Britt, "Applying Learning Principles to Marketing," *MSU Business Topics,* 23 (Spring, 1975), p. 9.
[14]"Dichter gives 10 points for effective ads," *Advertising Age,* 42 (November 22, 1971), pp. 57–61.

It may be practically impossible to learn how to skillfully use a new fishing lure by simply watching a commercial illustrating it, but this observation process does enhance an individual's comprehension of how he might catch more desirable fish by employing the lure.

AHA EXPERIENCES

The *aha experience* typically refers to a problem-solving situation where there is one correct or acceptable response. It is like saying, "Yes, I remember now." Britt characterizes this as follows:[15]

> The discovery in the "aha" experience is the result of a trial-and-error method in which the person attempting to solve the problem emits the most obvious response. This process continues until he finds the correct solution; and when he does, he feels as though he has "hit upon it."

This concept may be applied, for example, to the area of unplanned purchasing. The two instances that follow are illustrations of practical situations where this concept may be operational.

> *Reminder impulse buying:* This is a situation where a shopper sees an item and remembers that he/she needs the product.

> *Suggestion impulse buying:* This is when a shopper sees an item and then visualizes a need for it, even though no previous thought has been given to the product.

Supermarket checkout areas are a favorite setting to use in applying this idea.

MENTAL COMPLETING

Mental completing refers to the human tendency to remember incomplete patterns better than those that are complete. This involves the process of *closure*—the tendency of an experience to be organized into a whole or continuous figure or vision.

[15]S. H. Britt, p. 11.

This concept was used in advertising Salem cigarettes. Salem commercials were built around the jingle "You can take Salem out of the country, but you can't take the country out of Salem." In broadcast advertising the jingle was played one and one-half times. The silence after the second "You can take Salem out of the country, but . . ." encouraged the listener to complete the message. Even to the nonsmoker there was a compelling urge to complete the jingle.[16]

This section has illustrated the fact that various learning concepts that have been developed elsewhere do have useful applications in consumer behavior. However, there has been some risk in offering them—the tendency to oversimplify both the concepts and their usefulness. Even if such concepts are appropriately used, they do not guarantee success to the marketing manager for a number of reasons. For instance, it would be extremely difficult to determine the impact on generating profitable sales of Salem cigarettes that resulted from the clever use of closure noted above. Furthermore, what first meets the eye as an opportunity may actually be deceiving to the strategist.

In order to motivate people, it may take the recognition of deep emotional feelings or anxieties and a creative approach to soothing them. A good example of this comes from the appeal once made by the Red Cross to the patriotism of possible blood donors which proved to be a dismal failure.[17] This failure was due to the fact that abstract, ideological appeals rarely result in immediate action. In researching the problem, it was determined that giving blood arouses unconscious anxieties. This was found to be especially true of men, by whom it was equated with giving away part of their personal strength and virility.

Consequently, these underlying feelings squelched the impact of the information about the critical need for blood and the information concerning the rapid regeneration of blood in the body. Therefore, to get men to give blood it was vital to make them feel more masculine; that is, it is important to show that a man has virility to spare and that the personal sacrifice actually is a sign

[16]S. H. Britt, p. 10.
[17]P. Zimbardo and E. B. Ebbesen, *Influencing Attitudes and Changing Behavior* (Reading, Massachusetts: Addison-Wesley Publishing Co. Inc., 1970), pp. 109–110.

of his masculinity. This was accomplished in part by giving each donor a pin in the form of a white drop of blood, the equivalent of a wounded soldier's Purple Heart medal. The recommended changes in tactics resulted in a sudden and dramatic increase in blood donations.

Summary

Learning can be defined as those changes in responses and response tendencies due to the effects of experience. The learning process can be broken down into five key components: drive, cue, response, reinforcement, and retention. *Drive* is any strong internal stimulus that impels action, such as hunger, thirst, or one that is acquired through experience. A *cue* is an external stimulus from an environmental source that affects individual market actions or response tendencies. *Response* is the result of the interaction of drive, cue, the variables of the CCU, and environmental forces and can take several forms. *Reinforcement* occurs when the outcome of a response matches the anticipated benefits, satisfying the initial needs. *Retention* is the remembering of learned material and experiences over time; it is influenced by numerous factors.

Many learned theory concepts can be applied to consumer behavior. The creation of meaning for words such as "EXXON" that essentially have no meaning is a concept known as *semantic generation.* Continued use of a meaningful word, causing it to become less meaningful is *semantic satiation. Covert involvement* is the consumer's internal response to stimuli, such as feeling the benefits to be gained from a product by just thinking about it. *Vicarious practice* can occur when the consumer sees an object of attention in use. *Aha experiences* occur in problem-solving situations where there is one correct or acceptable response, such as unplanned purchasing. *Mental completing* is the human tendency to remember incomplete patterns better than complete ones. Indeed, the learning process is fundamental to consumer behavior.

1. Because learning is so basic to human existence, is it an appropriate area for marketing managers or other executives to attempt to manipulate? Explain your answer.

2. Many consumer goods are sold in a highly competitive environment where competing promotional messages are in plentiful supply. Under such circumstances, how can one firm use any learning concept to its own advantage?

3. Identify each of the following as a drive, cue, response, reinforcement process, or evidence of retention.
   a. shopping at J. C. Penney's
   b. gaining enjoyment from attending a professional baseball game
   c. recommending to a friend that she try your preferred brand of shampoo
   d. being concerned about one's personal health
   e. seeing an ad for 7-Up.

4. Is there reason to believe that because children generally have had much less experience than have adults, that they are likely to be more receptive to the use of vicarious practice in advertising appeals? Explain the reasons for your answer.

5. Give an example to illustrate the use of each of the following learning concepts in attempting to appeal to the consumer to conserve energy.
   a. semantic generation
   b. covert involvement
   c. aha experience
   d. mental completing.

6. How can consumer learning generally work to the disadvantage of a particular firm? Give an example to illustrate your answer.

7. Describe a purchase experience that you personally have been engaged in recently. Identify how learning was involved in this experience. Is it possible to determine what was the drive, cue, response, and the act of reinforcement in this situation?

8. Do consumers ever become so set in their ways that learning a new idea is nearly impossible? If so, give an example to illustrate how this could happen.

9. Is it possible to "unlearn" something? Does this affect consumer behavior? Explain.

10. Can a fear appeal be used successfully in advertising to get consumers to learn the benefits of a particular product or service? If so, give an example.

Case 1

The Superb Company has recently developed a coffee substitute which it claims smells, tastes, and looks like freshly brewed coffee. However, it does not have any of the unpleasant side effects that are often associated with drinking coffee. During extensive taste testing, consumers were unable to distinguish between the imitation and real coffee.

Although the new imitation product is an excellent substitute for coffee, it must be prepared differently by the consumer. The substitute must be boiled for at least 5 minutes before serving.

What difficulties might be encountered in gaining consumer acceptance of this new product?

How could a name be selected that would connote the benefits of the product and its distinctiveness?

Case 2

The NO-STICK brand has been successfully used for years to identify a coating process made available by Progressive Industries, Inc. This coating is used on various cooking utensils to reduce the chances of food sticking to them. Recently the firm has begun to apply the coating to many other consumer products including range surfaces, garden tools, razor blades, and table tops.

How can Progressive capitalize on their previous success in their most recent venture?

What problems might they encounter in generating consumer interest in other applications of the NO-STICK process?

Outline

Evaluative Criteria

Few areas of consumer behavior have more operational significance from a manager's point of view than the bases used by those in a target market to judge an organization or its product offerings. This chapter concentrates upon evaluative criteria—those specifications used by the consumer to compare and evaluate goods and services, brands, and places of business. The location of the evaluative criteria in the decision-process model is shown in Figure 9.1.

Actually, evaluative criteria are a group of product features or performance characteristics, such as price and dependability, that consumers value and expect to find in a particular product, brand, retail outlet, or other organization with which they anticipate dealing during some reasonable period of time. The use of such criteria is not limited to those situations where a product or service is being considered for purchase; they are applied more broadly in decision making. For instance, administrators of charitable organizations have considerable interest in the criteria used by their prospective donors in deciding which causes to support and the amount of the contribution that will be made. Political

FIGURE 9.1.
Evaluative Criteria

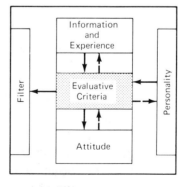

Source: J. F. Engel, D. T. Kollat, and R. D. Blackwell, *Consumer Behavior,* 2nd ed. (New York: Holt, Rinehart and Winston, Inc., 1973), p. 247. Reprinted by permission of the publisher.

candidates also try to identify those issues or factors that are the most instrumental in voting decisions. This, too, is an attempt to determine and be sensitive to the relative importance of evaluative criteria used by individuals in comparing alternatives in a decision-making situation.

Determining evaluative criteria is necessary but not sufficient. The consumer analyst must also identify and understand the evaluative criteria as they are perceived by the consumer. For example, if price is found to be important to consumers, does this mean that the very lowest price is sought or is it some target price that is considered fair and appropriate? As mentioned earlier in the text, the consumer's reality is his perception of the circumstances that surround him. This includes perceived features in whatever it is he or she is interested in—motorcycles, automobiles, tennis shoes, restaurants, clothing, books, and so forth. Therefore, a manager's knowledge is inadequate if it only includes determining what features or performance characteristics are sought by important market segments and is not clear as to what these mean in an operational sense or how the product is viewed in terms of these criteria. Furthermore, it is of major importance that a manager know how well his product offering compares to competitive brands in the eyes of the consumer.

An example of the importance of knowing the makeup and meaning of the evaluative criteria can be related to the purchase of suntan preparations. Assume that research has shown that ease of application is one of the most sought after features and that the branded products available can be easily grouped in terms of how they are applied. One group of products are creams, available in either tubes or jars. The other major group of products are packaged in aerosol cans. The producers of all these products believe they are easy to use, and in a functional sense, this may be true. However, if consumers in the primary target market only associate ease of application of a suntan preparation with a creamlike substance, this is the reality that must be dealt with. This does not necessarily suggest that aerosol cans should be abandoned, but it does pose a difficult belief to overcome and would affect the marketing strategy used. Just such a difficulty as this appeared when toothpaste was made available in aerosol cans as an alternative to tubes.

Variability in Evaluative Criteria

The features or performance characteristics sought in a product or service vary among different market segments as well as for a given individual under different circumstances. For instance, it is safe to say that what a typical teenager seeks in entertainment is different from what most senior citizens expect. Also, any given teenager's entertainment desires may vary in different situations. On a warm summer afternoon their entertainment desires may only be fulfilled by a picnic at the park with friends, while on another evening attending a movie alone is a most satisfying experience.

DIFFERENCES IN CRITERIA AMONG CONSUMER GROUPS

Various consumer groups may use substantially different evaluative criteria in assessing any given product. These differences, once identified, can become the basis for the formation of unique marketing strategies to be used in appealing to the respective market segments. This is illustrated by the situation in the following paragraph.

Several years ago it was discovered that women held two major views with respect to their reason for using perfume. One group viewed perfume as something that enhanced their natural beauty. The other group considered perfume a means of covering up unpleasant or offensive odors.[1] It is very likely that different evaluative criteria will be used by women within each of these two major segments in comparing alternative brands of perfume. For instance, a mild fragrance would probably be sought by the first market segment, while a bolder scent would be pleasing to the latter group. The importance of price is also likely to vary between these two customer groups. Differences like these can be incorporated in a firm's advertising strategy, package design, brand name selection, pricing scheme as well as other phases of their marketing program.

[1]D. Yankelovich, "New Criteria for Market Segmentation," in *Readings in Marketing Management,* P. Kotler and K. K. Cox, eds. (Englewood Cliffs, New Jersey: Prentice-Hall, Inc., 1971), p. 97.

INDIVIDUAL USE OF DIFFERENT CRITERIA

The evaluative criteria used by an individual and the relative importance of their contents at some point in time can change under different circumstances. This variation is discussed under two possible conditions: (1) purchasing for personal consumption versus buying for others and (2) the impact of environmental situations.

Purchasing for Personal Consumption Versus Buying for Others

When a person is buying an item for personal use that he or she has had experience with, a particular evaluative criterion is usually called to mind. This is then used in the process of choosing among alternative brands. However, if the same individual is making a purchase for someone else, such as a gift, a somewhat modified set of evaluative criteria is likely to be employed. This will probably include an attempt to consider what the recipient would look for in the product, but it is also likely to include some price limit as to the maximum amount that can or should be spent on this gift. The following situation illustrates such an occasion.

If you were to buy a flower arrangement for a table decoration for a party that you are giving, certain criteria would come to mind that you would use in making the selection. These would include your personal preferences for particular flowers as well as the colors that would complement the table decorations. However, if these flowers were intended as a gift for a parent's birthday and they were to be sent FTD, a different set of criteria would be used.

The same kind of variation in criteria can be observed when a parent is purchasing an item such as golf clubs for himself and also for his young son or daughter. If the parent is buying a set of clubs for himself and is an experienced golfer with a serious interest in the sport, the quality of the clubs will probably be considerably more important than the price. However, if the clubs are for a son or daughter who is just a beginner, price may be quite important. Under these latter conditions, the parent is uncertain as to whether the interest will continue and, consequently, wants to limit his investment while still providing an opportunity for the young person to learn something about the sport.

The Impact of Environmental Situations

Research shows that it is ordinarily possible to identify a list of what might be called ideal or preferred product features or operating characteristics for whatever product a firm markets. One study found, for example, that homemakers in one major market sought the following attributes in a cake mix: ease of use, economy, consistent results, and tastiness.

These are listed in the order of importance to the homemakers studied. As such, these four characteristics represent their evaluative criteria under "normal" circumstances. However, if some of these homemakers are faced with the responsibility of making a cake for a very special occasion, such as a wedding, some variation may take place. In the situation posed, it is likely that the fourth characteristic—tastiness—moves to the top as the most important consideration.

The consumer lives in an environment that poses many different circumstances, and to make the assumption that once established the evaluative criteria become rigid and not subject to change is inconsistent with reality. Nevertheless, it is possible to identify the evaluative criteria used by consumers in various market segments in the majority of buying situations. These criteria represent the most consistently used means of comparing alternatives and can greatly assist the marketing manager in developing strategy that will emphasize these.

How Evaluative Criteria Are Formed

The form that evaluative criteria take is the result of a number of forces. These can be classified into four separate groupings as follows: (1) *personality*—the individuality that is observable in the form of rather consistent modes of behavior that are characterized in various ways, such as aggressive, persuasive, innovative, and complacent patterns of behavior; (2) *social factors*—the family, peer groups, social class norms as well as other group influences that come to bear upon the individual; (3) *demo-*

graphic factors—the influence of variables such as age, education, income, and geographic area of residence; (4) *market forces*—the efforts of business firms and other organizations that have a direct impact in shaping the evaluative criteria of individuals. The nature of each will be discussed, with the major emphasis placed on market forces because these are more subject to the control of the marketing manager. The marketing strategist is wise to be aware of the first three, for they can be of considerable value in providing a direction for his efforts.

PERSONALITY

Individuality can influence the content of a person's evaluative criteria. Some people, for instance, are more willing to assume risk than others. This willingness to assume risk, in turn, can have a substantial effect on how they make choices. For a stock broker, it could be beneficial to segment prospective customers using this characteristic because it helps shape the evaluative criteria people use in selecting securities.

Innovativeness is also a personality characteristic that has important implications for consumer behavior. It, too, is likely to be related to one's willingness to assume risks of various kinds, particularly those associated with new product usage. For those who are truly innovators, it may mean that newness itself is a key component of their evaluative criteria. It appears that considerable personal gratification comes to some people simply by being one of the first to try a new product or service. Nevertheless, newness is unlikely to be the only basis for making any buying decision.

SOCIAL FACTORS

Each of the major social forces have been discussed in earlier chapters. However, it is important to visualize their relevance in shaping the criteria used by individuals in evaluating alternative products and services. This can be illustrated here with respect to the influence of the family environment.

The interest of a young man in auto mechanics and tinkering with motors is likely to have been affected by his father. If, for example, the young man's father did most of his own automobile maintenance work and shared his know-how with his son, the son will probably show similar interests. Such interests are likely to be reflected in the criteria used in selecting auto parts and accessories as well as the extent to which maintenance services are purchased.

Other social forces that can have a substantial impact on how products or services are assessed include the influence of friendship groups, social class norms, the work environment, and opinion leaders.

DEMOGRAPHIC FACTORS

A large proportion of marketing research effort has sought to differentiate prospective customers on the basis of demographic characteristics. These typically include age, education, sex, household income, occupation, household size, and geographic place of residency. As mentioned earlier, the development of the family life cycle concept has resulted from the combining of selected demographic variables into groupings that provide further insight into behavioral patterns.

From the illustrations used in Chapter 6, it is apparent that evaluative criteria are subject to variation as family composition changes through time. However, even a single demographic variable can have an effect on the content of one's evaluative criteria. For instance, the amount of formal education completed can have a substantial impact on an individual's ability to read and comprehend information. As a result, those with very little formal education generally rely more on radio and television media for information and may not develop very sophisticated evaluative criteria.[2] The consequences of this may show up in many ways, for instance, in their inability to include any nutritional factors in the criteria they use in food selection and meal planning.

[2]C. E. Block, "Prepurchase Search Behavior of Low-Income Households," *Journal of Retailing,* 48 (Spring, 1972), pp. 12–13.

Income, too, can have a direct and noticeable effect on evaluative criteria. For example, the concept of a fair price for a product may vary considerably across income groups. Furthermore, price considerations are likely to be among the most important selection criteria for low income groups. It is not uncommon for senior citizens on social security to use price rather than style or color as the most important factor in assessing alternative brands of women's clothing.

MARKET FORCES

The efforts of business firms and other organizations can have a substantial impact on the formation of an individual's evaluative criteria. For instance, environmental groups such as National Wildlife Foundation, the Audubon Society, and the Sierra Club have encouraged consumers to avoid clothing and other products that make use of rare species of animals. In other situations the influence has come from organizations such as the Better Business Bureau, Consumers' Union, and the Consumer Product Safety Commission. One significant promotional effort undertaken by the CPSC in cooperation with private business encouraged consumers to exercise great care in using their rotary lawn mower and to purchase only rotary mowers that meet minimum safety requirements. Of course, advertising and other marketing efforts that business firms employ also influence the criteria consumers use to assess products and places of business. The area of influence subject to the greatest control by the marketing manager or public administrator is their marketing strategy and the tactics they use in its implementation. Therefore, this effort is discussed in some detail in the following paragraphs.

In addressing this subject, Boyd, Ray, and Strong indicate that a manager has two possible strategy alternatives that focus on the evaluative criteria used by consumers in a firm's target market.[3] These two are presented below with illustrations of their application.

[3]H. W. Boyd, Jr., M. L. Ray, and E. C. Strong, "An Attitudinal Framework for Advertising Strategy," *Journal of Marketing,* 36 (April, 1972), pp. 29–33.

Add Characteristic(s) to Those Considered Salient for the Product Class

Through the use of salesmen, advertising, or publicity, a firm can make potential customers aware of one or more product features or attributes that were not previously considered; some may be entirely new features. This strategy has been successfully employed in a number of situations. For example, such a method has been used by promoting additives in gasoline, fluoride in toothpaste, vitamins in cereals, bleach in detergents, and butter or other fats in turkeys to make them self-basting.

This strategy has been used most frequently when a product is in the maturity stage of its life cycle; that is, it has enjoyed considerable market success and competitive brands have begun to look very similar. Such a strategy is often combined with a modification in the physical features of the product. The combined effort of altering the physical product and the employment of promotional strategy to encourage the consumer to notice this change with the intent of their considering it as an important buying criterion can extend the profitable life of the product. Of course, it is extremely important to keep in mind that the basic assumption made by the firm using this approach is that their brand is superior with respect to the product feature or attribute being promoted. For instance, it would be absurd for an oil company to promote a de-icer additive as an important product feature if their brand of gasoline had an inferior de-icer as compared to its competitors.

Increase or Decrease the Rating for a Salient Product Class Characteristic

A firm that found that its brand rated well on a product characteristic that was not of great importance to consumers can try to change the weight given this characteristic. It may be, for example, that one brand of ice cream has all natural ingredients, but this feature does not appear to be too important to consumers. The firm whose brand this is may wish to try to increase the weight placed upon this product feature. This could be a particularly attractive strategy if key competitors could not make the same claim.

Under some circumstances a firm may choose to try to reduce the importance that consumers place on a certain product feature or operating characteristic because of their brand's inability to show up favorably on this dimension. In promoting some of their full-size models, U.S. auto manufacturers have played down the importance of fuel economy and emphasized the roominess of the standard-size models.

Evaluative Criteria Are Not Always What They "Ought" To Be

Almost everyone has an opinion about what to look for when buying commonly used products and services, and from time to time we are asked for our advice as to what these important features include. A number of rather objective criteria are typically offered in response to such an inquiry. Frequently these include some statement about a product's price, durability, range of features, warranty, adaptability, and ease of obtaining service. In many product purchases these kinds of features are undoubtedly key considerations in the consumer's mind. Also, consumers as a whole probably believe that these are what evaluative criteria ought to be.

However, there are other evaluative criteria that are hardly ever discussed among consumers and it is likely that many would even deny their existence. These latter criteria are essentially subjective in nature; that is, they are much less well defined and more difficult to measure. Nevertheless, there is sound evidence to show that consumers do include dimensions such as eye appeal, style, status, aesthetics, and prestige when evaluating many products. Furthermore, it is not difficult to understand why these are relevant because some are the kind of things that enrich life and raise an experience above the ordinary.

For a consumer analyst, it would be naive to simply focus on either the objective or subjective criteria to the exclusion of the others. The real challenge is to correctly identify the whole set of evaluative criteria of prospective customers and to determine the relative importance of each of its components.

How Evaluative Criteria Can Be Identified

There are essentially two ways of determining the evaluative criteria that are used by important market segments. These are direct questioning and indirect questioning. Each of these may be employed with some or considerable in-depth probing.

DIRECT QUESTIONING

Direct questioning involves a series of inquiries that ask in a rather straightforward manner on what basis the person being questioned makes a particular buying decision, that is, what product features or performance characteristics he or she seeks in a given product or service. For instance, a number of studies have been done in an attempt to determine what prospective students and their parents look for in a college or university. It may be that, through direct questioning of a representative group, the curricula offered, the geographic location of the school, and its tuition emerge as the three issues of most importance. However, this list itself does not completely specify the content of the evaluative criteria for selecting a school. This point can be illustrated with respect to the location dimension. It may be that, all other things being equal, parents and prospective students may have a strong preference for schools within a 150-mile drive from their home. This information now gives practical meaning to the specification of location as a criterion.

Another illustration can be used to illustrate a different dimension of the content issue. The term *convenience* often appears among evaluative criteria but not always with the same meaning intended. For instance, "convenience" as a criterion in the selection of a fast food restaurant may mean a location close to home or possibly the minimum distance a person is willing to travel to find such a restaurant whenever he or she is hungry for a hamburger and French fries. Still another meaning could focus on the speed of the service received once a person is in the door.

To properly identify the evaluative criteria and accurately determine their relative importance by direct questioning takes careful planning and structuring of the questions used. It may also require a series of questions to get to the real meaning of each dimension, as the above examples illustrate.

INDIRECT QUESTIONING

Some experienced analysts believe that consumers are often unable to accurately list the bases they use in the selection of products or services. Those who offer this argument contend that what may happen is that a list of evaluative criteria are given by the consumer when he or she is asked, but that these represent what are socially acceptable reasons for buying a product—not necessarily the real reasons. Furthermore, some products and services are particularly difficult to discuss openly and, therefore, any inquiry regarding these must employ some indirect approach.

As a means of avoiding these kinds of difficulties and obtaining the actual evaluative criteria, various indirect questioning procedures can be used. One approach that has been successful is to ask those being questioned what they believe others they know seek in the product. For example, ''What do your neighbors look for in a house paint? In other words, on what basis do they judge the various brands available to them?'' The assumption made in following this procedure is that people will reveal their own feelings even though they are being asked about someone else's behavior. A similar approach to the one just described frames the questions in yet another way: ''What would you suggest that a new family in your community look for in selecting a church?''

Questioning individuals in small groups can also facilitate the discovery of their evaluative criteria. An experienced moderator can ask probing questions that nurture personal interaction and the discussion of deeply held ideas and notions. For instance, it may be discovered that color and texture preferences serve as subconscious bases for the evaluation of packaged goods. Obtaining such information could stimulate interest in reviewing packing schemes for a firm's product line.

This indirect questioning procedure could also take the form of asking people to compare brands of products on various attributes. Their responses can then be scaled for more precise comparisons. The most recent work of this nature uses multidimensional scaling and offers considerable promise as a means of more accurate differentiation of important evaluative criteria. However, this subject is beyond the scope of this book.

Indirect questioning procedures are ordinarily used to supplement or check the accuracy of the results obtained from the more direct methods of inquiry. It is important to keep in mind that considerable expertise is necessary to make good use of this approach.

Other Practical Considerations in Focusing on Evaluative Criteria

The points that follow cut across several topics discussed earlier in this chapter. They also serve as a final reminder of the operational significance of evaluative criteria to the marketing manager.

1. Although the number of features used to compare alternative brands of a product may be unlimited, consumers usually have about five or six key considerations that they rely on.

2. Evaluative criteria are usually formed over an extended period of time and are always subject to change based on new information and consumer experience. Nevertheless, criteria remain reasonably stable from year to year. In other words, rapid change in what people seek in particular products, services, and business establishments is not typical.

3. Obtaining some measure of the relative importance of each item in the evaluative criteria is essential. Some product features or operating characteristics may be considerably more relevant than others. The relative importance of various elements of the criteria is probably more subject to change over short periods of time than is the substance of the criteria itself.

4. In some product groups competitive brands or business establishments are perceived to be very similar on most features that consumers seek; therefore, characteristics of lesser importance become the real basis for differentiation. For example, when a consumer is selecting a drugstore to fill a doctor's prescription, assume that he is looking for a high level of professional expertise and judgment in the pharmacist, a fair pricing policy, and a convenient location. To many consumers, pharma-

cists may be perceived to be of essentially equal competence because of state licensing laws with requirements to use fresh, quality ingredients and to charge about the same price for prescription drugs. If this is their belief, then convenience of location emerges as the key differentiating characteristic and, consequently, the basis for their selection of a drugstore.

5. When consumers cannot judge a product's features directly, surrogate or substitute means of evaluation are frequently used. For example, national brand names may be relied on for quality. One of the reasons some people buy St. Joseph brand of aspirin is because they seek high quality in such drugs and apparently believe that they can trust in these national brands.

Some consumers also use price as a guide to quality; that is, they believe that you essentially get what you pay for in a purchase.

6. It is not unusual to find circumstances where a consumer's evaluative criteria are so specified that only one brand meets the features sought. This is particularly true when subjective criteria are involved. For instance, to some people their required product features and subjective considerations such as style and prestige in an automobile can be met only by a Volvo. If there are no major constraints on their purchasing a Volvo, they are likely to be very loyal buyers.

Some manufacturers of multiple product lines have tried to encourage the situation described above by specifying the use of one of their products with another. Kraftco, for instance, specifies on the box of its macaroni dinner that Parkay margarine be used in preparing it, hoping that consumers will use only this recommended brand.

7. Evaluative criteria may be applied in steps; that is, some consumers go through a rough screening of alternative brands using relatively general criteria preceding their making finer comparisons based on more rigorous standards. For instance, some individuals will only buy domestically produced products; Consequently, their initial comparisons will quickly sort out products with a foreign origin. This will be followed by a judging of the remaining brands on their features and performance characteristics such as price, durability, and aesthetic appeal.

Summary

This chapter concentrates on a portion of the central control unit—evaluative criteria. These are specifications used by the consumer to compare and evaluate goods and services, brands, and places of business. Evaluative criteria can vary substantially among segmented consumer groups. In addition, the individual consumer's evaluative criteria can vary considerably when buying for someone other than him or herself or when involved in other environmental situations.

Four major forces influence the form that evaluative criteria will take. The first is *personality*—an individual's uniqueness that is observable in his behavior patterns. The second is *social factors* or family and other group influences. The third is *demographic variables* such as age, education, or income. The fourth is *market forces* or the efforts of a firm or group to influence the individual's evaluative criteria. The market force influence may be implemented either by adding characteristics to those considered salient by the product class or by increasing or decreasing the rating for a salient product class characteristic.

Evaluative criteria are not always objective but can include many subjective dimensions such as eye appeal or status.

Direct questioning can be used to identify a consumer's evaluative criteria if the questions are planned carefully and reveal true, complete answers. Questioning indirectly by asking a consumer for his perception of another consumer's evaluative criteria can often reveal the original consumer's own criteria.

In concluding the chapter, several other practical considerations of evaluative criteria are noted.

QUESTIONS AND ISSUES FOR DISCUSSION

1. To what extent do consumers use more well-developed evaluative criteria in selecting expensive products than in choosing among less expensive items? Give an example.
2. What are some common evaluative criteria used to assess the following products and services?

chewing gum
color television
original art work
a medical doctor

3. Assume that you wanted to be the true "economic man," that is, what might be called perfectly rational. What criteria would you personally use to evaluate the following?

automobile
college
auto mechanic
breakfast cereal

4. Since evaluative criteria vary among people assessing the same good or service, how can a marketing manager use these in planning his or her marketing strategy?
5. Are there situations where evaluative criteria are developed after the purchase is made? If so, give an example.
6. Can consumers be taught what is "good" evaluative criteria in buying specific products? For instance, can a book on buymanship be helpful to a person in selecting a new electric range?
7. How is the experience that one has had with a product likely to affect the evaluative criteria used to assess its replacement? Give an example.
8. What are some products or services that are evaluated strictly on a subjective basis? Why is this the case?
9. Do consumers usually get what they pay for? When is price the most important criterion in selecting a product?
10. Give some examples of products that are evaluated today on bases substantially different from those used five years ago.

SITUATIONAL PROBLEMS

Case 1

The four members of the Byrd family have decided that it is time to redecorate their living room. After much discussion and having looked through various shelter magazines, they have come to some agreement. The room will have a contemporary theme and include dominant shades of blue and green. Each major piece of furniture will be selected by one member of the family, subject to the review of the other members. No more than $2,500 will be spent on the entire room this year. What are the objective and subjective evaluative criteria used by the Byrds?

Assuming that the Byrds are a typical, suburban, middle class family, how can this information be helpful to a marketing manager?

Case 2

The Safety Equipment Company manufactures a line of fire extinguishers for home use as well as an alarm system for fire and break-in detection that any handyman can install. The extinguishers are priced from $15.95 to $49.95 and the alarm systems start at $425. Although the Company has enjoyed a healthy sales volume, management believes that business could be substantially better. A recent study covering six major urban areas uncovered the following statistics:

15% of the households have a fire extinguisher
3% of the households have some form of smoke, fire, or break-in alarm system
83% of all respondents strongly agreed that homes should have a fire extinguisher
37% of all respondents strongly agreed that homes should have some kind of alarm system.

Most respondents expressed concern for the safety of their family and said that they would like to have an easy-to-use, inexpensive, reliable, and portable fire extinguisher. Those who were most interested in an alarm system lived near the central city and were very frightened by the increasing crime rate.

What are the evaluative criteria that are likely to be used to select each of these two products?

How can the Safety Company management use the information from this study in planning their advertising strategy?

10

Attitudes and Attitude Change

OUTLINE

The concept of attitude is one of the most prevalent and important concepts in consumer behavior and, indeed, in the social sciences generally. Interest in attitudes emanates from the belief that knowledge of attitudes permits accurate prediction of consumer behavior. "Attitude" will be defined precisely in the next section, but generally a consumer's attitudes can be thought of as his basic orientation for or against various alternative products, services, retail outlets, etc. Because attitudes form a coherent system of evaluative orientations, they are an important component in the consumer's Central Control Unit.

Nature of Attitudes

The term "attitude" is so common both in behavioral science research and in everyday living that precise definition is essential. "Attitudes" can be explored by defining their role in the CCU, identifying their composition, clarifying their organization, and specifying their functions.

THE MEANING OF ATTITUDES

Everyone has on occasion been asked to express his or her assessment of something. For example, "How do you like your new Vega?" or "How do you feel about free checking?" or "How do you feel about the use of sex in advertising?" Thus, although few can provide a precise definition of "attitudes," most have a reasonably clear intuitive understanding of what they are. Interestingly enough, even though there is general agreement on the meaning of "attitudes" at the intuitive level, there is little agreement at the theoretical level.

According to one widely accepted definition, *attitude* is a mental and neural state of readiness to respond which is organized through experience and exerts a directive and/or dynamic influence on behavior.[1] This definition is too broad for marketing

[1]G. Allport, "Attitudes," *Handbook of Social Psychology,* C. Murchison, ed. (Worcester, Massachusetts: Clark University Press, 1935), pp. 798–884.

purposes, however, because "attitude" in this sense is more appropriately considered as a component of personality. In marketing, "attitude" is used to refer to a consumer's assessment of the ability of an alternative to satisfy his purchasing and consumption requirements as expressed in his evaluative criteria. Thus, the consumer's response to the question "How do you like your new Vega" (i.e., the consumer's attitude toward his Vega) reflects his evaluation of the Vega based on the evaluative criteria he considers to be important.

As you will recall, evaluative criteria are a function of the consumer's stored information and experience. This relationship, as indicated by the solid lines in Figure 10.1, causes attitude to become the focal variable of the central control unit. The attitude variable's importance is further enhanced by the fact that once formed, attitudes affect evaluative criteria and stored information. This feedback effect of attitudes is shown by the dashed lines in Figure 10.1.

THE STRUCTURE OF ATTITUDES

An attitude is an abstract concept. As a result of the abstract nature of an attitude, its structure or makeup cannot be directly observed. This, in turn, permits the existence of alternative views regarding the underlying structure of an attitude. Two alternative yet not fundamentally distinct views can be summarized in the following models: the classical psychological model and the multiattribute model.

The Classical Psychological Model

The classical psychological model, a widely accepted view, maintains that attitudes are made up of three basic components: (1) cognitive, (2) affective, and (3) behavioral.[2] The cognitive component refers to the manner in which a consumer perceives information about a product, service, advertisement, or retail outlet. This component includes beliefs a consumer has about the support services a retailer offers as well as beliefs about the relative merits of the product. In other words, this attitude component

---

[2]D. Krech, R. S. Crutchfield, and E. L. Ballachey, *Individual in Society* (New York: McGraw-Hill Book Company, 1962), pp. 137–269.

FIGURE 10.1.
Attitude

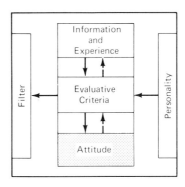

Source: J. F. Engel, D. T. Kollat, and R. D. Blackwell, *Consumer Behavior,* 2nd edition (New York: Holt, Rinehart and Winston, Inc., 1973), p. 267. Reprinted by permission of the publisher.

includes considerations such as whether Coke or Pepsi tastes better, which has more carbonation, which has a better after-taste, and which is a better thirst quencher.

The *affective* component is the consumer's overall feeling of like or dislike for an attitude object (i.e., product, service, adver-tisement, retail outlet). Generally, marketing analysts use verbal statements to measure the affective component. Statements such as "I really like the taste of Gator Aid," and "The slacks look great, but I just don't like the way they fit me" illustrate consumer expressions of the affective component. The affective and cogni-tive components are considered to be highly correlated; that is, consumer analysts have observed that a consumer's beliefs and feelings toward a particular product are typically consistent.

The *behavioral* component is the consumer's action tendency or expected behavior (i.e., intention). This "likelihood of buying" component is relevant to the product's normal purchase cycle. Thus, if a consumer indicates an intention to buy a Yamaha motorcycle, it is only reasonable to expect him to buy that brand the next time he buys a motorcycle. Marketing strategists have been particularly concerned about developing accurate and timely measures of the behavioral component because of the relationship between a consumer's action tendency and his actual purchase behavior.

The conception of attitudes as being comprised of three major components has had considerable impact on the thinking of consumer analysts and an especially pronounced impact in the area of advertising. The classical psychological model provided the basis for a conception of advertising effectiveness called the "hierarchy of effects" hypothesis.[3] This model became widely accepted because it provided a concise and lucid explanation of how attitudes were changed through advertising. The relationship between the three attitudinal components and the consumer's movement from unawareness to purchase is illustrated in Figure 10.2. Essentially, then, this model suggests that not only are attitudes made up of three components but that these components are arranged in a particular order; that is, a consumer must have awareness and knowledge of a product (cognitive component) before a liking and preference (affective component) for it can occur. The validity of this model has been the subject of extensive research and debate.[4] There is, for example, some indication that an alternative hierarchy of effects may exist under certain consumption situations. The fact remains that the hierarchy of effects model is conceptually founded on well-established psychological theory. Furthermore, this model, highly regarded by practitioners, has provided considerable direction for the development of promotional strategy.

The Multiattribute Model

The past decade has been characterized by the emergence of multiattribute models of attitudes.[5] These models consider attitudes to consist of two components: beliefs about the attributes

[3]R. L. Lavidge and G. A. Steiner, "A Model for Predictive Measurements of Advertising Effectiveness," *Journal of Marketing,* 25 (October, 1961), pp. 59–62.

[4]K. S. Palda, "The Hypothesis of a Hierarchy of Effects: A Partial Evaluation," *Journal of Marketing Research,* 3 (February, 1966), pp. 13–24.

[5]M. Fishbein, "An Investigation of the Relationship Between Beliefs About an Object and the Attitude Toward That Object," *Human Relations,* 16 (August, 1963), pp. 233–240.

FIGURE 10.2.
Hierarchy of Effects Model.

Related Behavioral Dimensions	Movement Toward Purchase
Behavioral	Purchase ↑ Conviction ↑ Preference ↑
Affective	Liking ↑ Knowledge ↑
Cognitive	Awareness ↑ Unawareness

Source: R. J. Lavidge and G. A. Steiner, "A Model for Predictive Measurements of Advertising Effectiveness," *Journal of Marketing,* 25 (October, 1961), p. 61. Reprinted from the *Journal of Marketing* published by the American Marketing Association.

of an object and an evaluation of those beliefs. For example, the attitude a consumer has toward a Mercedes is a function of her beliefs about the attributes (e.g., styling, performance, durability, etc.) a Mercedes possesses and the importance these attributes have for her. If a consumer evaluates the Mercedes high on the attributes that are important to her, she will have a very favorable attitude toward it. More specifically, multiattribute models consider an attitude to consist of a number of beliefs about the attributes and the importance of those attributes. The general model can be represented algebraically as follows:

$$A = \sum_{i=1}^{n} b_i a_i$$

where

A	= the attitude toward a product, service, or brand
b_i	= the belief that a particular attribute is associated with a particular product, service, or brand
a_i	= the evaluation of the product, service, or brand on that attribute
n	= the number of product attributes

Thus, the importance of each attribute and the evaluation of the attribute must be determined. The sum of the rating for each product attribute is the consumer's attitude.

The application of the multiattribute model of attitudes appears very complex but is actually not. In applying the model the marketing strategist must determine the major product features (attributes) and how consumers evaluate his product on each of those features. For instance, the manufacturer of a sporty compact may determine that the key product features in order of importance are: (1) good gas mileage, (2) dependable transportation, (3) low price, (4) quality workmanship, (5) contemporary styling, and (6) rapid acceleration. Information on the importance of these product features is then combined with the consumer's evaluation of the sporty compact on those features. The information on the importance of the product features is combined with the evaluation of the compact on those features to obtain the consumer's attitude toward the car.

The importance of applying the multiattribute model of attitudes can be readily illustrated. For instance, a particular brand of automobile may be evaluated very favorably on acceleration and styling, but consumers can still have only a mildly favorable attitude toward the car because those product features are not very important to them. In fact, consumers may have a small set of product attributes that have an overwhelming impact on the decision; that is, regardless of how other attributes are rated, a favorable rating on one or two particular attributes may determine whether or not the consumer purchases the product. Thus, the marketing strategist must determine the importance of the various product features and the evaluation of his product on these features in order to determine the attitude consumers have toward his product. Those product attributes that are determined to be particularly important then become the focal point for developing product and promotional strategies.

The Functions of Attitudes

This section focuses on the functions that attitudes serve. An understanding of why consumers hold the attitudes they do and the purposes that attitudes serve can facilitate the marketing analyst's understanding of consumer behavior. Attitudes have traditionally been viewed as serving four functions: (1) the adjustment function, (2) the ego-defensive function, (3) the value expressive function, and (4) the knowledge function.[6] Each of these will be discussed in the following paragraphs.

THE ADJUSTMENT FUNCTION

The *adjustment function* emphasizes the adaptive tendency of consumers. Consumers tend to adapt or adjust their attitudes to reflect the behavior viewed as favorable by their friends and associates. As a result of this adaptive tendency consumers develop favorable attitudes toward products, brands, and retail outlets that provide the expected level of satisfaction and unfavorable attitudes toward those that do not provide the expected level of satisfaction. In this manner a consumer learns to adjust to his environment and develop somewhat enduring response patterns that enable him to enhance the satisfaction experienced from consuming products and services. For example, a new soft drink may be perceived as having a good taste. If the drink lives up to the consumer's expectation, he may develop a favorable attitude toward the soft drink and decide to drink it regularly. Thus, the consumer's attitudes tend to provide direction to the behavior that provides satisfaction.

THE EGO-DEFENSIVE FUNCTION

The *ego-defensive function* refers to the human tendency to avoid situations or forces inconsistent with one's ego or self-image. Consumers develop and maintain attitudes toward prod-

[6]D. Katz, "The Functional Approach to the Study of Attitudes," *Public Opinion Quarterly,* 24 (Winter, 1960), pp. 160–204.

ucts, brands, and retail stores that protect them from acknowledging their limitations. For instance, even the purchaser of the Edsel maintains an attitude toward that product that permits his self-image to remain intact.

THE VALUE-EXPRESSIVE FUNCTION

The *value-expressive function* refers to those attitudes that reflect a consumer's values, that is, attitudes that express to society those values that are consistent with the consumer's self-image. Whereas the ego-defensive attitudes tend to protect the consumer, the value-expressive attitudes tend to enhance the consumer's self-image. For example, if Gant shirts connote high quality, workmanship, and styling, the consumer who prefers that brand expresses his preference for that value to society when he buys them. Furthermore, those consumers who consider that value important will probably be loyal to Gant shirts.

THE KNOWLEDGE FUNCTION

The *knowledge function* of attitudes is to provide consistency and stability in the way an individual perceives the world around him; that is, attitudes serve the function of providing a stable frame of reference for understanding and adapting to the chaotic world. Consumers are simply not able to engage in conscious problem solving with respect to every purchase decision; consequently, the knowledge function of attitudes can be instrumental in the formation of routine product evaluations and purchase decisions.

The Organization of Attitudes

Jonathan Whiteshed, a self-proclaimed wine connoisseur, has long preferred French wines because of their superior aroma, body, and taste. An associate of Jonathan's recently gave him a copy of Wines Internationale which contained the most recent ratings of wines by international experts. Despite the low ratings received by Jonathan's favorite French wines, he continues to prefer them to all others.

Was Jonathan's refusal to change his attitudes unusual? Not at all. Consumers' attitudes are characterized by an enduring tendency to maintain consistency and resist change from influences of various types. Moreover, the basic components of attitudes (i.e., the cognitive, affective, and behavioral dimensions discussed earlier) also must maintain consistency. Most consumers appear to have this basic tendency to maintain consistency. In fact, most people have a psychological ability that permits them to screen out and distort reality in order to maintain this consistency. Thus, for a marketing strategist to effectively utilize his marketing effort it is necessary to understand the process by which a consumer maintains consistency among the components of an attitude and among his various attitudes.

CONSISTENCY AMONG ATTITUDE COMPONENTS

Research on the internal organization of an attitude suggests that most individuals can tolerate only limited inconsistency between the affective and cognitive components.[7] When consistency is attained between the cognitive and affective components, the attitude is said to be in a stable state which persists over time. If the information a consumer receives about a product (cognitive component) is contrary to his beliefs about that product (affective component), inconsistency will result. Although most consumers can tolerate some inconsistency, at some level of inconsistency reorganization of attitude components must occur. Consistency among attitude components can be achieved by (1) rejecting the stimulus input that introduced the inconsistency, (2) modifying the stimulus input to make it consistent with the other component, or (3) making some sort of accommodation so that a new attitude emerges with internal consistency. For instance, the consumer who purchased a metal tennis racket may experience inconsistency after reading an advertisement claiming metal rackets to be inferior to wood rackets. The consumer can relieve this inconsistency by rejecting the

[7]M. J. Rosenberg, "Inconsistency Arousal and Reduction in Attitude Change," *Current Studies in Social Psychology,* I. D. Steiner and M. Fishbein, eds. (New York: Holt, Rinehart and Winston, 1965), pp. 123–124.

validity of the claim or by modifying the claim (e.g., the claim is true for some brands).

CONSISTENCY AMONG ATTITUDES

Every consumer maintains basic values and social relationships that are considered to have high personal goal relevance. Each of these can serve as a significant anchor for attitudes, in that only those dispositions that reflect a positive orientation toward the consumer's conception of himself are formed and retained.

Attitudes that are closely related to the consumer's self-concept and basic values are said to have *centrality.* Attitudes with central anchoring points, in turn, tend to become organized so that a change in one affects the others. Therefore, the person strives to attain balance in his attitudinal structure, making attitude change difficult:

> Insofar as a person's attitude toward something is imbedded in a large latticework of attitudes—and such things as the amount of stored information about the object, its personal goal relevance and psychological centrality are all indicators of such imbedding—any attempt to change the attitude must come to grips with the fact that this attitude is anchored by the other attitudes in the system. Such an attitude does not exist in a vacuum; if it changes, then other compensatory changes must follow to restore balance.[8]

A striving toward maintenance of balance and resistance to change, on the other hand, is greatly reduced when attitudes are peripheral to the self-concept, basic values, and other significant focal objects. Thus, although a professor's attitude toward the importance of higher education may be highly resistant to change, his attitude toward Budweiser beer may be readily changed.

The question may be asked as to whether attitudes toward products and services ever attain such a degree of centrality that change is resisted? This can happen on occasion, although it must be admitted that products and services generally reflect far less personal commitment than do attitudes with high personal

[8]T. M. Newcomb, R. H. Turner, and P. E. Converse, *Social Psychology* (New York: Holt, Rinehart and Winston, 1965), p. 136.

goal relevance (e.g., religion and family). However, some marketing strategists would contend that attitudes toward brands of coffee often attain high centrality. Many housewives supposedly are of the belief that their competence as a cook and even as a wife is determined in part by the quality of the coffee they serve. When one brand is perceived as being satisfactory, the resulting attitude is likely to be so imbedded that change is unlikely.

The probability of change varies inversely with attitude strength. In addition to centrality, the other basic determinant of strength is the amount of stored information and past experience that underlies the rating of the alternative. In other words, "attitudes about an object are more subject to change through contradictory incoming information when the existing mass of stored information about the object is smaller."[9] When centrality and/or stored information both are high, on the other hand, attempts to bring about change may well result in selective attention, comprehension, and retention.

The Measurement of Attitudes

Information on consumer attitudes is becoming increasingly important to marketing decision making. Effective utilization of information on consumer attitudes requires an understanding of how consumer attitudes are measured. There are a number of methods of measuring attitudes, each of which has strengths and weaknesses. A detailed review is beyond the scope of this book. Rather, the purpose here is to demonstrate a particularly useful method of measuring attitudes that is based on the multiattribute model discussed previously.

Use of the multiattribute model requires the determination of the importance of each product attribute and the evaluation of that attribute for a specific product. This rating is performed for each product attribute (evaluative criterion), and the summed score is the consumer's attitude toward the alternative. This procedure is demonstrated in the data presented in Table 10.1. The values presented in Table 10.1 are the result of having five

[9]T. M. Newcomb, p. 91.

TABLE 10.1

An Example of Brand Attitudes as a Rating Along Evaluative Criteria

(a) *Frequency of Attribute-Importance Ranking*

Attribute	Ranking (in percent)				
	1st	2nd	3rd	4th	5th
Kills germs	49.3	31.9	11.9	5.9	1.0
Taste/flavor	15.1	22.6	43.0	18.5	0.7
Price	4.7	12.2	22.9	52.8	7.4
Color	0.2	0.3	1.1	9.3	89.1
Effectiveness	30.9	33.1	21.0	13.4	1.6

(b) *Average Consumer Ratings of Mouthwash Brands on Relevant Attributes*

Brands	Average Score on				
	Kills Germs	Taste/ Flavor	Price	Color	Effectiveness
Micrin	2.22	2.46	2.60	1.85	2.21
Cepacol	2.40	2.92	2.70	2.29	2.36
Listerine	1.63	2.86	2.29	2.27	1.64
Lavoris	2.31	2.38	2.50	1.81	2.27
Colgate 100	2.35	2.52	2.68	1.87	2.32

Source: Reproduced with permission from J. F. Engel, W. W. Talarzyk, and C. M. Larson (eds.), *Cases in Promotional Strategy* (Homewood, Ill.: Irwin, 1971), pp. 90–91.

brands of mouthwash evaluated on five product attributes. The data indicate that germ-killing power and effectiveness were evaluated as the most important attributes. A summary score, the overall attitude, can be computed, but frequently the detailed ratings are more useful for strategy development. For example, examination of these data indicate that Listerine is the most preferred brand and, correspondingly, it has the highest ratings on the two most important attributes. The lower average rating scores indicate that the given brand was more satisfactory on the attribute. (A scale of 1 to 6 was used with 1 referring to very satisfactory on the attribute and 6 indicating very unsatisfactory.) Listerine, for example, was perceived to be more satisfactory than the other brands on the "Kills Germs" attribute with an average score of 1.63, whereas Cepacol was cited as the least satisfactory on this attribute with an average score of 2.40. Furthermore, Cepacol consistently has the lowest rating on all five attributes. Additional data from this study indicated that Cepacol was most preferred by those with advanced degrees (masters and Ph.D.'s). Unfortunately for the producer of Cepacol, this segment is very low in the consumption of mouthwash. Once the marketing analyst has determined the consumer's attitude toward her company's brand, she must determine how to improve it in the eyes of the consumer on the important attributes. Some physical changes in the product may be necessary. Alternatively, if the product is competitive in terms of the important product features, the appropriate course of action may be to modify the advertising strategy. In any event, the information on attitudes has contributed a great deal to the marketer's decision making.

One final comment is necessary. If the marketer can determine or has good reason to believe that consumers do not differ in the importance they place on the various product attributes, then information on the importance of product attributes is of limited value. In fact, in such an instance, information on the consumer's evaluation of the brand in question would be sufficient. For example, if all beer drinkers rate the following attributes of beer to be of equal importance: (1) carbonation, (2) aftertaste, (3) price, and (4) aroma, then this evaluation has no effect on the attitudes toward the alternative brands of beer. The marketing strategist need only concern himself with how beer drinkers evaluate his brand on those four attributes.

ATTITUDE CHANGE

Implicit in the preceding discussion is the assumption that attitudes affect both consumer information processing and behavior. Thus, one might logically conclude that a change in attitude will be accompanied by a change in behavior. Although the evidence is not conclusive, there is general agreement that attitudes and behavior are positively related; that is, most consumer analysts would agree that consumers who use smokeless tobacco also have a favorable attitude toward smokeless tobacco. A number of research limitations have, however, prohibited consumer analysts from determining the exact nature of the relationship between attitudes and consumer behavior. Consumer analysts have, for example, used a variety of methods to measure consumer attitudes. These methods can vary substantially in accuracy and, thus, affect the results obtained by the researcher. Another research limitation is the insufficient attention accorded to other considerations that intervene to affect behavior. The attitude component of the CCU is only one of several factors that affect consumer decision making. In certain instances other factors can intervene, causing a person to act in a manner which is not predicted by attitudes. For example, social norms, economic circumstances, consumer expectations, new product information, information on competing brands, and the store environment can affect the consumer's behavior.[10]

Consumer analysts now believe that behavioral intentions can be predicted from attitude plus other considerations that might enter in a specific situation.[11] Behavior can then be predicted from intentions. Thus, intention has become recognized as an intervening variable between attitude and behavior. This is especially appropriate because the behavioral component of attitude becomes relevant only when a problem is recognized and problem-solving activity has commenced. Thus, the behavioral component of an attitude becomes activated in the form of a consumer's intention.

The relationship between attitude, intention, and behavior is illustrated in Figure 10.3. Consumer attitudes can be estimated from ratings based on relevant evaluative criteria. When relatively enduring environmental factors such as social norms or real income are explicitly specified, behavioral intentions can be

[10]G. Day, *Buyer Attitudes and Brand Choice Behavior* (New York: The Free Press, 1970).

[11]I. Ajzen and M. Fishbein, "Attitudinal and Normative Variables as Predictors of Specific Behaviors: A Review of Research Generated by a Theoretical Model," paper presented at the Workshop on Attitude Research and Consumer Behavior, University of Illinois (December, 1970).

FIGURE 10.3.
Relationship Between Attitude, Intention, and Behavior.

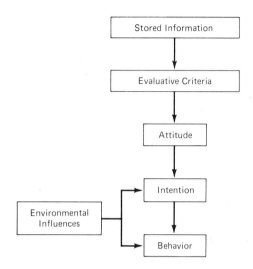

Source: J. F. Engel, D. T. Kollat, and R. D. Blackwell, *Consumer Behavior,* 2nd ed. (New York: Holt, Rinehart and Winston, Inc., 1973), p. 274. Reprinted by permission of the publisher.

predicted from attitudes.[12] For instance, a consumer anticipating a salary increase may plan to purchase a new automobile. However, if the anticipated salary increase is not realized, the intended purchase may not occur. The specification of the anticipated salary increase or other such conditions can improve the accuracy with which attitudes predict intentions. Finally, information on unexpected, temporary environmental influences such as an unexpected sharp increase in the price of food and housing can improve the accuracy with which behavior can be predicted from intentions.

[12]J. N. Sheth, "An Investigation of Relationships Among Evaluative Beliefs, Affect, Behavioral Intention and Behavior," unpublished paper (Urbana, Illinois: University of Illinois Press, 1970).

Thus, it can be concluded that attitude can accurately predict behavior when intention is used as an intervening variable. Intentions, in turn, predict behavior to the extent that moderating influences, such as adverse economic circumstances or new information on competing brands, are absent or at a minimum. When these moderating influences are operative, their influence must also be accounted for if behavior is to be predicted. Thus, attitude change is strategic to effective marketing because a change in attitude as expressed through behavioral intentions is usually reflected in a change in behavior.

ATTITUDE CHANGE AND MASS COMMUNICATION

The emphasis in this section is on the role of mass communication in changing consumer attitudes. Mass communication—the process of transmitting information via the various mass media such as television, radio, newspaper, and magazines—is a primary means by which marketing strategists attempt to influence consumer attitudes. In particular, mass communication provides the marketing strategist with the opportunity to influence the attitudes of a relatively large and diverse audience. Interpersonal communication—the information exchange that involves face-to-face contact between sender and receiver, such as that of a salesman and his client—is generally considered to be more effective than mass communication. In other words, interpersonal communication is more likely to result in the intended message being understood by the recipient. The superior effectiveness of interpersonal communication is normally attributed to the opportunity face-to-face communication provides for instantaneous feedback. In order to understand how mass communication influences consumer attitudes, the mass communication process must be examined.

The Mass Communication Process

Mass communication involves the same basic elements that characterize any form of communication; that is, mass communication (Figure 10.4) involves the communicator, the message, the channel, the receiver, and feedback. However, mass communication is unique in that the problems of delayed feedback,

FIGURE 10.4.
Mass Communication.

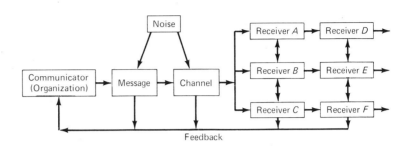

Source: Reproduced with permission from *Promotional Strategy,* by Engel, Wales, and Warshaw (Rev. Ed.; Homewood, Ill.: Richard D. Irwin, 1971 C.) p. 24.

inflexibility of message, and greater probability of selective processing by audience members present a threat to effective communication. Nevertheless, mass communication provides the marketing strategist with tremendous potential to influence consumer attitudes at a relatively low cost per individual.

Mass Communication and Information Processing
The role of mass communication in effective promotional strategies is particularly apparent when one considers how information is processed. The expanded model of information processing, illustrated in Figure 10.5, includes three broad phases: (1) exposure, (2) reception (attention, comprehension, and retention), and (3) attitude/behavior modification. Each stage is a necessary but insufficient condition for the succeeding stage.

The marketing strategist who seeks to influence the attitudes and ultimately the consumption behavior of a particular consumer group must first achieve audience exposure. Achieving audience exposure is primarily a problem of selecting the right media. After careful definition of the target audience in demographic terms, media audience data can be used to facilitate selection of those media which most closely reach the target audience.

FIGURE 10.5.
Expanded Information Processing Model

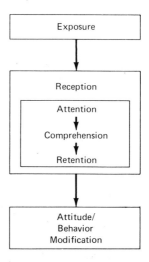

Source: J. F. Engel, D. T. Kollat, and R. D. Blackwell, *Consumer Behavior,* 2nd ed. (New York: Holt, Rinehart and Winston, Inc., 1973), p. 314. Reprinted by permission of the publisher.

Once the media have been selected, the concern shifts to assuring message reception. Numerous devices are available to the marketing strategist to facilitate the designated target audience's reception (attention, comprehension, and retention) of his communication attempts. For example, certain stimulus patterns such as contrast, intensity, and color are especially effective in enhancing the likelihood of message reception. The repeated use of any such stimulus pattern, however, is likely to reduce its effectiveness in stimulating reception.[13] One well-known example of the use of novelty and contrast is the Chiquita brand banana advertisements which usually depict the banana in such a way that it stands out clearly in dominant fashion against its

[13]R. Lynn, *Attention, Arousal and the Orientation Reaction* (Oxford: Pergamon Press, 1966).

background. The appearance of the banana in such positions as standing on end is novel, with the result that attention is more likely to be captured. This, of course, says nothing about the persuasive power of the message.

Size and position of communication are also frequently used to enhance message reception. Research on the impact of size and position suggest the following generalizations for marketing strategists:

1. Increasing the size of an advertisement increases the impact but less than proportionately.[14]
2. Readership of newspaper and magazine advertisements is unrelated to the side of the page (i.e., left or right hand) on which it appears.[15]
3. The greatest readership in magazines is usually attracted by advertisements on the covers or in the first 10 percent of the pages, but beyond this point location is a minor factor.[16]
4. Position on the page has no effect except when competing advertisements become especially numerous, in which case the upper right-hand position offers an advantage in newspapers.[17]

Marketing strategists have also come to recognize that, if used effectively, color can enhance message reception considerably. For example, color television commercials are on the average 50 percent more effective, as measured by message recognition, than are the same television commercials in black and white. Similarly, color newspaper advertisements have a much higher readership than do black and white advertisements.

Developing communications that achieve attention does not necessarily assure comprehension and retention. In fact, because consumers filter out communications substantially inconsistent with strongly held dispositions and because consumers modify the intended message, the marketing strategist has a

[14]R. Barton, *Advertising Media* (New York: McGraw-Hill Book Company, 1964), p. 109.
[15]"Position in Newspaper Advertising: 2," *Media/Scope* (March, 1963), pp. 76–82.
[16]"Position in Newspaper Advertising: 2," pp. 76–82.
[17]"Position in Newspaper Advertising: 1," *Media/Scope* (February, 1963), p. 57.

limited opportunity to change attitudes. Actually, the only strategy available is to design the communication in such a way that it is directed toward those dispositions and need states that are consistent with the action being suggested and oriented toward reinforcing these tendencies, thereby leading to the desired action.

The marketing strategist's ultimate goal in using mass communication is the modification of purchase behavior. As was indicated in the extended information processing model, this takes place through a change in attitude which, in turn, changes intention. All things being equal, the change in intention will be reflected in behavior. Thus, attitude change is a valid goal for promotional strategy, and mass communication can be an effective means of achieving this goal. There is a vast amount of literature on appeals and message variations that research indicates are effective in changing attitudes. The next section discusses these appeals and message variations.

Managing Attitude Change

Consumer attitudes tend to be relatively stable, especially if they are strongly held. However, they are not static, and thus much marketing effort has the goal of changing attitudes. Marketing effort can result in consumer attitude change, but such change can also result from nonmarketing factors. For example, consumer attitudes toward economy cars have changed considerably since the energy shortage and the accompanying increases in gasoline prices. The purpose of this section is to discuss some of the major ways in which marketing-controlled efforts, particularly mass communication, can contribute to attitude change. The topics discussed here are those that appear to have the greatest significance to marketing managers.

EFFECTS OF MESSAGE DISCREPANCY

The manager who wishes to change attitudes must answer several basic questions in order to develop an effective strategy. For instance, should an advertisement assert that the product in question is superior in every respect or should a more moderate position be taken? To what extent can an advertisement deviate from a consumer's own position and still induce attitude change? A decade ago consumer analysts would have contended that the more a message deviated from the recipient's own position the greater the likelihood that the consumer's attitudes would change in the desired direction. However, this position has been modified in recent years. Research now indicates that attitude change can be enhanced by advocating a discrepant position but beyond some point, increasing discrepancy will actually decrease attitude change. For example, an advertisement claiming that Ford automobiles are quieter and less expensive than Mercedes may very well produce attitude change regarding the quality of Ford automobiles. However, if the advertisement were to claim the Ford to be superior in every respect (performance, durability, workmanship, etc.), the discrepancy between the claim and the existing attitude might be beyond the consumer's limit and inhibited attitude change. Thus, the marketing strategist must conduct research to determine a discrepancy limit and make certain that the message stays within that boundary.

Consumer analysts have also found that attitude change is affected by the credibility of the communicator. Consumers seem to place greater confidence in a trustworthy source; that is, they are more receptive to a credible source, even when the message is substantially discrepant from their own position. The importance of having a highly credible source is particularly pronounced in advertising because the source is considered anything but impartial and unbiased.

EFFECTS OF MESSAGE CONTENT

The marketing strategist seeking to change attitudes has considerable latitude in the message content employed. The message can be designed to arouse the anxieties or fears of the consumer (fear appeals). Early research on fear appeals suggested that a marketer's attempt to stress the unfavorable consequences of not using a product would have an adverse effect on a consumer's attitude. In recent years research has suggested that there is a positive relationship between fear and persuasion but only in certain instances; that is, a favorable attitude toward a product can be developed by emphasizing the adverse consequences of not using the product in question but only when consumers do not perceive themselves as part of the market for the recommended product or brand.[18] Fear appeals have been used in recent years to promote such diverse products as mouthwash, toothpaste, candy mints, automobile seatbelts, nonsmoking, planned parenthood, and prevention of social diseases.

The amount of change advocated in the message has been found to have an effect on attitudes. The structured advertisement that tells a complete story logically and sequentially with a definite conclusion stated appears to be quite effective for many groups, at least in the short run. However, the unstructured advertisement that permits the audience to draw its own conclusion may be more effective in the long run, particularly with a highly intelligent audience. Thus, the marketing manager of a bank attempting to develop an image of friendliness would find the unstructured message to be more effective.

EFFECTS OF TWO-SIDED MESSAGES

Advertising messages have traditionally been one sided; that is, they have emphasized only the strengths of the advertised brand and have avoided the brand's weaknesses as well as the strengths of competing brands. Some recent evidence, however, suggests that under certain conditions two-sided messages may actually be more effective in changing consumers' attitudes. Thus, the advertisement promoting deodorant by comparing the strengths and weaknesses of the brand being promoted as well as those of the competing brands may be more effective than the advertisement that only discusses the strengths of the brand in question. In recent years the Federal Trade Commission has repeatedly urged advertisers to name competitors when comparisons are made in advertisements.

It is interesting to point out that the policy of corrective advertising instituted by the Federal Trade Commission in 1971 may

[18]J. J. Wheatley, "Marketing and the Use of Fear-or-Anxiety-Arousing Appeals," *Journal of Marketing,* 35 (April, 1971), pp. 62–64; B. Sternthal and C. S. Craig, "Fear Appeals: Revisited and Revised," *Journal of Consumer Research,* 1 (December, 1974), pp. 22–34.

have some unintended effects. The basic premise of the FTC is that manufacturers should be required to admit blame publicly in their advertisements once they have been found guilty of false and misleading appeals. (To date none have been found guilty but several have agreed to corrective advertising.) This admission in a certain percentage of its future messages presumably will serve to offset past misleading efforts. The result, however, may be to enhance the credibility of the advertiser in the consumers' eyes and hence increase his promotional effectiveness. This, of course, would be contrary to the result intended by the Federal Trade Commission.

Summary

Attitudes are the most important single component of the central control unit. *Attitude* is the consumer's assessment of the ability of an alternative to satisfy his purchasing and consumption requirements as expressed in his evaluative criteria. Two models exemplify current views of the structure of attitudes. The most widely accepted model, the classical psychological model, utilizes cognitive, affective, and behavioral components. The multiattribute model represents the consumer's attitude toward an object as the outcome of the interaction of the variables representing one's beliefs about the attributes of an object and one's evaluation of those beliefs.

Attitudes serve four basic functions: adjustment, ego-defensive, value-expressive, and knowledge. Consumers tend to maintain a degree of consistency in their attitudes. Internally, the cognitive, affective, and behavioral dimensions must be mutually agreeable. Also, people tend to maintain rather consistent attitudes.

To utilize an attitude theory, the marketer must be able to measure the variables comprising the theory. This is shown for the multiattribute model. Also, attitude change has significance for the marketer because a change in behavior may follow a change in attitude if intention is an intervening variable and the environmental influences are absent or minimal. Mass communication enables the marketer to influence the attitudes of a large number of consumers at a low cost per individual. He or she is involved in exposing the proper target audience, ensuring reception of the desired message (through consumer attention, comprehension, and retention), and actual modification of purchase behavior.

The marketing manager is concerned with those methods used to effect attitude change. The controlled use of advocating discrepant positions and the use of credible communicators are beneficial to advertising. Also, messages using fear appeals or unstructured messages can be effective when properly employed. Finally, the two-sided message in which the advertiser admits that his product is not perfect can have positive results.

QUESTIONS AND ISSUES FOR DISCUSSION

1. "An attitude is an abstract concept. As a result, attitudes are interesting to the academician but are unimportant to the marketing strategist." Do you agree? Why?
2. How might the hierarchy of effects model help the manufacturer of tennis equipment develop an effective promotional program?
3. What function do attitudes play in the CCU? How do attitudes affect consumer information processing?
4. Distinguish between the classical psychological model and the multiattribute model. Which model holds the greatest promise for the marketing strategist?
5. Describe in detail how the multiattribute model might provide useful direction in the following instances:

   a. decision as to whether or not to modify the taste carbonation of Dr. Pepper
   b. decision as to whether or not to remodel a women's clothing store
   c. development of a promotional strategy for the United Way.

6. What are the major functions served by attitudes? Identify an example of each function. How can an understanding of the functions served by attitudes help the marketing strategist?
7. "Understanding consumer attitudes is intellectually gratifying but is not beneficial to the marketing strategist because

consumer attitudes are very difficult to change." Do you agree? Explain.

8. A marketing research study undertaken for a manufacturer of televisions indicated that 20 percent of the target market planned on purchasing a colored television within the following six months and 5 percent planned on purchasing a black and white set. How much confidence should be placed in the predictive accuracy of such intention measurements? Why?

9. A manufacturer of automobile tires has recently been informed that tests by an independent group have found his tire superior to all others in five of seven categories. Should this information be included in product advertisements? Why or why not?

10. A large, nationally known insurance company is considering a promotional campaign featuring the unfavorable consequences of not having adequate life insurance. Would you encourage the use of such a campaign? Why or why not?

SITUATIONAL PROBLEMS

Case 1

Fine Rackets, a manufacturer of quality wood tennis rackets, has experienced a declining market share for the past two years. Ken Buetell, marketing director, attributes the declining market share to the poor advertising program of Fine Rackets. The advertising emphasizes the quality and workmanship of Fine Rackets' product line and uses the print medium exclusively. Fred West, advertising manager, contends that the major problem is not the advertising but rather the limited product line. West contends that every competitor produces metal rackets, and these are the rackets purchased by the quality-conscious segment. Consumer research clearly indicates, West contends, that consumers prefer the durability, weight, and appearance of metal rackets. No advertising program can possibly overcome the disadvantages of an inferior product.

How might an understanding of consumer attitudes aid in determining the reason for Fine Rackets' declining market share?

How might an understanding of consumer attitudes aid in the development of a more effective marketing program?

Case 2

The White Mountain Company, a large producer of bicycles, has decided to discontinue its current advertising program. The company is considering the following two campaigns. The first campaign would feature a well-known athlete on a series of television commercials. Each commercial would be in a different setting and would emphasize the enjoyment bicycle riders experience. The second campaign would feature various typical bicycle riders who would discuss the fine qualities of White Mountain bicycles. They would, for example, indicate that White Mountain bicycles, although slightly more expensive than other brands, are well made.

How might an understanding of consumer attitudes and attitude change aid in selecting the most effective campaign?

Which of the two campaigns would you recommend for White Mountain?

PART IV

ANALYSIS OF THE CONSUMER DECISION PROCESS

Problem-Recognition Processes

The preceding chapters have focused on various aspects of the consumer decision processes. The key environmental influences on consumer decision making—culture, subcultures, social class, groups, and the family—and their influences on consumer decision making were discussed in Chapters Four, Five and Six. Subsequent to this, consumer information processing and the elements that comprise the individual consumer's psychological makeup were examined. In the discussion of each of these topics it was assumed that the consumer wanted to purchase a product. But how do consumers recognize the need to purchase a particular product or service? How does the consumer's unique psychological makeup influence the recognition of a consumption problem? Do environmental influences (e.g., culture, social class, etc.) affect the process of consumer problem recognition?

These questions and many others must be addressed if consumer analysts are to fully understand the mechanism that triggers consumer action. In other words, because the consumer must perceive a problem before a purchase is enacted, it is necessary to understand the process whereby a problem is recognized and the action results from the recognition. Unfortunately, problem recognition is not a simple act. Rather, it is a complex process that involves and occurs as the result of many variables.

The Nature of Problem-Recognition Processes

Problem recognition, depicted in Figure 11.1, occurs when an individual perceives a difference of significant magnitude between a desired state and an actual state. Statements such as "I need a Coke" or "I need a new sweater" are clear instances of consumers expressing their recognition of a problem. In the first instance—"I need a Coke"—the desired state is the absence of thirst. The actual state is a feeling of discomfort resulting from a physiological need for liquid. The recognition of the discrepancy between the desired state and the actual state will cause the consumer to initiate behavior to alleviate this discrepancy. In the second instance—"I need a new sweater"—the desired state and actual state are less clear. The individual may

FIGURE 11.1.
Problem Recognition Processes

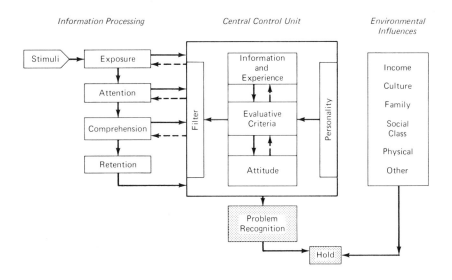

Source: J. F. Engel, D. T. Kollat and R. D. Blackwell, *Consumer Behavior,* 2nd ed. (New York: Holt, Rinehart and Winston, Inc., 1973), p. 352. Reprinted by permission of the publisher.

actually need a new sweater to keep warm; however, most likely the statement reflects the consumer's perception that a different, more stylish sweater would more accurately reflect the "real me."

The desired and actual states are quite complex, involving a number of variables. First, consider the desired state. By definition, there are one or more motives underlying this state. The motives that are prominent and the behavior perceived as having the potential to satisfy these motives are affected by personality characteristics, attitudes, values, and evaluative criteria. Since the consumer's central control unit is affected by culture, subculture, social class, group, and family influences, these variables, albeit indirectly, affect the desired state. Furthermore, there are instances in which the condition or performance characteristics of the product or service being used affect the desired state. For instance, the owner of a 1976 Mercedes can develop a considerably higher expected level of performance for automobiles (ideal state) than that of the owner of a five-year-old Chevrolet. The desired state is also affected by the consumer's desired resources, including current and expected income, and by marketing efforts such as advertising, personal selling, and product demonstration.

The actual state refers to the way the consumer perceives the existing state of affairs. The consumer's perception of the existing state of affairs involves many variables interacting in complex ways. In fact, the variables that affect the actual state are the same variables that influenced past purchases and might affect the desired state. Thus, the actual state is affected by the variables in the central control unit, by the environmental constraints on decision making, and by marketing efforts.

THE OUTCOMES OF PROBLEM-RECOGNITION PROCESSES

Problem recognition can result in two major types of outcomes: (1) hold, and (2) proceed to internal search and alternative evaluation. The hold outcome results when the consumer perceives a discrepancy between the actual and desired states but the difference is not of sufficient magnitude to affect behavior. That is, there is a minimum level of perceived difference that must be surpassed before problem recognition that triggers behavior change occurs. For instance, the consumer's desired state with respect to a bank's checking service may be totally free checking at a convenient location. The actual state may be low-cost checking at a conveniently located bank. There is clearly a difference between desired and actual states of affairs, but the discrepancy (low-cost checking) is probably not of sufficient magnitude to trigger search and alternative evaluation. If the actual state were high-cost checking at an inconveniently located bank, the discrepancy might be sufficient to cause the consumer to search for an alternative bank.

The level of perceived difference that is necessary to initiate search behavior varies among consumers and circumstances. The retired consumer with considerable free time might not be disturbed by an inconveniently located bank or long waiting lines in the lobby. However, the working mother of three young children might find the same distance and delay intolerable. Special circumstances can also affect the perceived discrepancy between actual and desired states of affairs. For instance, the possibility of a hamburger and French fries at a "greasy spoon" restaurant might normally produce a significant discrepancy between actual and desired places at which to dine out; yet, when very hungry and pressed for time, many people find such "cuisine" palatable, even gratifying.

The hold outcome can also occur when a significant discrepancy between desired state and actual state is perceived, but further problem-solving behavior is precluded. Such a condition can result from a lack of financial resources, time, energy, or the availability of appropriate alternatives. For instance, if the working mother of three young children had no alternative bank available, she would necessarily continue to do business with that institution; that is, even though considerable discrepancy exists between the desired and actual bank service, the fact that no alternative bank is available would preclude any change in behavior.

Many consumers have on occasion experienced problem recognition only to have further action constrained by the intervention of an external influence. A consumer may perceive considerable discrepancy between an actual state (ownership of a 1961 Ford) and a desired state (ownership of a 1976 Porsche) only to have further action (purchase of the Porsche) constrained by a lack of available income.

Similarly, behavior can be constrained by other factors such as time, energy, and the availability of appropriate alternatives. For instance, the household with both adults employed full time outside the home might perceive a significant discrepancy between the meals they actually prepare and the meals they would like to prepare. In this instance, the behavior to eliminate this discrepancy might be precluded by available time.

The second type of outcome that can result from problem recognition is internal search and alternative evaluation. As was detailed in Chapter 3, internal search and alternative evaluation can be followed by external search and alternative evaluation, purchasing behavior, and the decision outcome. Both types of problem-recognition outcomes are stored in the information and experience component of the central control unit (Figure 11.1) Thus, some problem-recognition processes are learned while others are not. In the case of learned problem-recognition processes, for example, those involving a physiological need such as thirst, the problem recognition becomes programmed and automatic. In the United States a considerable segment of the population is programmed to reach for a Coca Cola, Pepsi, or 7-Up when thirsty; that is, they have learned and stored the information that when they recognize a discrepancy between their actual state (thirst) and desired state (absence of thirst), Coke, Pepsi, or 7-Up will eliminate that discrepancy. Frequently problem-recognition processes are not this automatic; indeed, they can be quite complex.

Types of Problem-Recognition Processes

The preceding discussion attempted to explain the nature of the problem-recognition process. Implicit in this discussion was the notion that problem recognition varies substantially in relation to the extent of complexity involved. Problem recognition can be simple, somewhat complicated, or highly complex. The amount of complexity is considered to be a function of: (1) the time period involved, (2) the urgency of the need, (3) the number of influencing factors, and (4) the intensity of the consumer's attitudes and motives.

SIMPLE PROBLEM-RECOGNITION PROCESSES

Simple problem recognition refers to those strongly learned, highly programmed, and automatic types of processes. Although perhaps not arising in the same way, the consumer has typically experienced this general type of situation in the past. Assume, for example, that you are driving down the highway 100 miles from your destination when you notice the gas gauge is on empty. Gasoline is clearly necessary for the continuance of your journey.

Because there is a significant discrepancy between the actual state (an empty gas tank) and the desired state (an adequate supply of gasoline), a problem is recognized. This type of problem recognition (depletion of existing solution) is a very common occurrence. In fact, many of the problems that consumers recognize result from the depletion of the product being utilized to satisfy the problem.

SOMEWHAT COMPLICATED PROBLEM-RECOGNITION PROCESSES

This type of problem-recognition process refers to those characterized by more time, more influencing factors and, perhaps, more intense consumer attitudes. In brief, the problem-recognition process is more complex than in the previous case. Assume an individual has had a Harman-Kardon stereo system for a couple of years and has been completely satisfied with it. This individual reads a magazine advertisement for Pioneer stereo systems but does not think much about it and continues to be satisfied with her present system. During the next few weeks she continues to read advertisements on Pioneer systems. While visiting a friend, she listens to his Pioneer stereo system and finds it to be superior to her own in several respects. Her friend indicates that he has been very satisfied with the system's performance. On her next shopping trip, she stops at a stereo shop and finds that Pioneer stereo systems have been reduced in price by 40 percent. The factors described above might not have affected the desired state of this consumer. However, this consumer's desired state may have changed dramatically because of these impinging factors. There is no doubt, however, that the problem-recognition process is considerably more complex in this situation than in the previous one.

HIGHLY COMPLEX PROBLEM-RECOGNITION PROCESSES

Highly complex problem-recognition processes refer to those infrequent, unprogrammed types of processes that involve a considerable period of time, are affected by a number of factors, and involve strongly held attitudes. Assume that several years ago a consumer purchased a 1966 Chevelle. The car has performed well and the consumer is satisfied with it. He has seen advertisements for the new compacts (Pinto, Vega) but considers them too small and too expensive. One evening a friend gives him a ride home in his recently purchased Vega. He is amazed at the room in the Vega and likes the car. His feeling is intensified considerably during subsequent weeks when his 1966 Chevelle will not start, and he is forced to walk 11 blocks in a rainstorm. During the next few months he pays closer attention to the cars he sees. He pays closer attention to advertisements for cars and on two occasions visits automobile dealers for trial runs and price information.

Finally, he comments to his wife about the high price of gasoline, the likely impending repairs on his "old" Chevelle, and the possibility of a sporty compact. She reacts negatively, pointing out that the family has one car (a 1971 wagon) that is in excellent condition and that a new car is too expensive. She would prefer to save the money or use it for a nice vacation. Besides, she observes, he would be healthier if he walked to work—a routine which would eliminate the need for a second car.

A few weeks later the 1966 Chevelle breaks down, and it is estimated that it will cost $200 to repair it. The husband points out that spending $200 on that old junker is just wasting money. During the next few weeks the family gets by with one car and both husband and wife become somewhat irritated because of the inconvenience this causes. The next day the husband finds out he has received a $50 per month raise, and that evening he informs his wife of the raise. They discuss the matter at some length and eventually decide to buy a new car.

In this hypothetical although not unrealistic situation, problem recognition is far more complex than in the previous two cases. Problem recognition occurred over a considerable period of time as the result of the interaction of many factors, including marketing efforts (advertisements, dealership, price), environmental factors (price of gasoline), the ability to purchase ($50 raise), and the difficulty with the old car ($200 repair cost).

UNIQUE ASPECTS OF PROBLEM-RECOGNITION PROCESSES

The preceding discussion of problem recognition and the illustrative cases indicate that these processes differ in four major respects from the other concepts discussed in the previous chapters. First, problem recognition may be a more comprehensive process than are many of the concepts discussed previously. As the cases were intended to indicate, problem-recognition processes can simultaneously involve many variables, including perception, learning, attitudes, and family influences. Furthermore, the number of variables involved varies considerably from one situation to another.

Second, problem recognition includes the consumer's motives, but it is a considerably more complex process than motivation in that problem recognition includes the consumer's attitudes, values, and other such influences as well as motives.

Third, problem recognition involves a complex comparison and weighting process. The consumer assigns a relative importance to his needs, attitudes, and expected level of satisfaction. Moreover, the order assigned to the various needs and attitudes vary considerably from individual to individual.

Finally, problem recognition is not synonymous with product awareness. Problem recognition refers to an awareness of the difference between an actual state and a desired state. This recognition of a discrepancy may or may not have been precipitated by the awareness of a particular product or brand. Awareness is a more general concept that bears no particular relation to the phenomenon of problem recognition.

Determinants of Problem-Recognition Processes

The preceding discussion of problem recognition has illustrated the complexity of the phenomenon and has demonstrated that numerous factors affect the processes. The type and number of factors that affect problem-recognition processes vary from situation to situation. The number of factors that can affect problem-recognition processes in general is large, but in any given situation a single factor or small number of factors are the primary contributors to problem recognition. Detailed discussion of all possible determinants of problem recognition is impossible. However, detailed discussion of the primary determinants is necessary and appropriate.

Certain determinants produce problem recognition by affecting the consumer's desired state of affairs, whereas others affect the consumer's actual state of affairs. Certain determinants can, of course, affect both desired and actual states. The primary determinants of problem recognition and the state of affairs on which they are believed to have the greatest impact are presented in Figure 11.2.

FACTORS AFFECTING THE ACTUAL STATE

A consumer's actual state of affairs can be affected by the depletion of the previous solution, dissatisfaction with the previous solution, and marketing efforts. Although other factors can affect

FIGURE 11.2.
Factors that Affect Problem Recognition

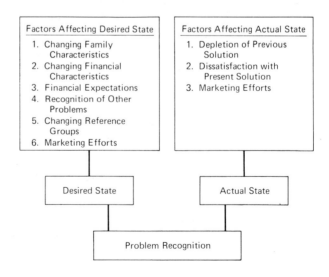

the consumer's desired state of affairs, these three factors are the most important determinants.

Perhaps the most frequent determinant of problem recognition is *the depletion of the previous solution* to a problem. Familiar examples are running out of gasoline, food, beer, toothpaste, and any other such products. The depletion of an existing solution to a problem produces problem recognition only if the consumer recognizes the depletion and if the underlying need still exists. Thus, the depletion of an ample supply of golf balls would not produce problem recognition if you have decided never to play golf again. However, the depletion of an ardent golfer's supply of golf balls would produce a state of problem recognition. The marketing analyst must estimate the likely depletion time of various market segments and the pattern of behavior used to replenish the depleted supply in order to assure availability of the product. Determining when users of a certain type of product will replenish supply is crucial to adjusting marketing efforts to encourage repeat purchases of users and to stimulate trial by nonusers.

Problem recognition can also result from a consumer's *dissatisfaction with the present solution* to a problem; that is, when a product breaks, wears out, or otherwise becomes unsatisfactory a consumer's desired state of affairs can be affected.[1] The purchase of a new automobile is, for instance, frequently triggered by the failure of the consumer's present automobile. A consumer can also become dissatisfied with the present solution to a problem because of the solution's price. For example, the high cost of renting a home or an apartment frequently triggers the problem recognition that precedes the purchase of a home.[2] The marketing analyst must monitor the satisfaction that consumers

[1]D. H. Granbois, "A Study of the Family Decision Making Process in the Purchase of Major Durable Household Goods," unpublished doctoral dissertation (Bloomington, Ind.: Indiana University Graduate School of Business, 1962), p. 84.
[2]R. T. Norris, "Processes and Objectives of House Purchasing in the New London Area" in *The Dynamics of Consumer Reaction*, L. Clark, ed., (New York: New York University Press, 1955), pp. 25–29; P. Rossi, *Why Families Move* (New York: Free Press, 1955); W. T. Kelly, "How Buyers Shop for a New Home," *Appraisal*, 25 (1957), pp. 209–214.

experience with his products in order to accurately focus marketing efforts.

The third factor that can affect the consumer's actual state and, consequently, trigger problem recognition is marketing efforts. An advertisement informing consumers that a certain type of lawn mower once believed safe is actually unsafe may affect the consumer's perception of the actual state and thus result in considerable discrepancy between his desired and actual states.

FACTORS AFFECTING THE DESIRED STATE

There are perhaps an infinite number of factors that affect a consumer's desired state of affairs. The most important factors affecting a consumer's desired state of affairs are: (1) changing family characteristics, (2) changing financial characteristics, (3) financial expectations, (4) recognition of other problems, (5) changing reference groups, and (6) marketing efforts.

Perhaps no factor that affects the desired state has so monumental and lasting an effect as *changes in family characteristics.* When a person marries, substantial changes occur in the desired state with respect to housing, home furnishing, leisure activities, and numerous other things.[3] The birth of a child substantially alters the needs and attitudes of the nuclear family and produces considerable changes in the desired state of affairs.[4] Indeed, new needs and commensurate redefinitions of desired states continually occur as the size and composition of the family changes. For instance, the promotion to corporate vice-president might affect the desired automobile, desired home, and desired club memberships.

Financial considerations, such as *changing financial status* and *financial expectations* can affect a consumer's desired state and, thus, trigger problem recognition. A salary increase, inheritance, or some other windfall can cause a consumer to substan-

[3]R. Ferber, "Family Decision Making and Economic Behavior," in *Family Economic Behavior: Problems and Perspectives,* E. B. Sheldon, ed. (Philadelphia: J. B. Lippincott Company, 1972), pp. 29–61.

[4]W. D. Wells and G. Gubar, "The Life Style Concept in Marketing Research," *Journal of Marketing Research,* 3 (November, 1966), pp. 355–363.

tially alter his desired state of affairs.[5] Such a change in financial status can, for example, cause the desired state to be ownership of a new Cadillac when the prewindfall desired state might have been a three-year-old Ford. Similarly, a financial disaster can precipitate a change in desired state of comparable magnitude in the opposite direction. The marketing strategist, obviously, cannot influence a consumer's financial status. However, changes in the financial status of sizeable market segments can present an opportunity to increase profit by adjusting the market offerings. For example, changes in the financial status of farmers can affect changes in the desired equipment on pickup trucks. Such a change might be met by producing trucks with fewer options and frills. Consumers' expectations regarding their financial status can also affect their desired state of affairs. The purchase of a new automobile by the second-semester college senior frequently results from a change in the student's desired state of affairs that is triggered by financial expectations upon graduation. Marketing analysts have clearly documented the importance of expectations in the period preceding the purchase of many durable goods.[6]

A consumer's perception of the desired state frequently results from the *recognition of another problem.* The desire for a new stereo system can affect the consumer's perception of the desirability of records or tapes currently owned. In other words, the consumer can become dissatisfied with the desired state of one product because of the recognition of problems in related areas. Marketing strategists frequently group or display related products in reasonable proximity where such a phenomenon may occur. For example, washers and dryers, beds and bedding, and furniture and carpeting are frequently displayed together.

The state of affairs perceived to be desirable can be affected by *changes in reference groups.* For example, reference groups

[5]F. T. Juster and P. Wachtel, "Uncertainty Expectations and Durable Goods Demand Models," in *Human Behavior in Economic Affairs,* B. Strumpel, J. N. Morgan, and E. Zahn, eds. (San Francisco: Jossey-Bass Inc., 1972), pp. 321–345.

[6]E. Mueller, "The Desire for Innovations in Household Goods," in *Consumer Behavior: Research on Consumer Reactions,* L. Clark, ed. (New York: Harper & Row, Inc., 1958), p. 37.

frequently influence the desired state of apparel. College gradu-
ates quickly learn that there is a conspicuous difference between
the types of clothing that were appropriate on a college campus
and the types appropriate for a career in business. The change
in reference groups from fellow students to aspiring executives
influenced the consumer's desired state of affairs and, consequently, the consumer perceives the existence of a problem.

Finally, various *marketing efforts,* including advertising, product displays, and personal selling, can affect a consumer's perception of the desired state of affairs and hence trigger problem
recognition. An advertisement informing the viewer of certain
distinctive product features can, for example, affect the viewer's
desired state of affairs. If the desired state of affairs is perceived
to be significantly discrepant from the actual state, the advertisement has triggered problem recognition. Indeed, the marketing
strategist's objective may be to focus marketing efforts in order
to stimulate problem recognition among certain market segments.

MARKETING IMPLICATIONS OF PROBLEM RECOGNITION

The preceding observations on the determinants of problem recognition suggest certain guidelines for the marketing strategist.
First, the marketing strategist must determine the unique aspects
of problem-recognition processes for the specific product in
question, because the determinants of problem recognition are
different for automobiles, sport shirts, and soft drinks. Consequently, the marketing strategist must identify the relative importance of the various determinants of problem recognition and
then focus marketing efforts to achieve the firm's objective. Second, the marketing strategist must recognize that consumers
differ substantially in their sensitivity to the factors that affect
problem recognition. Consequently, the marketing strategist
must identify the prominent problem-recognition processes associated with purchase of a particular product by the relevant
consumer segments.

Suppose that the Coca Cola Company identifies depletion of
the previous solution as the primary determinant of problem recognition relative to the purchase of Coke by people between the

ages of 16 and 21. This determination and the recognition that Coke is a convenience-type product would suggest that an intensive distribution strategy would be appropriate; that is, since dissatisfaction with the product is not a major factor triggering problem recognition, the company need not attempt to convince consumers of the relative benefits of their product. Rather, the company should concentrate on making the product available at as many locations as possible. However, the Coca Cola Company might find that the primary determinant of problem recognition in another consumer segment is dissatisfaction with the previous solution. The marketing strategy appropriate for this segment would differ considerably from that appropriate for the youth segment.

The Measurement of Problem-Recognition Processes

Consumer analysts now believe that problem recognition can best be measured by obtaining information on purchase intentions. As discussed in Chapter 10, purchase intentions have become recognized as the intervening variable between the attitudes and the behavior that is operative when a problem is recognized. Thus a consumer's indicated intention to purchase can be interpreted as an acknowledgement that a problem has been recognized and the consumer is in the early state of problem-solving activity. A consumer's expressed intention to purchase a product indicates that the consumer perceives a discrepancy between the desired and actual states, and consequently will be seeking to facilitate resolution of the problem.

Consumer analysts have used a variety of techniques to measure consumer purchase intentions.[7] The technique that has provided marketing strategists with the most accurate information on problem recognition is the purchase-probability scale.[8] The purchase-probability technique requests that consumers es-

[7]F. T. Juster, *Consumer Buying Intentions and Purchase Probability* (New York: National Bureau of Economic Research, 1966).

[8]D. H. Granbois and J. O. Summers, "On the Predictive Accuracy of Subjective Purchase Probabilities," in *Proceedings of the Third Annual Conference of the Association for Consumer Research* (Chicago: American Marketing Association, 1972), pp. 502–511.

timate the probability that they will purchase a particular product or brand within a designated time period on the following type of scale.

The predictive accuracy of this method is largely attributable to the fact that it sensitively distributes consumers with different levels of purchase intentions. Consumer analysts have demonstrated that purchase probability scales provide marketing strategists with accurate measures of problem recognition for numerous product categories, such as automobiles,[9] household appliances,[10] low-priced convenience items,[11] and several grocery-product categories.[12] The usefulness of purchase-intention information depends upon the specific product and brand in question.

Using Information on Problem-Recognition Processes

An executive of the General Electric Company has very ably demonstrated the usefulness of information on problem recognition in formulating marketing strategy.[13] Measures of problem recognition were obtained from members of the General Electric Consumer Panel by means of purchase-probability scales. This

[9]D. H. Granbois and J. O. Summers, p. 506.

[10]R. W. Pratt, Jr., "Understanding the Decision Process for Consumer Durables: An Example of the Longitudinal Approach," in *Marketing and Economic Development,* P. D. Bennett, ed., (Chicago: American Marketing Association, 1965), pp. 244–260.

[11]A. Gruber, "Purchase Intent and Purchase Probability," *Journal of Advertising Research,* 10 (February, 1970), pp. 23–27.

[12]S. Banks, "The Relationship Between Preference and Purchase of Brands," *Journal of Marketing,* 15 (October, 1950), pp. 145–157.

[13]R. W. Pratt, "Consumer Buying Intentions as an Aid in Formulating Marketing Strategy," in *Marketing and the New Science of Planning,* R. L. King, ed. (Chicago: American Marketing Association, 1968), pp. 296–302.

information was then used to identify promotional targets and allocate promotional efforts. First, the purchase probability scale must be grouped into larger categories. One of several possible groupings is as follows:

FIGURE 11.3.

Category	Purchase Probability Scale
I	Certain, practically certain (99 in 100) Almost sure (9 in 10)
II	Very probably (8 in 10) Probable (7 in 10)
III	Good possibility (6 in 10) Fairly good possibility (5 in 10) Fair possibility (4 in 10)
IV	Some possibility (3 in 10) Slight possibility (2 in 10)
V	Very slight possibility (1 in 10) No chance, almost no chance (1 in 100)

Once the categories have been determined, the marketing analyst estimates the percentage distribution of consumers across the five categories for the firm's brand and the major competing brands. In other words, General Electric must determine what percentage of its customers are in Category I, Category II, and so on. Subsequent to this, the marketing analyst must specify the following for each category:

1. The evaluative criteria used by consumers
2. The relative importance of the evaluative criteria
3. The evaluation of each brand on the evaluative criteria
4. Multiply the relative importance of each criterion times the brand's rating on that criterion.

The marketing analyst uses this information to estimate the potential economic value of each category. If a particular category evaluated the product in question high on the evaluative criteria considered important to consumers in that category, then that category would have a higher potential than if it had evaluated the product low on those evaluative criteria. The same procedure can be used to assess the value of each category.[14]

Once the marketing analyst has estimated the economic value of each category, media usage profiles can be constructed for each category. Promotional plans can then be developed that focus on those specific categories. Media can be directed toward the objective of moving people up one or more category levels. Copy can be conceptualized and developed to refer to differences in brand ratings on specific evaluative criteria between users and nonusers at each category level for the firm's brand as well as for competing brands. Finally, after the marketing program has been executed, purchase intention information can be evaluated to determine if the program has effectively moved people up into a higher category of purchase intention.

The preceding discussion has illustrated how information on problem-recognition processes can be used to more effectively direct marketing efforts. The increasing competition for organizational resources will undoubtedly lead to the development of yet more sophisticated means of utilizing this information.

Summary

A problem is recognized when the consumer perceives a difference of significant magnitude between a desired state and an actual state. Following the problem recognition, the consumer may "hold" and not change behavior or begin the process of searching for an alternative product or service. Types of problem-recognition processes vary substantially in complexity. Simple problem-recognition processes are strongly learned, highly programmed, and automatic. Somewhat complicated processes are characterized by more time, more factors impinging, and perhaps, more intense consumer attitudes. The highly complex processes are the infrequent, unprogrammed type that involve a considerable period of time, are affected by a number of factors, and involve strongly held attitudes.

[14]For a variation of this approach see G. Smith, "How GM Measures Ad Effectiveness," *Printers Ink* (May 14, 1965), pp. 19–29.

This chapter addresses the primary factors involved in the problem-recognition process. The factors affecting the actual state of affairs are: (1) the depletion of a previous solution to a problem, (2) dissatisfaction with the present solution to a problem, and (3) marketing efforts. The factors affecting the desired state of affairs are:(1) changes in family characteristics, (2) changes in financial status, (3) changes in financial expectations, (4) recognition of another problem, (5) changes in reference groups, and (6) marketing efforts. Problem-recognition processes can be measured by marketers by using the purchase-probability scale. A practical example of how the General Electric Company used problem-recognition processes to improve their marketing effort is cited.

QUESTIONS AND ISSUES FOR DISCUSSION

1. What is problem recognition? How does the consumer's unique psychological makeup influence problem recognition?

2. "Problem recognition is something over which marketers have no control. Therefore, the marketing manager's task is to identify the problem-recognition patterns relevant to his products." Do you agree?

3. Is problem recognition always followed by behavior that eliminates the discrepancy between actual and desired states?

4. The First Friendly Bank located in Library, Michigan (population 50,000), has experienced a declining market share for the past three years. The marketing director knows that Library has a very mobile population and that First Friendly has not gotten its share of new residents but is perplexed as to what action to take. How might an understanding of problem recognition help the marketing director?

5. Describe the problem recognition processes that might occur relative to the following products:

   a. Soft drinks
   b. Breakfast cereal
   c. Medical examination
   d. Tennis racket

6. How would the problem-recognition processes differ for the following types of people with respect to the products in Question 5:

   a. College student versus professor
   b. Middle-class mother of four versus lower-class mother of four
   c. Retired carpenter versus 25-year-old secretary.

7. How does problem recognition differ from motivation, needs, and product awareness?
8. Identify the factors that affected problem recognition for your most recent purchase of a nondurable product, durable product, and service. Were the factors that affected problem recognition the same in all three instances?
9. A major producer of golf clubs has just determined that the major factors affecting problem recognition for sporting equipment products are changing financial characteristics and dissatisfaction with the present solution. How might this information help the company more effectively allocate its marketing effort?
10. How have the factors that affect problem recognition for you changed in the past five years?

SITUATIONAL PROBLEMS

Case 1.

Albany, Incorporated, produces a complete line of televisions that are sold throughout the United States. In the past ten years the TV industry has experienced considerable growth. During this period Albany's sales have increased faster than those of the rest of the industry. Albany's market share during this period increased from 6 to 9 percent. However, in the past 16 months the TV industry, particularly Albany, has experienced serious difficulty. Albany's sales declined by 17 percent, and its share of the market dropped below 8 percent. Albany's market research director contends that a recent study suggests that consumers either don't recognize the need for a new TV or do recognize such a need but are constrained from resolving the problem.

How might an understanding of problem recognition and the factors that affect problem recognition assist the management of Albany?

Should Albany attempt to stimulate problem recognition? How might this be done?

Case 2.

Merit Brothers, a producer of quality outer apparel, has experienced stable growth for the past 25 years. Merit Brothers' management is gratified with the success it has experienced in outer apparel but recognizes that continual growth will require their penetration of new markets. In response to this recognition, the company has developed a complete line of men's leisure suits that will be distributed through the firm's existing channels. The uncertainty Merit Brothers' management perceived relative to the market for leisure suits precipitated a market analysis designed to provide a measure of problem recognition, identify promotional targets, and allocate promotional efforts. The market analysis provided the following information on consumer purchase probability:

Consumer Response	Percent of Consumers
1. Certain or almost certain to buy a Merit Brothers' leisure suit.	10
2. Very probable or probably will buy a Merit Brothers' leisure suit.	20
3. Good, fairly good, or fair possibility will buy a Merit Brothers' leisure suit.	30
4. Some or slight possibility will buy a Merit Brothers' leisure suit.	25
5. Very slight possibility or almost no chance will buy a Merit Brothers' leisure suit.	15

Should Merit Brothers' attempt to stimulate problem recognition relative to the leisure suits they plan on introducing?

How can this information on problem recognition be used to effectively direct marketing efforts?

12

Information Search and Alternative Evaluation

The American consumer, more than any other in the world today, is exposed to information from numerous sources. The following are a few statistics which illustrate the volume and extent of this exposure.

About 24 million pieces of direct mail advertising are mailed to Americans in a year. According to a U.S. Postal Service survey, 63 percent of all such pieces are opened and read.[1]

In a typical day 40 million people turn to the classified sections of their newspaper: 45 percent look at ads for merchandise, 42 percent go over real estate listings, 35 percent pay attention to automobile offerings, while 33 percent look at employment opportunities.[2]

Approximately 5.5 billion copies of consumer magazines are published each year with a total audience of more than 116 million adults.[3]

Despite such mass exposure, there is considerable evidence to show that when it comes time to make a purchase, often there appears to be relatively little deliberate search undertaken for purchase-related information. For example, in one study it was found that about one consumer in ten checked advertisements before shopping for shoes or personal accessories. Even when more costly items are sought, such as a television set or household furniture, there is evidence to show that only about half of the consumers look at ads before shopping. Another study revealed that small-appliance purchasers visited only one store and made their buying decision in about a week.[4]

Most of what has been observed and reported above should not be used to characterize the American consumer as an irrational, frivolous person. Actually, there are several explanations for such behavior. First, exposure to information and persuasive messages is a continuous process. This constant flow of infor-

[1]"The New World of Advertising," *Advertising Age,* 44 (November 21, 1973), p. 119.

[2]"The New World of Advertising," p. 64.

[3]"The New World of Advertising," p. 74.

[4]S. H. Chaffee and J. M. McLead, "Consumer Decisions and Information Use," in *Consumer Behavior: Theoretical Sources,* S. Ward and T. S. Robertson, eds. (Englewood Cliffs, New Jersey: Prentice-Hall, Inc., 1973), pp. 386–387.

mation enables people to accumulate knowledge about various goods and services even before they need or want it. Furthermore, this exposure also helps consumers clarify what it is they might want or what product could conceivably assist them in resolving some particular problem, should it ever arise. This means that consumers are in a state of readiness to buy many different products before they are specifically sought.[5] For most of us, it is not difficult to recall some situation where this readiness was consciously noted, for instance, finding that an all-night drug store located conveniently to your home now carries a few grocery items including bread and milk. The chances are that these products will only be purchased here at some off hour when a pressing need arises. Nevertheless, the information is stored and available for quick recall when necessary. Outdoor advertising along the highway often serves this same function. It is not unusual in some areas to see a sign that reminds you that there is a Howard Johnson's restaurant 75 miles ahead. The sign may be noted briefly in passing without interest. However, 65 to 70 miles later, the restaurant is sought as an opportunity for a refreshing break.

There are several other logical explanations as to why consumers appear to engage in little search prior to making a purchase. Such information gathering can add substantially to the cost; for example, trips to various stores and the studying of ads and searching through catalogues takes considerable time and even money for direct expenses such as gasoline and parking. Furthermore, because these activities take time, their consideration forces postponement of the purchase. This delay can be bothersome if there is an urgent need for the item or if there is a strong desire to have it. To some, wedding rings would be in this category, while to others it would be a motorcycle or a new dress.

The gathering of information can add to personal frustration in yet another way. Consumers can become overloaded with facts, figures, and persuasive statements so much so that it distracts

[5]J. D. Clarton, J. N. Fry, and B. Portis, "A Taxonomy of Prepurchase Information Gathering Patterns," *Journal of Consumer Research,* 1 (December, 1974), p. 35.

from their ability to make a satisfying purchase decision. Consequently, some people allot little time to gathering information beyond some minimum level.

Before going further, it is appropriate to more formally introduce the subjects covered in this chapter. As the title suggests, this chapter focuses on two closely related aspects of consumer behavior which are prepurchase search and the evaluation of alternatives. To the extent that it is possible, each of these topics are integrated into all of the major sections of the chapter.

Search and Alternative Evaluation Defined

Search as used in this text, is the purposeful attention given to the gathering and assembling of information related to the satisfaction of some perceived need, want, or desire. It is a prepurchase action in that it takes place before the product of interest is bought. The search process is proactive; that is, it is deliberate and has a certain momentum to it. Search may be either internal or external. *Internal search* is essentially a mental review of what an individual has experienced or has been exposed to and what has been learned and remembered. *External search* is the act of seeking information from any outside source by the individual who is engaged in the search process. The evaluation process usually takes place during search and involves the use of evaluative criteria in assessing that which comes to the consumer's attention. Also, as mentioned in Chapter 9, often these criteria are themselves modified as a result of the search experience.

The Place of Search and Alternative Evaluation in the Decision Process

It can be noted in Figure 12.1 that the search process follows the problem recognition. This means that some need or want has been consciously identified. These problems and the search they precipitate come in many forms. Three brief examples are given below to illustrate the relationship between problem recognition and search.

Having noticed that the window air conditioner in his bedroom has been running excessively, a man checks the filter and finds it to be in need of replacement. By this means he acknowledges that a purchase must be made. In this case the product cost is low, and the most likely concern in the search process is to locate the most

FIGURE 12.1.
Search and Alternative Evaluation Processes

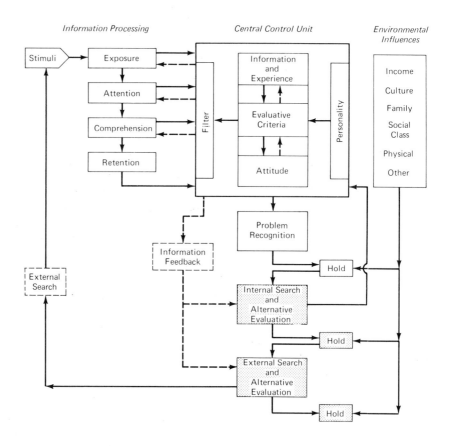

Source: J. F. Engel, D. T. Kollat, and R. D. Blackwell, *Consumer Behavior,* 2nd ed. (New York: Holt, Rinehart and Winston, Inc., 1973), p. 374. Reprinted by permission of the publisher.

convenient store where the filter of the correct size can be purchased. This does not mean that the search process will take little time; it just depends on the availability of the filter and the consumer's ability to locate it.

During the fall semester, a university student has become discontent with dorm life and has decided to move into an apartment in town. She has never had her own apartment but has observed the advantages that it has provided her friends. The problem she has recognized is that of dissatisfaction with dorm life and the resulting need to move. However, the search is likely to be considerably more complex and time-consuming than in the previous situation described. For instance, initially she will have to decide what kind of an apartment she wants. Then, through external search, she will be able to discover what is actually available in the town and obtain information regarding such issues as rental costs, lease arrangements, required security deposits, and whether she might be able to share an apartment with someone.

A local independent trucker who owns his own rig has just decided that he wants a new CB radio for his personal car. He purchased his first CB radio two years ago for his truck and has found it very helpful in cases of emergencies and in monitoring road and weather conditions. Although the product is somewhat complex and technical in this situation, the trucker has experience to rely on. Nevertheless, the search process may take him a substantial amount of time and involve the consideration of alternative product types and brands as well as comparison of the prices and service available at various retail outlets.

These three situations illustrate some of the variation that is likely to occur in search behavior and alternative evaluation as different circumstances arise. A number of factors directly affect the nature of the search process itself. These can be categorized as follows:[6]

1. *The uniqueness of the object sought, that is, the extent to which acceptable substitutes exist*   This can be illustrated by

[6]R. F. Kelly, "The Search Component of the Consumer Decision Process— A Theoretic Examination," in *1968 Fall Conference Proceedings: Marketing and the New Science of Planning,* R. L. King, ed. (Chicago: American Marketing Association, 1969), p. 276.

again referring to the three situations previously described above. In the case of the air conditioner filter, there is considerable similarity among alternatives. Therefore, once one is found, it will probably be purchased. However, the trucker faces more variety and, consequently, a greater need to engage in search. The manufacturers of CB radios and the retail outlets that stock them can have a substantial effect on this process by means of their promotional efforts. For instance, the issuance of a catalogue can reduce the need to visit some stores.

2. *The strength of the motivation that precepitated the search activity*   In the case of the university student who has become dissatisfied with dorm living arrangements, there is really no explicit indication given as to her level of discontent. If, for example, she is very unhappy and this dissatisfaction is reinforced by her parents after seeing her grades, she will be inclined to expend considerable effort in the search process. However, if the situation is quite different and her discontent is related to one particular situation that has essentially been resolved, her propensity to look for alternative in-town rental units may be extremely low.

Firms can play a direct part in stimulating a willingness to search. The heavy advertising of new products, for instance, can cause discontent with those currently used or at least encourage the consumer to consider alternatives. If one gives a quick thought to the breakfast cereal or snack food offerings currently available, this point is confirmed.

3. *Previous experience in searching for similar products or services*   The extent of the search that the trucker will engage in as he seeks to find a CB radio for his car will be affected by the fact that he already owns one and has had the benefit of the first purchase experience. For example, he may already know which stores carry equipment of the quality he is most interested in owning. He may also have catalogues from these outlets describing their product lines and showing current prices.

4. *General predisposition toward search*   None of the situations described earlier offer any details about the individual's willingness to personally engage in search. However, differences among consumers do exist, and to a large extent the observed variation has been related to perceived risk. For example, two people with similar backgrounds and experience facing essen-

tially the same situation often approach it differently. In a number of instances this can be explained by the fact that some people are simply more willing than others to assume a given amount of risk. In other cases, two individuals will perceive varying amounts of risk in a given situation and, hence, behave differently.

The impact of variation in perceived risk can be illustrated by observing two mothers who each face the same problem of needing to treat what looks like poison ivy on their young children. One mother is very apprehensive about using any over-the-counter drug before checking with her doctor. She fears a possible reaction in the child and is deeply concerned as to whether her diagnosis is correct. The other mother, who faces the same situation, simply goes to the drugstore and then after reading the labels of several branded lotions for the treatment of poison ivy, purchases one and applies it according to the directions.

In order to reduce risk, consumers often adopt one of several behavioral patterns. Some of the most common are identified below.[7] Buy only:

    a. a specific brand
    b. nationally advertised brands
    c. the cheapest brand
    d. the most expensive brand
    e. only a certain amount of the product
    f. only products with a plain and simple design.

As a means of further examining the consumer search process, the next two sections will deal first with internal search and alternative evaluation and then with external search and alternative evaluation.

Internal Search and Alternative Evaluation

Internal search is the conscious recall and consideration of specific information and experiences that appear to be relevant to the recognized problem that the consumer faces. In some situa-

---

[7]J. F. Engel, D. T. Kollat, and R. D. Blackwell, *Consumer Behavior,* 2nd ed. (New York: Holt, Rinehart and Winston, Inc., 1973), p. 379.

tions this search is nearly instantaneous while in others, thinking and pondering of ideas takes place over a considerable period of time. A simple illustration will explain how the latter occurs.

Assume that it is a Saturday morning and you have just recalled that next Monday is your mother's birthday. You are 225 miles from home. You have a gift in mind and rush out to the store to buy it. Things are going quite well, and at your first stop you are able to buy what you want and have it gift wrapped. You then hurry home to prepare the package for mailing. You do this as quickly as possible, but by now it is 11:45 A.M. Although the post office is only about a 10-minute drive away, in Saturday traffic it takes you nearly 20 minutes, and upon arriving you find the post office closed. This is a frustrating moment, but you do not know what to do except to drive home disappointed. You sit down and relax, trying to think of some way of getting that package to its destination by Monday. In a few minutes you have thought of two alternatives. First, there is a post office substation in a local supermarket that is still open, and second, you could send the gift by Greyhound Package Service. You recall having heard an advertisement for this service on the radio.

Almost everyone has had this kind of an experience. In this situation the two alternative means for getting the package to its destination on time were in memory but were not recalled without conscious effort and the lapse of some time.

It is important to keep in mind that nearly everyone in our economically advanced society is exposed to vast amounts of information, some of which is retained and available for recall at a later time. The way in which this information is dealt with and retained is of major concern to the consumer analyst. What is retained may have a lasting effect on an individual's behavior as a consumer. Consequently, managers of all organizations that are interested in consumer behavior must necessarily become aware of the information selection and retention process.

Specifically, the success and general helpfulness of internal search to the consumer is dependent on what information is retained. No one is receptive to and retains all that he or she sees, hears, touches, smells, or tastes. For example, there is evidence to show that during about 50 percent of television advertising, the average consumer tunes out the entire commercial.[8]

In terms of effectiveness as an information receiver and storage facility, man compares poorly to equipment such as a tape recorder. But man's coding ability—his capacity for insight, judgment, and the ability to identify meaningful patterns in messages—are superb. To a great extent, this remarkable ability is the result of a systematic selection of information and not a random process. People generally seem to have a unique set of rules and operating procedures enabling them to select information, keep it manageable, and yet still meet their needs.

Howard has offered a model of this selection process that includes three phases or steps in information handling.[9] These phases are illustrated in Figure 12.2.

Each of these components has a separate function and all three phases are described below:

Sensory memory: It receives all information to which it is exposed. Although this memory component is large and comprehensive at any point in time, total retention is extremely short. If the information in the sensory memory is not transferred from it to short-term memory in a matter of milliseconds, it is dissipated and lost.

FIGURE 12.2
Information Reception and Storage

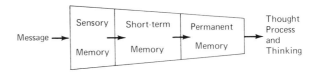

[8]J. A. Howard, "New Directions in Buyer Behavior Research," in *Combined Proceedings: 1971 Spring and Fall Conferences,* F. C. Allvine, ed. (Chicago: American Marketing Association, 1972), p. 376.
[9]J. A. Howard, pp. 376–377.

Short-term memory: This component retains its content somewhat longer than does sensory memory before it is lost. Some evidence suggests that if the message is transferred to long-term memory within 18 seconds, it can be satisfactorily stored.

Permanent memory: This is the component that affects consumer behavior. Another way of describing it is to think of this phase of memory as being made up of all the coded stimuli received from the various messages that penetrated the sensory and short-term memory components. These come from many sources including products themselves, packages, advertisements, and personal encounters with salesmen as well as with friends and family members.

The coded stimuli stored in long-term or permanent memory are what is recalled when internal search is undertaken. However, this does not explain why some information gets into long-term memory and other material does not. There are several factors that can affect what impressions and experiences move into long-term memory. Three of these are identified here.

1. *The capacity of the individual*   This is influenced by such characteristics as the person's intelligence, maturity (i.e., children cannot process information as fast and as accurately as can adults), personality, education, and social class. The last two factors may contribute to message receptiveness through their effect on an individual's language capacity. For example, the better educated member of the upper middle class probably has a vocabulary larger than that of the average lower class member. As a result, the former is better able to interpret messages.

2. *Familiarity with the subject*   The more familiar a topic or product, the more likely the individual is to already have some memory base for it. For instance, toasters are a familiar household product to nearly everyone whereas a stoneware-lined, electric slow-cooker branded as a Crock-Pot by Rival Manufacturing is comparatively less well known. All other things being equal, familiarity contributes to the ease of movement of information into long-term memory.

3. *Relevance of the subject or product*   This refers to the extent to which some bit of information is related to the individu-

al's perceived needs, wants, or desires. In short, consumers are more likely to give attention to what they believe they need to know and less or no attention to other information. Ad headlines that promise cost savings or increased miles per gallon attempt to attract attention through making the message appear extremely relevant.

There is evidence to show that consumers develop brand concepts in their long-term memory. These concepts are made up of: (1) *brand comprehension,* which is the denotative or literal meaning of a brand (e.g., Ivory as a brand of hand soap, including its physical attributes), (2) *attitude or connotative meaning of a brand* (i.e., the subjective feelings that an individual has about a brand, such as its status appeal), and (3) *brand confidence,* which refers to the extent to which the consumer is comfortable or certain about his or her evaluation of the brand.

Internal search and alternative evaluation usually produce one of three outcomes. First, if the process generates satisfactory results, that is, an acceptable resolution to the recognized problem, the consumer will likely forego external search and proceed to the purchase stage. Second, internal search and alternative evaluation may convince the consumer that there is no viable way of solving the problem, and so the process is halted. The third outcome is the recognition by the consumer that there is a need for further information and, therefore, it is necessary to undertake external search and further evaluation.

External Search and Alternative Evaluation

As indicated earlier, external search is the expenditure of deliberate effort to seek information from various outside sources. This phase of search is a means of supplementing the consumer's existing knowledge. Any source may be used, but there are several that are most frequently consulted. These include salesmen, advertisements, packages, showroom visits, and friends and family members. The propensity for an individual to engage in such search is discussed in the following section.

THE PROPENSITY TO ENGAGE IN EXTERNAL SEARCH

The energy expended by an individual in external search is dependent on several factors. The following are some of the most important.[10]

Individual Reactions to a Given Problem

Some problems appear to need immediate attention. To certain individuals, for example, the loss of their watch would require quick action. They may simply feel unable to function without it. To others, seeing their automobile gasoline gauge register one quarter full will precipitate a similar feeling of urgency. In this same sense, the use of the brand name Die-hard for a Sears' auto battery quite likely has a special appeal to some people because of their fear of not being able to start their car.

Modes of Tension Reduction

Some personal tension always accompanies problem recognition, but the general patterns that people use to relieve this internal stress vary among individuals and to some extent by situation. Some consumers, upon recognizing a need for a particular product, must actively begin going from store to store in search of the product and related information to ease their tension. The very act of getting out into the market relieves their stress. A careful study of the newspaper ads appears to ease the tensions of some homemakers as they face the weekly grocery shopping.

To other consumers, it seems as if their tension is lessened only by making a purchase. Any time expended in search is simply seen as a delaying action and, consequently, may even increase the level of anxiety.

The differing natures of problem situations precipitate varying patterns of relieving tension. For example, any delay in the choice of a dentist when you have a toothache is probably going to be avoided. Therefore, search may amount to no more than calling a friend for the name of her dentist or frantically calling each dentist in the telephone directory until one is located who will see you immediately.

[10]R. F. Kelly, p. 278.

Perception and Handling of Risk or Uncertainty

As mentioned earlier, the ability and willingness of people to assume risk varies considerably. Inability to resolve a recognized problem through internal search will result in different behavioral patterns.

Research has suggested that some consumers can be characterized by their risk-handling styles and the means that they use to reduce their perceived risk. Two such consumer groupings classified by risk-handling styles have been identified as *clarifiers* and *simplifiers.* Clarifiers, when confronted with some confusion, seek additional information in order to better understand the context in which a decision can be made. Simplifiers, facing the same amount of confusion, selectively screen out information that is not consistent with their predispositions, thus simplifying the context within which the decision is to be made.[11]

The use of brand names that strongly suggest specific product benefits may be particularly helpful to the simplifier. They are short and to the point. This can be illustrated by considering the brand names of several sedatives and stimulants including Sleep-Eze, Cope, Compoz, and No Doz.

As the result of some personal initiative and considerable encouragement from governmental agencies, consumer interest groups, and Congress, business firms have taken several significant steps to reduce perceived risk among consumers by facilitating search and the evaluation of alternatives. Three of the more recent examples are given below.

Unit Pricing.   A considerable number of grocery stores are now providing shelf-pricing information that gives price per some standard unit, such as per ounce or pound. This can be helpful to consumers in making price comparisons among brands of a given product such as canned green beans, cooking oil, and dry milk. It also provides a quick means of determining how much of a premium, if any, is being paid for national brands. Then, too, it

[11]D. F. Cox, "The Influence of Cognitive Needs and Styles on Information Handling in Making Product Evaluations," in *Risk Taking and Information Handling in Consumer Behavior,* D. F. Cox, ed. (Boston: Division of Research, Graduate School of Business, Harvard University, 1967), pp. 370–393.

is a way of finding out just how economical the "super size" is over the "large" of some brand.

Nutritional Labeling.   A list of the nutrients contained in a serving of many processed foods is now available on their labels. Such information can serve as a means of determining how each food item can be used to build a balanced diet through meal planning and careful shopping.

Interest Rate Information.   As the result of federal legislation, interest rates must be communicated in a uniform manner to each consumer by the financial institution involved before a loan is made. Although many questions remain as to the total effect of this effort, it has been a substantial step in the direction of more openness.

PHASES OF EXTERNAL SEARCH

The external search process can be divided into two parts, based on how the search experience takes place.[12] This is illustrated very simply in Figure 12.3 and is then discussed in the paragraphs that follow. The process is shown as funnel shaped to emphasize that it is a means of beginning with broad considerations and then gradually refining the search and evaluation process until a satisfactory conclusion is reached.

**FIGURE 12.3
Phases of Ex-
ternal Search**

Preliminary
Search
Effort

Concluding
Search
Effort

[12]R. F. Kelly, p. 276.

Preliminary Search and Alternative Evaluation
The search that is initiated after it is recognized that internal search has not resolved the problem is called preliminary search. The length of this phase varies depending upon the circumstances faced, but it typically produces the following results.

1. *A redefinition of the desired product or service attributes* This often occurs because there is a reconciliation between what may be called the idealized product or service—what was conceived of as being sought—and what is observed as being available in the market.

This includes becoming aware of specific product features and operating characteristics as well as other dimensions such as warranties, available credit terms, and the service that can be expected from the supplier. In planning their product and service offerings, firms that practice the marketing concept have sought to identify consumer preferences in terms of what is perceived to be the "ideal product." This has then been followed by the use of strategy in producing and positioning their offerings in the market to deliver the most acceptable product to the identified market. Quite obviously, some "ideal products" are not profitable to produce and market, while others require some modifications before marketing. For example, some French-designed clothing for women would be very appealing to the mass market in the United States, but it usually cannot be produced and distributed profitably to the American consumer until it is modified. Some modifications are often required so that the items can be mass-produced and sold at acceptable price levels through stores such as J. C. Penney's, Macy's, Famous Barr, and Sears.

2. *Consumer's first acknowledgment that there are constraints imposed in the search process* These constraints come in various forms. For example, in some communities there are only one or two retail outlets that carry certain merchandise. It may be that the item of interest is a small household appliance —a personal size television set with a 10-inch screen. Prior to beginning the external search process, it was assumed that all appliance stores and the local discount house carried these sets. However, upon visiting several of these stores and calling the others, only two stores were found to stock them.

Another constraint may be the terms available. It is possible that a young couple looking for their first home soon discovers that every bank and savings and loan association in their town requires a 20 percent down payment as a condition of securing a loan. This poses a considerable obstacle given their housing preferences. This may be reconciled by deciding to wait until some future time with the idea that additional savings can be accumulated, assistance can be sought from their parents in the form of a short-term loan to supplement their savings, or possibly their housing preferences can be modified.

3. *More concise assessment of personal resources available*

This includes a recognition of the time and energy necessary to carry out the search activity as well as those resources needed to obtain the product or service sought.

It is often hard to estimate what it will take to adequately search out information about a product or service that is being considered for purchase. But once the search process gets under way, one begins to realize the number of alternative brands available, which stores should probably be shopped, and just how much time this could take. It seems as though most people are likely to underestimate what it takes to engage in a satisfying search experience.

For instance, a student arrives on the campus of a large state university with plans to purchase a 10-speed bicycle. This will help him greatly in getting around the campus. However, the student is new in the community and, furthermore, has never owned a 10-speed. His plan is to make this purchase the first day or two after he arrives. He considers this a major investment and has set aside $150 for this purpose but hopes to spend less. In this case, extensive search is probably going to be necessary to identify where bicycles are sold, the models and makes available, and the features of greatest importance; to gather pricing information; and to inquire about warranties as well as the service that can be expected. This student soon realizes that two days are not enough time to accomplish what he wants to do and that his $150 may not even be adequate.

Business firms assist in resolving such consumer problems by various means including advertising, placing stores in convenient locations, publishing catalogues that can be kept at home for quick reference, providing salespersons to point out and explain product features, and labeling and designing packages that allow a full view of the product while still protecting it. It is through exposure to these sources during the preliminary search that many consumers clearly formulate some order in their preferences regarding specific product features. In addition, it is common for the consumer to add some features to those sought initially and to drop others from further consideration.

It is also during this preliminary search process that consumers assemble the range of brands that can feasibly be looked upon as true alternatives. This list of alternatives has been called a consumer's *evoked set* or *consideration group.* This group nearly always is a subset of all the brands available. For instance, a young man looking for motor oil at a discount house quickly observes that there are over a dozen different brands on the shelves in the automotive section. Upon giving this some thought, he eliminates all but the recognized national brands. He reasoned that this is for his new car and he wants to be sure of the quality. Furthermore, by changing the oil himself, he can save considerable money, more than enough to buy what he considers to be a top quality product. Not only has this young man eliminated the private brands, but he also has implicitly excluded any national brand that is not on the shelf at the discount house.

This concept of the formulation of an evoked set or consideration group has important implications for the marketing manager. First, in a very real sense, if the firm's brand is not in the consumer's consideration group, it will not be given any attention. Therefore, an important marketing strategy objective is to move a given brand into the evoked set of more consumers. This is a very measurable objective to establish. For example, it is possible to develop a research study that asks members of an identified target market which brands they ordinarily consider before making a purchase of a particular type of product. The question could be just as easily framed in terms of selecting a store. For instance, "Which stores are you likely to visit when you are looking for a new pair of dress shoes?"

Another extremely important factor to acknowledge regarding the evoked set is that those brands in the set represent the real competition. Again, if a brand is not in a consumer's evoked set, it is not given attention. Therefore, not only must a firm work to establish its brand as one that is ordinarily considered when purchasing that type of product, but it is necessary to recognize its competitors in the mind of the consumer.

Concluding Search Effort and Alternative Evaluation

After the preliminary efforts have been expended in external search, the process itself must be drawn to a close. As in preliminary search, there is no uniform amount of time or effort given to this concluding phase. This will vary depending upon the circumstances. However, there are several possible identifiable results of this latter phase.

1. The consumer has identified an acceptable product or service that resolves the recognized problem. This means that whatever needs, wants, and desires are present, apparently these can be satisfied in some acceptable manner by making a purchase of a particular item. At this point a decision is usually made to discontinue the search process; often this is followed quickly by a purchase.

2. The consumer has not been able to locate an acceptable product, service, or store alternative given the evaluative criteria used. However, a decision is made to discontinue search anyway. This may be the result of simply running out of time or patience or a recognition that there are no acceptable alternatives currently available.

3. No acceptable alternative is found, but a decision is made to continue searching. In some cases, the complete search cycle is repeated; that is, internal search is again undertaken with the possibility of it being followed by further external search and alternative evaluation.

FACTORS AFFECTING THE IMPACT OF EXTERNAL SOURCES

There is no limit to the number and variety of sources consulted during external search and the accompanying evaluative process. However, several factors can be associated with the impact of the messages received. Some of the most important are discussed in the following paragraphs.

Perceived Image of the Source

There are at least three ways in which the perception of the source can influence its impact. These are considered under the topics of medium image, vehicle image, and personal or organizational image.

Medium Image. *Medium* is the means or channel used to reach the consumer. Television as well as radio, salespeople and newspapers are media. Various studies have been undertaken in an attempt to determine what differences in consumer perceptions exist with respect to the overall effectiveness of various media. The results from one such study are reported here to illustrate some of the findings.

The findings summarized below were obtained in a series of nationwide surveys conducted over a 15-year period by Roper Research, Incorporated, for the Television Information Office, a television industry trade association.[13] These data show that

TABLE 12.1
The Relative Desirability of Media

Most Want to Keep	12/59 %	11/63 %	1/67 %	1/71 %	11/72 %	11/74 %
Television	42	44	53	58	56	59
Newspapers	32	28	26	19	22	19
Radio	19	19	14	17	16	17
Magazines	4	5	3	5	5	4
Don't know or no answer	3	4	4	1	1	1

Source: Television Information Office, *Trends in Public Attitudes Toward Television and Other Mass Media: A Report by the Roper Organization, Inc.* (New York: Television Information Office, National Association of Broadcasters, 1975), p. 5.

[13]Television Information Office, *Trends in Public Attitudes Toward Television and Other Mass Media: A Report by the Roper Organization, Inc.* (New York: Television Information Office, National Association of Broadcasters, 1975), pp. 4–5.

consumers have different expectations with respect to various media. For example, in an effort to measure the relative desirability of four major media, the following question was asked: "Suppose that you could continue to have only one of the following —radio, television, newspapers or magazines—which one of the four would you *most* want to *keep?*"

Vehicle Image. The term *vehicle,* as used here, refers to a specific source such as *The Wall Street Journal* or *Business Week.* Quite obviously all magazines are not alike; neither are all newspapers, or all television programs, etc. Consequently, these perceived differences can have an impact on the receptiveness of consumers to their messages. For example, the major news magazines such as *Newsweek, Time,* and *U. S. News and World Report* have a certain authoritative manner. Their total character is substantially different from that of *Woman's Day* and *Family Circle.*

As the result of such differences, consumers expect to obtain certain kinds of information from each vehicle. Furthermore, some products and services are out of place in some media. For instance, the news magazines previously mentioned are more likely to be perceived as appropriate sources of information on such topics as life insurance and books to read than they are as sources of information on food items or fabric softener.

Personal or Organizational Image. Individuals and organizations that are engaged in communicating with consumers precipitate an image or characterization in the mind of their audience. This, too, can affect the impact of their message.

Testimonials—the inclusion of product or service users in promotional messages—have been a favorite technique of many businesses. The intent of the sponsor in using such a technique varies widely. However, there are at least a few common reasons that can be pointed out quickly. First, it provides an endorsement of the product or service by a source who is generally considered to be more credible than the sponsor. In a sense, it is also a way of personalizing the product and its benefits. In addition, it can be a means of suggesting the product's superiority. For example, the racing car driver's use of STP may vividly illustrate to the average consumer the operational significance of his expertise in selecting an oil treatment. Some consumers might conclude that if he uses STP, it must be good. The concern for accuracy and truthfulness in advertising has recently led the FTC to propose guidelines for using testimonials.

The use of individuals in promotion is not the only time when the image of the message source is of importance. Business organizations themselves have images. Firms such as IBM, Xerox, General Electric, and Hallmark have worked hard to establish and maintain a favorable public image. Consequently, slogans such as that used by Hallmark—"When you care enough to send the very best"—can have real market benefits in terms of message receptiveness.

The public endorsement of some products by certain associations, groups, or professional organizations can increase the receptiveness of consumers to the respective messages. For instance, the American Optometric Association name has been used in conjunction with the promotion of Quasar's television control mechanism for automatically adjusting the brightness of the television picture as room lightness changes. The American Dental Association's endorsement has long been used on Crest toothpaste, and the NFL has licensed various firms to use the league's name on specific "official" products.

The Consumers Union has an outstanding record of testing products, publishing the results in *Consumers Report,* and making "best buy" recommendations. Although firms are forbidden from mentioning the Consumers Union findings in their promotional messages, millions of Americans have used *Consumers Report* as a source of product- and service-related information.

Various magazine and newspaper columnists have earned reputations as extremely reliable sources of information regarding a number of different goods and services. For example, sports writers' comments and recommendations have proven helpful to consumers in selecting such products as fishing lures, ski equipment, and tennis shoes. It is just as likely for a home and garden writer to suggest that certain products be used in protecting bushes from insects.

The fact that consumers frequently seek prepurchase information from friends and relatives reflects their concern for the image of the source. These personal sources are relied on for several reasons. The more important include their perceived credibility, the fact that they are readily available, there is little or no cost associated with their use, and because these personal sources offer an opportunity to discuss features of the product or service that may be of particular interest to the prospective buyer. The extent to which these same benefits can be found in a commercial source will greatly enhance its value to the consumer.

Clarity of the Message Presented

The word communication comes from the Latin word *communis* which means common. When we attempt to communicate with someone or some group, we are trying to establish a "commonness" with them, and language is the currency of human communication.

In this process of communication, the likelihood that the keynote idea as perceived by the source—for example, the business firm—will get to its destination is determined to some extent by the effect of certain obstacles it faces en route. For instance, there is usually some unwanted interference that comes to bear upon the message. This includes audible noise, such as static on the radio, or the distraction resulting from a doorbell ringing during a television commercial. It can also result from what is typically called "clutter." In the broadcast media this term refers to the unwanted distractions from nonprogram material: other commercials, promotional announcements, credits, and public service announcements.

The extent of this latter kind of interference was brought to light by a spot-check conducted in December 1971 by the American Association of Advertising Agencies. The Association found 50 percent more commercials and 33 percent more commercial minutes at this time than was found in a similar study conducted in 1963. Under these conditions, it is appropriate for advertisers to question the capacity of their messages to affect behavior in the intended way. A study conducted by Daniel Starch and Staff, Incorporated draws specific attention to the appropriateness of this concern. In the Starch study the recall of commercials was measured in 1971 and found generally to have dropped an average of 22 percent from those determined in a comparable study done a year earlier.[14]

The clarity of a message is also influenced by the extent to which the message source and destination have common frames of reference.[15] Figure 12.4 illustrates the importance of this.

The communicator as the source can only form a message out of his or her experiences, and the intended receiver can only understand and interpret a received signal in terms of his or her own experience. The area of commonness shown in Figure 12.4 is where a meaningful exchange can take place. For example, the benefits of a quartz crystal watch or a videodisc machine (the visual equivalent of the phonograph) could not be presented effectively to anyone who has never before heard either of the terms.[16]

HOW TO INCREASE CONSUMER RECEPTIVENESS TO MESSAGES

There are several ways in which business firms and other interested organizations can influence receptiveness to their messages. Three of the most important means are appropriate timing, media selection, and message formulation.

Timing Considerations

Timing, as the term is used here, refers to getting the message to the target market at times when it is likely to have a significant impact. Important factors in timing are the natural buying cycles and at what stage the consumer is in the purchase process.

For example, in considering a buying cycle, products such as garden seeds and Christmas cards are seasonal items and, for the most part, are purchased during relatively short identifiable periods. For seeds, catalogues typically are mailed during the

[14]P. Webb and M. L. Ray, *The Effects of Television Clutter: An Experimental Investigation* (Cambridge, Massachusetts: Marketing Science Institute, 1974), p. 3.

[15]W. Schramm, "How Communication Works," in *Dimensions of Communication,* L. Richardson, ed. (New York: Appleton-Century Crofts, 1969), p. 6.

[16]"Videodiscs: The expensive race to be first," *Business Week* (September 15, 1975), p. 58.

FIGURE 12.4
The Importance of Commonality

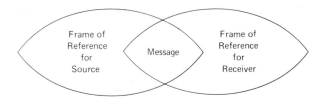

winter while Christmas cards must be promoted and sold in the late fall.

Another aspect of timing that is more difficult to deal with focuses on the position of the consumer in the buying process. For instance, if the purchase process is viewed simply as a hierarchy of effects including awareness, interest, desire, and action, it is ordinarily appropriate to deliver different messages to consumers at each of the various stages. In some cases it is possible to segment a market on the basis of stages in the purchase process. Using information from an organization such as Welcome Wagon can pinpoint families that are not aware of the services that some firms offer in their new neighborhood.

Media Selection

There is considerable evidence to show that various media have different audiences, meaning that they reach different groups. Without even obtaining any specific figures, most people would expect to find substantial variation between the readers of *Redbook* and *Popular Mechanics.* There may be less confidence in one's personal ability to specify differences among the viewers of Lawrence Welk's program and Monday night football, but differences would be expected nevertheless.

Fortunately, there are considerable data available to managers who need to make media selection decisions. For instance, The Standard Rate and Data Service publishes a wealth of information about media reach and related cost data. A. C. Nielson does continuous ratings of television programs, and many radio and television stations as well as most magazines and newspapers provide information to perspective advertisers on their respective audiences.

Other forms of analysis have provided a more vivid picture of the relationship between product usage and media exposure patterns. Psychographics—the study of the interrelationship among consumer activities, interests, and opinions—offers an interesting example. One such study focused on eye make-up users.[17] It found that users tended to be young and well educated and to live in metropolitan areas. Product usage rates were much higher for working women than for full-time homemakers and substantially higher in the western part of the United States than elsewhere. Further analysis showed the person also to be a heavy user of other cosmetics such as liquid face make-up base, lipstick, hair spray, perfume, and nail polish. She also turned out to be an above average cigarette smoker, gasoline purchaser, and long-distance telephone user. With respect to media, the eye make-up user was found to like television movies and the "Tonight Show," but she did not like panel programs or westerns. She read fashion, news, and general interest magazines, but did not read publications such as *True Confessions.*

Studies of this nature add an important dimension to the way in which various media are evaluated. There is no doubt that an audience's quality, as well as its size, should be considered. In using psychographic analysis, one study found the *Playboy* reader, for example, to be basically the male counterpart of the eye make-up user, while the man who read *Reader's Digest* emerged as the essence of conservative middle-class values—pro-business, antigovernment welfare programs, anti-union power, and politically active. In the same study, the *Time*-only reader, as compared to the *Newsweek*-only reader, emerged as less concerned about job security, less worried about government and union power, less worried about the threat of communism, and generally more favorably disposed toward advertising.[18]

[17]W. D. Wells and D. J. Tigert, *Activities, Interests, and Opinions Working Paper* (Chicago: Graduate School of Business, University of Chicago, September, 1969), pp. 3–4.
[18]W. D. Wells, p. 8.

The concern for effectiveness in reaching a particular audience has led to considerable innovativeness on the part of some nonprofit organizations. For example, the development and distribution of *True to Life* magazine was the result of the efforts of the staff and students of the Emory University Family Planning Program.[19] In a unique approach to health education, they used a confession magazine format for a health information aid. Two titles from the table of contents illustrate the approach: "Mama Made Me Do It, but She Wouldn't Tell Me Why!" and "How I Spent My Summer Vacation—and Nearly Died Three Months Later!"

The *True to Life* magazine presented information about birth control and other health and social issues. The characters woven into the stories demonstrate how individuals can take control of their own lives. *True to Life* was distributed to high schools, hospitals, Planned Parenthood affiliates, and other health, social, and educational agencies.

Even though the above examples focus on the mass media, it should not be assumed that these are the only alternatives. Certainly the use of salespeople is a medium of major importance. In fact, more money is spent in personal selling than in advertising or other forms of promotion. Salespeople must be carefully integrated into a firm's marketing effort. Also, the use of dealers and their representatives are another channel through which information reaches the consumer. In the move toward self-service, there has been a tendency for some people to overlook the significance of personal sources of information. Even the major discount houses and supermarkets that epitomize American self-service retailing have clerks available for answering customer questions and for aggressively selling products such as appliances and furniture.

Message Formulation

It has been said, "The medium is the message," and some do believe that the environment within which a message is offered

[19] *True to Life,* M. Crow, ed. (Atlanta: Emory University School of Medicine, Department of Gynecology and Obstetrics, Division of Research and Training in Maternal Health and Family Planning, September, 1970).

is so important that often it overwhelms what is actually written or said. If this were true, it would simplify the preparation of messages. Unfortunately, however, it is not true.

Prepared messages become a critical part of what the consumer receives and moves into memory; therefore, they must be formulated with great care. For instance, there is little doubt that some positive responses have been effected by the simple statements "Look, Ma, no cavities" used by Procter and Gamble in their Crest toothpaste ads, and from "Only a dentist can give her a better fluoride treatment," used by Colgate-Palmolive. They may even have contributed to the dominance of these two brands of the $500-million toothpaste market.

It is interesting to note the creative strategy that was used by Lever Brothers to penetrate this market with Aim toothpaste. In 1971 Crest and Colgate had 73 percent of the total market when work was begun on Aim. After considerable study and market analysis, it was decided that there were several differentiating features of the Aim brand that would be important to consumers. However, these needed to be communicated effectively to a target audience essentially made up of mothers with children living at home. The tone of the message needed to be serious, informative, and authoritative because tooth decay, dental health, and dentist bills are major family concerns. It was then decided that attention would be focused on the fact that Aim was new, contained a therapeutic level of stannous fluoride, was in a modern gel form, and had more brushing incentives. These incentives included a pleasing color, flavor, texture, and appearance.[20]

The decision was made to use a slice-of-life setting for the message to create as nearly as possible the situation that was likely to occur in many Crest-user homes. The message theme used was "Take Aim against cavities"—a strategy that proved very successful.

An equally challenging task faced Burger King in its attempt to gain on the giant McDonalds. Briefly it was a task of taking one

[20]C. Fredericks, "Aim Toothpaste vs. Crest and Colgate," in *How Do You Tackle The Leaders: Paper from the 1974 Regional Convention of the American Association of Advertising Agencies* (New York: American Association of Advertising Agencies, 1975), pp. 3–13.

simple fact uncovered through consumer research—that fast-food customers hate to wait for special orders—and turning it into an opportunity. A simple, direct message seemed most effective, and "Have it your way" was promoted in a memorable campaign.[21]

Of course, getting the message across was not the only critical marketing task. The total strategy had to demonstrate to the public that no matter what they might order at Burger King, it will be served promptly in a pleasant manner. This message was delivered to consumers through television advertising, restaurant signs, and printing on packages as well as through personnel. The 38 percent sales jump in one year suggests that Burger King's prime prospects—people 18–49 years old, many of whom live in families with children aged 12 and under—liked the idea.

Summary

Information search is the purposeful attention given to the gathering and assembling of information related to the satisfaction of some perceived need, want, or desire. Alternative evaluation uses evaluative criteria in assessing the alternatives that come to the consumer's attention. In the consumer decision process, search and alternative evaluation follows problem recognition. Several factors significantly affect the search process: (1) the uniqueness of the object sought, (2) the strength of the motivation that caused the search activity, (3) previous experience in searching for similar products or services, and (4) one's general predisposition toward search.

The consumer search process is carried on both internally and externally. *Internal search* is the conscious recall and consideration of specific information and experiences that appear to be relevant to the problem. This information is drawn from the long-term or permanent memory that Howard describes in his information reception and storage model. Internal search and alternative evaluation will cause the consumer to either proceed to the purchase stage, decide not to purchase, or commence external search and further evaluation.

[21]R. Mercer, "Burger King vs. McDonalds," in *How Do You Tackle the Leaders,* pp. 27–39.

External search is the expenditure of deliberate effort to seek information from various outside sources. The extent to which the consumer engages in external search depends upon: (1) the way the individual looks at a given problem, (2) his or her modes of reducing the tension accompanying the problem recognition, and (3) his or her ability and willingness to assume risk. Two phases make up the external search—the preliminary search effort and the concluding search effort. The preliminary search typically produces: (1) a redefinition of the desired product or service attributes, (2) a firm acknowledgement by the consumer that there are constraints imposed in the search process, and (3) a more concise assessment of available personal resources. The concluding search effort can result in the consumer's either finding the problem-solving product or service, not finding it and discontinuing the search, or not finding it and continuing the search.

The impact of the external search is affected by the consumer's perceived image of the source (communicator) and by the clarity of the message. The image of the source is influenced not only by the person or organization doing the speaking or writing but also by the images of the vehicle and medium used. An important contributor to message clarity is the field or experience common to the source and the receiver. Consumer receptiveness to messages can be increased by: (1) timing the message to reach the market when it is most likely to have significant impact, (2) selecting the media that the target audience is most likely to be using, and (3) formulating the message itself with great care.

QUESTIONS AND ISSUES FOR DISCUSSION

1. Some contend that change takes place so rapidly in our society today that it makes most product information obsolete soon after the consumer receives it. To what extent is this true? How is the constant introduction of new products likely to affect the consumer's search process?

2. A U. S. Postal Service survey was referred to on the first page of this chapter. It indicated that 63 percent of all direct mail pieces are opened and read. How could a nonprofit

organization such as Planned Parenthood develop a direct mail piece that could be expected to obtain a much higher level of readership?

3. How successful could a firm expect to be if it concentrated on making the best possible product for a price no higher than its competitors and if it relied strictly on its satisfied customers and its label to tell of the product's superiority? Consider this question with respect to each of the following products: mouthwash, musical instruments, homemade candy, and cameras.

4. How would the prepurchase search and alternative evaluation process probably vary for families at different stages of the family life cycle? Answer this question for each of the following situations:

Product/Service	Stages of Family Life Cycle
a. Medical doctor in a new town	Newly married couples; full nest II
b. Family clothing store	Full nest I; full nest III
c. Living-room furniture	Full nest II; empty nest I
d. Supermarket	Bachelor state; solitary survivor, retired

5. Is it reasonable to say that most people make poor choices of products and services if we compare their decisions to the "best buy" available in their community? Explain your answer.

6. Assume that you are responsible for teaching a class in how to be a good shopper. How would you go about explaining to your students how to carry out their prepurchase search and the evaluation of alternatives? Would these suggestions vary by product, age of those in your class, the income of the students, or how much experience they have had with the product?

7. How can the following buying patterns reduce the risk that a consumer takes in making a particular purchase?

   a. Consistently buying one brand
   b. Selecting the cheapest brand available
   c. Buying the most expensive brand available
   d. Purchasing only products with a plain and simple design.

8. How helpful and practical would each of the following be in assisting consumers in their search for information and in their evaluation of various competitive brands?

   a. That many products be packaged in uniform amounts (e.g., all soup cans would be 10 ¾ oz., peanut butter jars 18 ¼ oz., and canned corn 12 ⅓ oz.)
   b. That all containers have even amounts in them (e.g., the soup referred to above would be either 10 oz. or 11 oz.), but that different brands could have varying amounts in their packages
   c. That the federal government test and rate all consumer goods with a retail price over $10.00, with the resultant rating appearing on the product.

9. How appropriate are each of the media listed below likely to be for promoting Preparation H (hemorrhoid treatment); Memorial monuments (grave markers), and Jockey brand men's underwear? Give reasons for your answers.

   a. *The Wall Street Journal*   f. *Field and Stream*
   b. *Readers' Digest*   g. Billboards
   c. National television   h. Local radio
   d. Salespeople   i. *Seventeen*
   e. *Esquire*   j. Direct mail

10. Testimonials are often used to promote goods and services as well as political candidates and charitable causes. If you were asked to suggest three or four simple rules of thumb that would assist in making testimonials successful, what would you offer? Give reasons for your suggestions.

**SITUATIONAL
PROBLEMS**

Case 1.

The Top Line Chemical Company, a leading producer of household products, has just completed research and development work on a new home scouring powder. When compared with other cleaners now on the market through consumer-use tests, it was rated far superior in its cleaning effectiveness. However, in other research, it was discovered that consumers usually select such cleaners on the basis of the product's smell (strong smelling products are preferred), price (low price is important), and cleaning effectiveness—in that order. Furthermore, brand loyalty is reasonably high among the heavy users of scouring powders.

Top Line Chemical's new product is somewhat more expensive (10 percent more costly) than its competitors' products, and it has a naturally pleasant odor. Plans are underway to test market this new cleaner in Chicago in about three months.

What recommendations would you make to the company's management as it develops its plans for the Chicago market test?

What difficulties are they likely to encounter in gaining consumer acceptance? How might these be overcome?

Case 2.

The Midwest Egg Producers' Association, an organization of people whose business is dependent on egg sales, has become increasingly concerned about the charges made against eggs because of their cholesterol content. The members feel that it is time that a concerted effort be made to get the true story about eggs to the public. It is their opinion that eggs are one of the very best natural foods available anywhere. The nutritional value of eggs far exceeds that of a host of other food products. In addition, eggs are economical and, therefore, they can greatly assist homemakers in their efforts to offer their family a balanced diet at a reasonable cost.

The Association's executive board has discussed their members' concerns on two separate occasions and has made a list of several questions that they feel must be answered before proceeding further. These questions follow:

    a. What group or groups should be singled out to receive the "egg story?"
    b. Can two or three key issues be identified that, once explained, will make people think more favorably toward eggs?
    c. How can the Association get the consumer's attention so that the Association's story can be told?
    d. What is the best way to present the Association's message in a believable manner so that it will be remembered?

How would you respond to the Midwest Egg Producers' executive board's questions?

Purchasing Processes

According to some, purchasing processes include all the means by which consumers make buying decisions—everything from the initial need recognition to and including the purchase, consumption, and postpurchase evaluation. However, this is not the perspective taken here. In this chapter the intention is to consider purchasing processes in a more limited sense.

As used here, *purchasing processes* include the purchase act itself and those encounters that comprise the immediate surroundings of the act of buying. In a very fundamental sense a number of these latter activities are actually the final phase of the search process, but because they are so closely associated with making a purchase, they will be given special attention. Often these purchasing processes can be described simply as consumer-retail environment interactions. These include, for example, what one encounters upon entering a service station to buy gasoline or a sporting goods shop to purchase a volleyball net.

Figure 13.1 shows the complete consumer behavior model and clearly identifies purchasing processes in relation to both search and outcomes. To a large extent these outcomes are actual purchases. Consequently, purchasing processes involve the final aspects of the refinement of the evaluative criteria and their application by the consumer in a market setting where there is an awareness not only of what is desired, but also of what is available.

In treating the subject of purchase processes, the chapter is divided into two major sections. The first focuses on the selection of a store or place of business where the consumer intends to make a particular purchase. The second part of the chapter pays attention specifically to the in-store environment and to how it can influence consumer behavior.

Store Selection as a Purchasing Process

Choice of a store or other business establishment is one of the important decisions that consumers make as they approach the final act of buying. Store selection itself is a purchase process, and Figure 13.2 is a conceptualization of how consumers go

FIGURE 13.1
Complete Model of Consumer Behavior Showing Purchasing Processes and Outcomes.

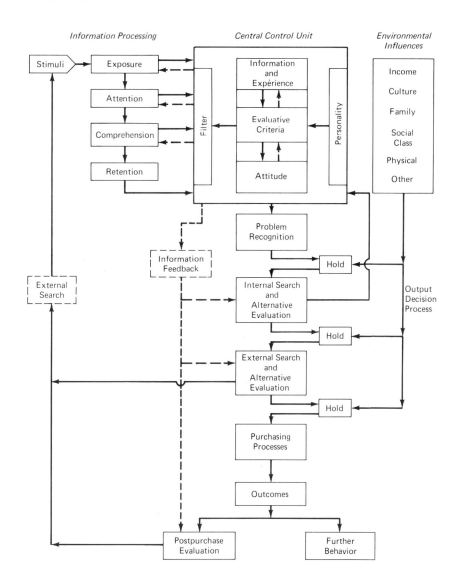

Source: J. F. Engel, D. T. Kollat, and R. D. Blackwell, *Consumer Behavior,* 2nd ed. (New York: Holt, Rinehart and Winston, Inc., 1973), p. 58. Reprinted by permission of the publisher.

about making such selections. Essentially four sets of variables are involved: (1) evaluative criteria, (2) perceived characteristics of the stores under consideration, (3) the comparison processes, and (4) the classifying of stores as either acceptable or unacceptable. The actual choice is the result of the process of comparing perceived store characteristics with the consumer's evaluative criteria.

As consumers make store choices and proceed to patronize those selected, learning is going on. That is, if the shopping experience within the "acceptable stores" is satisfactory, the choice will be reinforced. As a result, over time the need to search for particular types of stores is greatly reduced. It can reach the point where certain need arousal sends the consumer to one of a very limited number of stores. For instance, it is not unusual for consumers to develop a pattern of regularly patronizing a particular dry-cleaning establishment. This may have been

FIGURE 13.2
Store-Choice Processes.

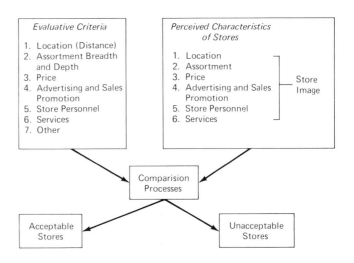

Source: J. F. Engel, D. T. Kollat, and R. D. Blackwell, *Consumer Behavior,* 2nd ed. (New York: Holt, Rinehart and Winston, Inc., 1973), p. 443. Reprinted by permission of the publisher.

the result of a rather long trial-and-error process or of simply finding an acceptable cleaner on one trial. Whatever the initial selection process involved, at some particular point there was the feeling that on the basis of the given evaluative criteria, this one establishment was satisfactory. It is likely that patronage will continue in a rather habitual manner as long as the relationship continues to be satisfactory.

Store loyalty of this sort is rather widespread. It is often possible to find a considerable amount of customer loyalty as reflected in regular visits to a specific supermarket, beauty salon, barber shop, clothing store, auto repair shop, and drugstore. Medical doctors and dentists also enjoy a very high level of patient loyalty. *Patronage routine*—regularly returning to a given store or service outlet—can be quite appealing to the consumer because it reduces uncertainty and the time necessary to complete a purchase as well as enhancing one's general feeling of belonging. Such benefits pose a formidable competitive challenge. Therefore, it is usually much easier for a merchant to maintain his present customer base than to attract business from competitors.

GENERAL DETERMINANTS OF STORE CHOICE

The specific evaluative criteria used in store choice vary significantly depending on the type of product or service being sought. For instance, the criteria used to select a photo shop where a new camera is to be purchased are usually much more varied than those employed in seeking to buy a can of spray enamel for repainting an old desk. Nevertheless, there are certain determinants that are used more than others. These include: (1) location, (2) depth and breadth of assortment, (3) price, (4) advertising and word-of-mouth communications, (5) sales promotion, (6) store personnel, (7) services, (8) physical attributes, and (9) store clientele—who else shops there.

The operational impact of these various determinants is affected by consumer perceptions. These perceptions form what has been called store image. Put simply, *store image* is a composite of the dimensions which consumers perceive as the store or service establishment; it is often what makes one business different from its competitors in the eyes of the consumer.[1] The next section pays specific attention to what has been called "image" and to the importance of this phenomenon in studying consumer choice processes.

STORE IMAGE AS A FACTOR IN CONSUMER DECISION MAKING

The cluster of dimensions whose presence and importance compose an image vary from one store to another. Tangible dimensions typically involve such factors as having low prices, adequate parking, and sufficient salespeople. Intangibles that are not easily measured but are of importance are characterized by descriptions such as "a friendly store," "a place where I feel comfortable," and "it's an exciting place to shop." How these dimensions are actually put together to form an image of a particular establishment and the relative importance of each dimension depend on the store's management and on the views of the consumers who shop there. For example, the way in which one type of customer perceives Nieman Marcus or R. H. Macy can be markedly different from the manner in which others view them. In today's consumers' market, it is impossible to be "all things to all people." A firm's management must decide which segments of the consumer market it can successfully serve and then try to develop an image that is consistent with the preferences of these consumers.

Two short cases are presented here to illustrate what is meant by a retail store's image and how this image can be related to a firm's market success. These cases include a composite of experiences of several different organizations that have been combined into two representative situations. They employ the analysis framework suggested by May.[2]

[1]E. G. May, *Management Applications of Retail Image Research: Marketing Science Institute Working Paper* (Cambridge, Massachusetts: Marketing Science Institute, 1973), p. 21.
[2]E. G. May.

Case 1

Subject Area: Sewing Machine Sales and Service Department Image

Type of Company: A major midwestern department store in a large metropolitan area. Its direct competition included three other full-line stores, all of which were significantly larger in total size.

Issue: A sizable number of customer complaints were being received with respect to the store's sewing machine sales efforts and their related service operation. The complaints were steadily increasing, and specific references were being made to the use of bait-and-switch tactics.

Objective: To determine the image of the sewing machine sales and service department among recent customers (those who had done business with the department during the previous six months) as well as among noncustomers.

Research Methods: A sample-survey procedure was used to reach a representative number of both recent customers and noncustomers. Telephone interviewing was employed. A series of questions were included to determine how people chose among departments offering these products, what were the most important considerations, and how all four department stores in the area compared on these evaluative criteria.

Findings: The research findings revealed the following about the store studied:

1. It had a considerably poorer sewing machine service image than did its major competitors.
2. The store's salespeople in this department were considered aggressive and often even rude.
3. The sales area and its displays were poorly arranged and messy as compared to the competitors' facilities.
4. Phone calls to the department were frequently met with long delays as people waited for answers to simple questions.
5. Its prices were considered the lowest in town.

Conclusion: Further analysis of the sales and service volume of this department showed that its sewing machine sales were greater than those of its three competitors combined. In addition, it appeared that most complaints came from people who had purchased a machine during November or December and from those who had sought warranty work. It was also discovered that their competitors had recently experienced some increase in the number of complaints in their sewing machine and service departments.

Action: Management decided to take no immediate action. This department had shown one of the best growth and profitability records in the whole store. It was hoped, however, that in the future additional space could be allocated to this department.

Case 2

Subject Area: Image of Young Women's Ready-To-Wear and Related Merchandise

Type of Company: A women's specialty store in a southern university community of about 60,000.

Issue: A lower level of sales in various accessory departments of this shop as compared to the sales of similar items in two local competitive stores. These accessories included such items as jewelry, scarves, hosiery, and handbags.

Objective: To determine the image of the three women's ready-to-wear shops and to compare them. Some explanation was sought for the lower level of accessory sales in the store sponsoring the study.

Research Methodology: A sample-survey was conducted using a questionnaire inserted in the local newspaper followed by personal interviews of members of selected sororities at the university.

Findings: The study revealed that:

1. Both customers and noncustomers of the sponsoring store found the two competitors to have a more appealing store layout. People could better visualize the interrelationship among the display items in these stores.
2. The two competitors' lines were considered to be more complete. A shopper was just more likely to find what she wanted.

Conclusion: The store that initiated the study was larger and had divided its offerings into separate departments, each having a clerk who was responsible for its displays and sales. This had led to the development of these departments into rather separate entities. Consequently, even though the selection was the largest in town, the customer was not able to see the merchandise as parts of a coordinated whole.

Action: The individual departments were disbanded and consolidated into one coordinated unit, making use of various display areas for different accessories. The store manager assumed responsibility for developing display themes throughout the store that emphasized the interrelatedness of the merchandise.

The impression might be conveyed by these cases that once an image is determined, management can proceed to deal with other matters. This is not possible because store image is a dynamic concept; that is, even maintaining an existing image takes effort. If, for example, a men's apparel store is noted for its fashion leadership, its merchandising practices must be consistent with this character.

Unfortunately, the Great Atlantic and Pacific Tea Company did not realize this fact until its dominant position in the food business had seriously deteriorated. A&P management recognized that it might have overemphasized low prices during the last few years and, as a result, sacrificed its company pride. However, the food chain has recently responded with a concerted recovery effort. The first line of its $70 million advertising campaign sums up the prevailing theme—"The time has come to put price and pride together again."[3]

Once a business establishment has been selected, the purchase act follows. The next section pays specific attention to these encounters.

In-Store Purchasing Processes

Three situations are introduced here to illustrate what are frequently identified as purchasing processes that occur after a store has been chosen. After each situation is described, the various aspects of the purchasing process in that consumer–retailer interaction are identified. Then, following all three situations, a section is devoted to discussing the ways in which the components of the purchasing process affect consumer behavior and why marketing managers should take an interest in this phenomenon.

[3]"A&P apology kicks off drive; phase 2 will stress service," *Advertising Age*, 46 (September 22, 1975), pp. 1, 76.

Situation I: A young woman in her early twenties enters a local Ford dealer's showroom. For her this is one of about six different visits that she has made to various car dealers during the past month. It is the second time that she has been here. Upon entering, she looks for Gil Crawford. Mr. Crawford was the salesman whom she talked to last week, and he had been quite helpful to her in narrowing her choice of cars down to a couple of compact models—one a Chevrolet and the other a Ford.

She was here today to ask a few remaining questions and to determine if the $2595 cash price that she had been quoted was their lowest. She had brought her checkbook because she felt that she needed to make a final decision within the next couple of days. She had gathered about as much information as she could use and really did not want to spend much more time shopping around.

Upon seeing this young woman, Mr. Crawford recognized her, and they exchanged friendly greetings. However, he was with another customer and asked if she could wait a few minutes. She agreed and walked around the showroom before sitting down in the lounge area. Various banners were hanging from the ceiling and there were signs announcing that it was spring sale time. While waiting, she picked up a magazine called *Ford Times* and read a short article. This article described several inexpensive auto trips that could be taken along the East coast.

Mr. Crawford approached her and asked what he could do for her today. She proceeded to ask him a question about Ford's warranty and another concerning body color options that were available. He was able to answer these quickly and then said, "I have just the car for you. It was delivered yesterday and I think you will like it." Actually, the car was almost exactly what she had in mind, but it had an AM/FM radio that she had not planned on buying.

She then asked for his best price. After checking his price book, Mr. Crawford replied, "I can sell you this car with its special trim and deluxe radio for $2635. She responded by offering to pay $2575, but no more. Furthermore, if Crawford were to agree, she would give him a deposit today. He checked with his sales manager and found that the lowest acceptable price was $2595. Upon hearing this, the young woman thought for a moment and said, "All right, I will take it for $2595."

This brief encounter and the purchase that followed include several activities and circumstances that make up the purchasing process. These are identified below.

1. Deciding to go back to this particular Ford dealer
2. Going into the showroom and looking for Gil Crawford, the salesman
3. Observing the interior atmosphere of the dealership, including taking notice of the various signs.
4. Sitting down in the lounge area and reading the article in the *Ford Times*
5. Looking at the car that the salesman said he thought she would like
6. Asking for the salesman's best price
7. Making a counter offer to the salesman
8. Deciding to purchase the car shown to her
9. Giving the salesman the deposit.

Situation II: An elderly man enters the Safeway supermarket near his home. Just a short distance from the entrance, he notices several shopping carts filled with various canned goods. Attached to the carts are signs that identify these items as weekend specials. He stops for a moment looking over the sale items and then proceeds on into the main part of the store. There is the soft sound of music in the background, and as he moves down the first aisle, he sees fresh strawberries in pint containers displayed along with shortcake and whipped topping. These berries are certainly appealing, for they are the first of the season. However, what he really came in for was a quart of milk and some luncheon meat. He picks up these two items and also a container of strawberries and then makes his way to the checkout. He pays for these groceries with food stamps. The items are put into a bag and he leaves.

Here, too, there are a number of dimensions to the purchasing process that are identifiable.

1. Entering the Safeway store.
2. Taking notice of the canned goods on sale as well as the display of strawberries and related items.
3. Being aware of the background music.
4. Selecting the three items for purchase.
5. Choosing among the available brands of milk and luncheon meat.
6. Going through the checkout.
7. Paying for his purchases with food stamps.
8. Having his purchases put into a bag.

Situation III: It is September, and the Sears' Christmas catalogue, called the *Wish Book,* has just arrived in the Daugherty home. The children can hardly wait to study the toy section. One child has a birthday coming up in mid-October and, therefore, she wants to get her list of gift suggestions together quickly. This is soon done and brought to the attention of the rest of the family during dinner.

She has been careful to separate her suggestions into three groups, according to their costs. She has done this because she knows from experience that her mother and dad are willing to buy her a gift more expensive than what her younger brother could afford. Furthermore, it was strongly suggested that she make only modest requests of her aunts and uncles.

Shortly after these suggestions are made known, her mother and dad decide to call the Sears' catalogue department and place their order. This is done, and the two items ordered are picked up later in the week at the local store and charged to their account.

Here, as in the previous two situations, there are several aspects of the purchasing process that can be noted. These are listed below:

1. The child's looking over the catalogue and making a list of suggested gifts.
2. The discussion of the various gift suggestions during dinner.
3. The parents' selection of two items from their daughter's list.
4. Calling the local Sears' store and placing the order.
5. Picking up the items and charging them to their account.

Each of these three situations has described a set of circumstances that portray a consumer-retailer encounter following individual problem recognition, the formulation of evaluative criteria, and varying amounts of search. These circumstances include a cluster of factors and related interactions that make up the immediate or near environment within which the actual purchase takes place. Because each of these factors and accompanying interactions may have had some influence on the purchase outcomes, they are of considerable interest to the consumer analyst. The ways in which the various aspects of these purchasing processes affect consumers can be summarized under the following topics: (1) serving as a reminder; (2) creating a favorable atmosphere; (3) resolving questionable issues; and (4) gaining closure. Each of these will be discussed in the following sections, and examples from the three situations will be used to illustrate their possible impact.

SERVING AS A REMINDER

It would make it easier for the consumer analyst and probably for the consumer, too, if all or most purchases were made as the result of a clearly identifiable sequence of steps. Such a sequence would include the conscientious recognition of a particular problem and a deliberate pattern of action to resolve it in some practical manner. Although it is recognized that consumer behavior is essentially reasoned behavior, that is, purposeful, often the consumer needs some nudge or other assistance in directing him or her toward want-satisfying action.

Consumers may need to be reminded that they actually need or want some particular product. For instance, to certain shoppers the layout of their favorite supermarket serves as a shopping list of a sort. Going up and down the aisles and noting what is in each section of the store brings to mind items that have not been explicitly written down on a list but that, nevertheless, are desired. Just glancing at the cash register in the beverage store may remind you to buy some snack food that you had nearly forgotten. The very act of browsing through a clothing store can bring to your attention the desire to buy a new tie to match a shirt received recently as a gift or remind you that those favorite brown slacks are showing wear and should be replaced.

Each of the three buying situations described earlier included reminder factors. Furthermore, a number of these are subject to the direct control of the merchant and, consequently, can be modified to vary their possible effects on the consumer. In Situation I the various hanging banners and signs in the Ford dealer's showroom reminded the young woman that this was the time to buy—cars were on sale. Even the placement of a magazine like *Ford Times* in the lounge area could have contributed favorably to moving the consumer closer toward making a purchase. The article she read reminded her of the fun she should have traveling in her new car. The salesman's pleasant greeting may have brought to her mind that this is a friendly and cordial place, one that she would likely get good treatment from after the purchase.

This latter experience could have served to strengthen her feeling that this was a wise stop to make.

In Situation II the elderly man took note of the canned goods on sale as he entered the store. This may have reminded him of a need for these items. Although he did not buy any of them on this trip, he could return later and do so. These sales displays may also have served to remind him of the fact that the prices at the supermarket are low as compared to others nearby. The display of fresh strawberries did bring to his mind how good these can taste, and they were sufficiently attractive to him to make the purchase. However, even though he noticed the shortcake and topping on display with the berries, no purchase was made. Retail experience shows that such combination displays can often promote greater interest in all items in the display.

Some of the purchase processes in Situation III also served as reminders. The receipt of the *Wish Book* itself is a reminder to begin planning for Christmas. Its arrival in September served to encourage the Daugherty girl to put together a list of gift suggestions if she wanted to express her preferences to her family. Using the catalogue in this way again brought to the attention of this family that a large number of items can be purchased from the convenience of their home.

Many companies take very seriously the opportunities that exist within the store to remind the customer to buy their brand. This interest is substantiated by the fact that United States firms spent an estimated $2 billion on point-of-purchase advertising in 1973. The following figures note the estimated annual expenditures of five major firms on point-of-purchase advertising:[4]

General Motors	$44,000,000
Procter and Gamble	9,000,000
Coca Cola	16,000,000
Bristol Myers	7,942,000
General Foods	4,000,000

The possible impact of in-store reminders is exemplified by considering the findings from one study of the buying behavior of 6795 shoppers in 16 mass-merchandising stores in several

[4]H. S. Gorschman, "New Dimensions in Unhidden Persuasion," *Journal of the Academy of Marketing Science,* 1 (Fall, 1973), pp. 110–111.

geographic areas. Unplanned purchases were made by 30 percent of all shoppers. Of these unplanned purchases, 81 percent were a national or regional brand; 24 percent of these items were first-time purchases; and 48 percent were of a brand that had not been bought before.[5]

Some merchants have become very creative in developing reminder techniques. One display for a baking products company utilized a device that released the pleasant odor of its cinnamon cake inside the supermarket. This allowed the shopper to make a buying decision after having had the opportunity to inspect the package, note the price, read the point-of-purchase advertising, and smell the product's aroma.

CREATING A FAVORABLE ATMOSPHERE

The environment within which goods are offered for sale or services rendered can be a substantial part of what interests the consumer. For example, nearly everyone likes to try a new restaurant, often just to sample the experiences that are available there.

In a very real sense, the environment or atmosphere is a part of what the consumer buys. Too frequently the business person has neglected atmosphere as a viable marketing technique. According to Kotler, *atmospherics* involves the conscious designing of space and its various dimensions to effect certain responses in buyers.[6] Of course, consumers perceive an atmosphere in a business establishment whether or not one has been consciously developed.

In Situation I the perceived atmosphere was apparently one of friendliness that nurtured a feeling of confidence in the dealership. This perception may even have included the belief that the salesman had the consumer's best interest in mind. In Situation II the supermarket was probably like many others; yet it most likely had some characteristics that set it apart from its competitors in the area. Factors that can contribute to atmospheric differences among supermarkets include the general cleanliness of the store, the quality and freshness of its meat and produce, the

---

[5]H. S. Gorschman, p. 113.

[6]P. Kotler, "Atmospherics as a Marketing Tool," *Journal of Retailing,* 49 (Winter, 1973–74), p. 50.

width of the aisles, the extent to which the shelves are well-stocked, the helpfulness of the employees, and even the background music and the color of the interior walls.

One might be tempted to conclude that Situation III has no atmospheric dimensions. However, this is not the case. The format of the catalogue itself creates a unique environment for shopping. In addition, the mailing of the *Wish Book* makes use of the home as part of the purchasing atmosphere. In recognizing this opportunity, some catalogue merchandisers have even suggested that a person sit down in front of the fireplace or some other comfortable spot and browse through the offerings. If children grow up with fond memories of paging through such catalogues, this may have a substantial impact on their purchasing patterns later in life. Consequently, even the atmosphere created via a catalogue can be a powerful marketing tool.

Atmospheres are likely to be most important under certain conditions. Four of these are identified below.[7]

1. Atmospherics is a relevant marketing technique primarily in situations where the product is purchased or consumed and where the seller has design options. For example, atmospherics are more likely to be important to a restaurant with sit-down facilities than to one that only has a carry out service. Also, manufacturers of consumer goods are less likely to be able to use atmospherics than are retailers.

2. Atmospherics becomes an important marketing tool as the number of competitive outlets increase. This becomes another means by which one business can be differentiated from another. Furthermore, this kind of competitive action is more difficult for competitors to counter than are price changes or even assortment carried.

3. Atmospherics is a more relevant marketing tool in industries where product and/or price differences are small. Savings and loan associations often seek differentiation through the use of atmospherics because regulatory requirements necessarily result in considerable similarity among them. Their efforts typically take shape through the skillful use of interior decor and related promotional strategy.

[7]P. Kotler, pp. 52–53.

4. Atmospherics can be a helpful technique when a firm's offerings are aimed at a distinct social class or at buyers with particular life-styles. The May Company basement, with its unique merchandising strategy, is likely to appeal to the working class. Consequently, its atmosphere must be consistent with bargain-basement retailing. This environment is in considerable contrast to other departments in the very same stores that cater to a more upper middle-class clientele.

RESOLVING QUESTIONABLE ISSUES

The retailer-consumer interaction offers a unique opportunity to deal with unresolved questions that the consumer might have about the product or service under consideration. As pointed out in the last chapter, the search process can bring the consumer to the realization that initial expectations must be modified in light of what is available and personal resource limitations. Such confrontation with reality can be disturbing and can raise doubts as to whether certain personal needs or desires can be satisfied.

The retail store is often the only place where these questions can be answered. The consumer needs assistance to resolve these difficulties. Such assistance may be provided by the merchant through salespeople, product usage and care labels, assembling an assortment of products for customer inspection and visual comparison as well as through point-of-purchase advertising.

In Situation I the young woman who entered the local auto dealership had some specific questions in mind. These were quickly answered to her satisfaction by the salesman. In neither Situation II or III were specific questions identified, although there were implicit questions nevertheless. In Situation II, for example, the elderly man's entering the supermarket with two items in mind poses the question as to whether his preferred brands or enough variety will be available. Furthermore, in this specific situation he no doubt had some definite price expectations because he was using food stamps to make his purchases. In Situation III there apparently was considerable excitement on the child's part as she approached the catalogue expecting to find a number of acceptable gift possibilities. The issue as to whether any acceptable items could be found in the catalogue could only be resolved by searching through it. However, past experience with the Sears' catalogue as well as the attractive cover and related promotion by the company suggest that this is a gratifying way to shop.

Unfortunately, it is not an unusual experience for consumers to enter business establishments with specific questions in mind only to find no satisfying means of resolving them. The striving for greater efficiency in mass retailing has led many firms toward greater emphasis on self-service, which in turn has made the retailer-consumer encounter more impersonal. Consequently, the consumer has had to depend on point-of-purchase advertising, package descriptions, personal inspection of the product, or even on the opinion of someone else to help make the final evaluation. In some cases, where clerks have been made available in large mass-merchandising outlets, the service has been so poor that customers buy in spite of the 'assistance' and not because of it.

An important point for businesspeople to be aware of is that those who enter their establishment are frequently serious prospects; they have been through a self-selection process. For example, most of those who walk into a shoe store are acknowledging that they have an interest in the shoes in that store.

GAINING CLOSURE

Closure refers to the process of bringing consumers to the point where the evidence before them conclusively suggests that the product or service being offered should be bought. Or stated more simply, it is moving the consumer to the point where he or she says, "Yes, I'll take it."

To the business firm, all expenditures of time and money to get the prospective customer to the point of a "near sale" are wasted if a satisfactory level of profitable sales is not generated. This suggests that there is some truth in the old saying that "Nothing happens until somebody sells something."

However, gaining closure does not mean selling people goods or services that they do not want. It is quite the contrary; it means providing the consumer with exactly what is wanted and proving so beyond a doubt. This is consistent with the marketing concept.

Gaining closure is so important that some businesses have specialists who take over from the regular salespeople after there is evidence that the consumer is nearing a final decision. Other firms help their sales staff develop closing techniques through extensive sales training.

Of course, obtaining closure takes more than a salesperson's asking for the order. It is presenting goods or services in such a way that the prospect will find that what is being given attention represents the culmination of the search process. As a result, the purchase act becomes a natural step to take.

To a large extent, the whole series of events in Situation I that occurred after the young woman entered the auto dealership seemed to move her toward the purchase. This included the pleasant atmosphere, the point-of-purchase advertising, the friendliness shown her, the way in which her questions were answered, and the salesman's showing her the car that he believed she would like. It appeared as if it was quite natural for her to say, "All right, I will take it."

In Situations II and III closure has also been obtained but in a more subtle manner. In the supermarket, for example, having the desired items conveniently available and in an attractive setting at an acceptable price contributed to gaining closure. The special display of three related products also encouraged the elderly man to purchase one item that he apparently had not planned to buy when he entered the store. In Situation III the catalogue format, the extensive selection of merchandise, the ease with which orders could be placed, and the apparent knowledge from past experience that orders would be filled promptly and satisfactorily are all likely to have contributed to gaining closure.

Summary

Purchasing processes include the purchase act itself and those encounters which are a part of the circumstances that make up the immediate surroundings of the act of buying. This chapter examines the consumer's selection of a store and the in-store environment.

Store selection itself is a purchasing process involving the comparison of the store's perceived characteristics against one's evaluative criteria and then the classification of the store as either acceptable or unacceptable. Common criteria used are location, depth and breadth of assortment, store personnel, etc. The image of a store should be made consistent with the preferences of the consumer group that the store management desires to serve.

Once the store is selected, the in-store purchasing processes commence. Three buying situations are related in some detail in the chapter. It is significant to note the effect that various aspects of these purchasing processes have on the consumer. First, techniques to serve as a reminder to the consumer, such as point-of-purchase advertising, are quite effective and precipitate substantial unplanned purchases. Second, creating a favorable atmosphere for purchase is effective, especially under certain conditions. For example, when the product or price differences are small, atmospherics can be the deciding factor for the consumer. Third, the retailer-consumer interaction can be beneficial to both parties by resolving questionable issues that the consumer has in mind. Lastly, gaining closure is proving beyond a doubt to the consumer that he has been provided with exactly what he wants and having her or him acknowledge, "Yes, I'll take it."

QUESTIONS AND ISSUES FOR DISCUSSION

1. Is it reasonable to assume that a store's image is similar to an individual's personality and that neither changes very much over time?

2. How could atmospherics contribute to the creation of the following:

   a. A budget men's shop
   b. A feeling of security as well as friendliness and customer concern in a bank
   c. An exclusive women's health spa.

3. Identify the major components of the purchasing process when you have been the buyer of each of the products or services listed below.

   a. A small convenience good, such as a newspaper
   b. Auto repair service
   c. A small appliance when brand was an important consideration.

4. Is it in the best interest of the public to have firms create an image of their retail establishments? Shouldn't they just try to serve their customers in the best possible manner? Explain.

5. How can the layout of a store or of a particular department in it contribute to generating profitable sales? Describe what you would call a good layout of a sporting goods' shop. Give reasons for your suggestions.

6. Closure is a concept that has operational significance in a number of aspects of marketing. Give an example of how closure could function in each of the following:

   a. In an advertisement for sunglasses
   b. As part of a display in a hobby shop
   c. When a door-to-door volunteer calls for contributions to the Heart Fund.

7. How could one go about determining the evaluative criteria that consumers use to select particular stores in which to shop? Is it likely that these criteria are well established in the consumer's mind?

8. How true is the following statement? "During inflationary periods with high unemployment, consumers generally will sacrifice store atmosphere for low prices."

9. Some say that today the package, serving as the "silent salesman" in self-service retailing, is probably the most influential component of the purchasing process. Evaluate this observation.

10. Some large retailers appear to spend millions of dollars on advertising to get the consumer into their store only to lose the sale because of the poor expertise of their salespeople. What is their rationale in following this practice?

Case 1.

Discount Auto House is a high-volume, low-margin retail outlet with stores in six West coast cities. It takes pride in providing a massive array of goods in one location and in operating an associated catalogue sales' department for ordering items not stocked in the stores. Each of the 20,000-square-feet stores has essentially the same layout. Self-service displays make most items easily accessible to the shopper.

The store's management sees an opportunity to better serve their customers and of increasing the sales of more profitable specialty items, such as the latest customizing kits, by hiring several salespeople for each store. These employees would circulate throughout the store answering shoppers' questions and encouraging customers to consider specialty items. For example, the new "kits" referred to range in price from $700 to $3000 and are increasing rapidly in their appeal.

Would sales personnel be an appropriate addition to Discount Auto House Stores?

What problems might arise?

How would these salespeople be likely to affect the purchasing processes in these stores?

Case 2.

The First Security Federal Savings and Loan Association has assets of nearly $100 million. It is located in a metropolitan area and has two suburban branch offices. Until this year, FSF had experienced a very consistent growth rate. However, recently two of its major competitors have become very aggressive in their efforts to attract savings dollars. Both have made extensive use of various premiums such as blankets and dinnerware to lure savers away from the local banks and FSF.

Historically, FSF management has taken a strong position against using any premiums to attract business. They believe it cheapens a financial institution's image. Furthermore, they have asked their customers on two different occasions through mass mailings about their interest in premiums. In each case, very few customers expressed any interest in premiums. At this time FSF pays the highest interest rate allowed by law, as does its two competitors. It also has modern offices located conveniently in the largest suburban areas. Its competitors have similar facilities in equally convenient locations. A recent image study has shown that FSF customers are very satisfied with the service that they are receiving from the Association.

How much can the use of a tactic such as offering premiums affect a firm's image?

What would you recommend that FSF management do to regain its growth position in this market?

Postpurchase Processes

Joe Martin strolled leisurely across the campus reflecting on the events of recent weeks. Seven weeks ago Joe had received a job offer from General Foods. As soon as the offer was firm, Joe had decided to buy a new car. He read numerous automotive magazines, *Consumer Report,* talked with friends, and test drove every type of car in his price range. Joe liked the appearance, handling, and E.P.A. gas mileage ratings of the Pinto. Both local Ford dealers offered to sell Joe the Pinto he wanted at approximately the same price. Joe decided to purchase the Pinto from the Vern Wilson Ford dealership because he heard that Vern Wilson had a good service department. Once Joe had selected the car there were only a few details remaining to complete the transaction. In particular, Joe had to select a bank to obtain financing and an insurance company and agent to obtain auto insurance. The ancilliary aspects of the transaction required more effort than Joe had anticipated but he finally completed the transactions.

As he approached the student union Joe saw Charlie Stallers sitting on the steps. Charlie, who was also graduating next month, had recently purchased a Vega. "Hey, Charlie," Joe said, "how's the Vega?" "Hi, Joe. The Vega's running great. I drove to Chicago last weekend and got 35 miles per gallon." "Hey, that's great, Charlie. I'm not even getting 30 miles per gallon with my Pinto."

The Nature of Postpurchase Processes

The situation described in the preceding paragraphs illustrates a key element of the consumer decision process that has not yet been discussed in detail. In particular, the situation illustrates that the consumer decision process does not culminate with the decision to purchase. The decision to purchase a product or service can, as illustrated in Figure 14.1, result in two types of outcomes: further purchase-related behavior, and postpurchase evaluation. The first type of outcome, further purchase-related behavior, refers to the fact that many purchase decisions necessitate further actions by the consumer. For example, the decision to purchase

FIGURE 14.1.
Postpurchase Processes.

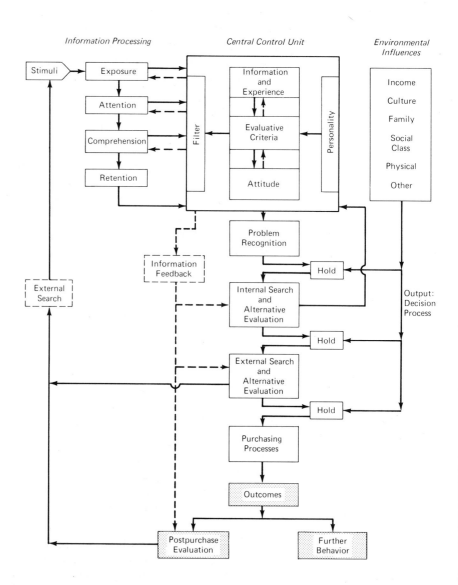

Source: J. F. Engel, D. T. Kollat and R. D. Blackwell, *Consumer Behavior,* 2nd ed. (New York: Holt, Rinehart and Winston, Inc., 1973), p. 530. Reprinted by permission of the publisher.

an automobile may require that the consumer procure a loan to pay for the auto. Since there are typically several sources for obtaining a loan, the consumer must make a decision as to the type, terms, and source of the loan. As in the situation described previously, the purchase of an automobile is typically followed by further purchase-related behavior, such as the purchase of auto insurance.

The decision to purchase a product or service can also result in postpurchase evaluation. *Postpurchase evaluation* is the consumer's evaluation or assessment of the purchase decision that was made. Consumers prefer to believe that the purchase decision made was the best possible decision, but the information available seldom permits such unequivocal assurance. More typically, the consumer must use insufficient information and less than careful scrutiny of available information as the basis for the evaluation of purchase alternatives. The postpurchase evaluation may cause the consumer to search for additional information to relieve doubts about the purchase decision. The additional information can lead to the reconsideration of the evaluative criteria. While postpurchase evaluation is typical, the most common outcome is satisfaction rather than dissatisfaction with the purchase decision. Satisfaction with a purchase decision serves to reinforce existing attitudes and evaluative criteria, tending to strengthen the probability of a repeat purchase under similar circumstances in the future.

Further Purchase-Related Behavior

As indicated in the previous section and illustrated in Figure 14.1, one type of outcome resulting from the purchasing processes is further purchase-related behavior. *Further purchase-related behavior* includes the near limitless variety of additional actions that can result from the purchasing processes. The types of action that result depend on the particular situation and on the consumer; consequently, the number of possible actions can be large. There are, however, three types of further purchase-related behaviors that are of significance to marketing strategists.

TYPES OF FURTHER PURCHASE-RELATED BEHAVIOR

The three types of further purchase-related behavior that are of particular importance to the marketing analyst are: (1) purchase-related financial outlays, (2) recognition of interest in related products and services, and (3) product installation and use considerations.

The decision to purchase a product or service precipitates a financial outlay that for some purchase decisions (e.g., automobiles, homes, major durables) present genuine problems for the consumer. In certain instances the decision concerning the most appropriate method of payment can trigger extended problem solving for the consumer. For example, the decision to purchase a stereo system can trigger the evaluation of the following alternative methods of financing: (1) installment credit, (2) bank financing, (3) personal sources, and (4) complete payment at the point of purchase. The decision with respect to financial payment is among the most important that are confronted in many buying situations. The tremendous success of bank cards (e.g., Master Charge, Bank Americard, etc.) and retailer-sponsored installment credit (e.g., Sears, Penney's, Wards) suggests that consumers prefer to simplify the financial payment decision as much as possible.

A second type of further purchase-related behavior that can be triggered by the purchase decision is the interest in related products and services; that is, the purchase of a particular product can generate interest in the purchase of related products. For example, the purchase of a new sofa can trigger the recognition that other furniture items (e.g., chairs, tables, lamps) are necessary to properly coordinate the entire room. The purchase of a new home frequently results in the purchase of numerous household items such as major appliances, draperies, and other furniture items. The recognition of this phenomenon by marketing strategists has resulted in the existence of home furnishing centers rather than furniture departments. In other words, marketing strategists frequently provide consumers with the opportunity to procure related product items at the same time the major purchase decision is made.

The third major type of further purchase-related behavior is product installation and use considerations. Once a consumer decides to purchase a product, the product must be prepared for use. For many types of products the preparation for use is a simple task. For example, the purchase of a shirt typically requires the consumer to simply remove the package, remove any tags, and, perhaps, iron it before use. The preparation for use can, however, be considerably more complex. As most parents can attest, the preparation of products for use that occurs on birthdays and holidays can provide a formidable challenge to the most able "engineer." Even after a product is prepared for use, a period of learning may be necessary to acquire the skills necessary for proper use. A bicycle, for example, must not only be assembled but, as in the case of the novice, the consumer also must learn to ride it. Each of these situations can require considerable time, thought, and effort, to say nothing of the consternation that can result if inadequate directions are provided.

MARKETING IMPLICATIONS

The major focus, in many instances the sole focus, has been on the purchasing process. The many activities that frequently follow the purchase decision have been ignored or given only incidental consideration. However, the recognition that a consumer's concern over financing and credit arrangements can be a barrier that delays or even prevents a purchase dictates the development and implementation of aggressive marketing practices. Retailers have long been aware of this fact, and many offer such a variety of convenient credit arrangements that the need for extended problem solving by the consumer relative to financing is virtually eliminated. The introduction and widespread use of the various bank cards (e.g., Master Charge and Bank Americard) further attests to the consumer's preference for simplifying the financial payment decision. There are differences in how bank cards are used by different market segments. For instance, consumers in the higher income categories tend to use them for convenience purposes, while lower income consumers tend to use the cards as installment credit.[1] Nevertheless, the widespread use of bank cards suggests a rather pervasive preference

[1]H. L. Mathews and J. W. Slocum, Jr., "Social Class and Commercial Bank Credit Card Usage," *Journal of Marketing*, 33 (January, 1969), pp. 71–78.

for simplifying the financial payment decision. In essence, then, the marketing strategist must determine the financial payment alternatives preferred by the relevant consumer segments and, to the extent possible, make them available.

As indicated previously, the purchase decision can trigger an interest in related products and services. Even though few marketing analysts would deny that this presents considerable opportunity to the perceptive decision maker, many opportunities are not capitalized on because decision makers fail to recognize the extent to which one purchase can lead to another. One strategy might be to prepare accompanying literature that suggests possible accessories, companion products, and so on. For example, the camera manufacturer might include information on the advantages of certain film, the merits of certain attachments, and the capabilities of alternative camera lenses. The automobile dealer should recognize that the purchase of a car triggers numerous other purchases such as a state inspection, licenses, insurance, and financing. Even if the auto dealer is not able to provide all of these related items for the consumer, the dealer's assistance in obtaining them could certainly contribute to the consumer's satisfaction. The dealer might offer to arrange for the state inspection as well as obtain and pay for the car license. Although the activities suggested would result in a minor increase in cost, they might add substantially to the satisfaction experienced by the consumer, producing favorable word-of-mouth communications to friends and relatives.

The recognition of a decision that triggers the purchase of related products can provide considerable opportunity for increasing a firm's profitability. The purchase of a tent, for example, will typically trigger the purchase of numerous related products such as camping stoves; lanterns; sleeping bags; air mattresses; special pots, pans, and dishes; tent heaters; and many other items. The Coleman Company of Wichita, Kansas, recognized this some years ago and is now a leading producer of virtually every product associated with camping. In essence, then, the marketing analyst must identify the various related products that might be associated with the purchase of a given product. The identification of such can assist considerably in the development of a growth strategy, the identification of new product opportunities, and the more effective merchandising of existing product lines.

Manufacturers all too frequently assume that their responsibilities to the consumer terminate with the decision to purchase. There is, however, considerable indication that timely, proper installation and adequate instruction in the proper use of a product can contribute substantially to the satisfaction experienced by a consumer. Furthermore, the lack of these postpurchase activities can result in consumer dissatisfaction and, consequently, negative word-of-mouth communications about the product to friends and relatives. Consider, for example, the dissatisfaction experienced by the consumer who purchases central air conditioning to make the months of July and August somewhat tolerable for his family only to have the company delay installation to September. The probability of this consumer recommending this company to friends or neighbors, if not zero, certainly approaches zero. Contrast that with the sailboat company that includes as a condition of sale free instructions in the operation and maintenance of sailboats. The satisfaction a consumer derives from the purchase of a sailboat is directly related to his use of that product, and the company that demonstrates and encourages proper use of the product increases the likelihood of having satisfied consumers.

The marketing effort should be based on an awareness of how the product fits into the consumer's life-style and of the essential conditions of product use.[2] On this basis, the seller should facilitate the consumer's efforts to the extent possible in order to maximize the satisfaction gained from the product.

Postpurchase Evaluation

As was indicated in the initial section of this chapter, purchasing processes can result in two outcomes: further-purchase related behavior and postpurchase evaluation. The preceding section

[2]H. W. Boyd, Jr. and S. J. Levy, "New Dimensions in Consumer Analysis," *Harvard Business Review* (November–December, 1963), pp. 129–140.

focused on the former, whereas this section focuses on the latter.

NATURE OF POSTPURCHASE EVALUATION

Postpurchase evaluation—the process by which a consumer assesses the result of a purchase decision—frequently follows a purchase decision. This evaluation process results from the fact that consumers make purchase decisions that frequently involve substantial monies with insufficient information. Because the purchase decision is normally made on the basis of insufficient information, the consumer cannot be certain that the decision made was the best possible decision. Furthermore, consumers frequently lack the technical knowledge necessary to thoroughly evaluate alternative products available in the marketplace. Few consumers, for example, possess an adequate understanding of electronics to intelligently evaluate alternative brands of color televisions. Thus, the assurance of complete, comparable product information will not assure that the consumer will select the best alternative. The lack of the knowledge necessary to intelligently evaluate product alternatives results in uncertainty as to the correctness of the decision made and, thus, the tendency for postpurchase evaluation.

The postpurchase evaluation stage of the consumer decision process serves two primary functions. First, postpurchase evaluation enables the consumer to appraise the astuteness of his decision making in the marketplace.[3] This purpose has been discussed and illustrated in the previous paragraph. Second, the postpurchase evaluation provides a vital feedback to the CCU as to the extent to which a purchase serves to reduce a problem. Thus, a positive evaluation of a purchase decision will increase the likelihood of similar purchase behavior occurring in the future. Indeed, this positive evaluation of a purchase experience tends to produce and strengthen loyalty to a particular brand.

The other variables in the CCU are also affected by positive evaluations of purchase decisions. Evaluative criteria, for exam-

[3]R. J. Holloway, "An Experiment on Consumer Dissonance," *Journal of Marketing,* 31 (January, 1967), pp. 39–43.

ple, are learned and, thus, strengthened or weakened in importance by the consumer's evaluation of purchase decisions. Similarly, consumers acquire or learn attitudes that are reinforced or changed, at least partially, by the feedback resulting from the postpurchase evaluation. Suppose a consumer has delineated the following evaluative criteria relative to the purchase of an automobile: (1) gas mileage, (2) dependablity, (3) comfort, and (4) styling. Also suppose, as the consumer decision model would contend, that this consumer evaluates the available alternatives on these criteria and develops a strong positive attitude toward the Ford Granada. If after this consumer has decided to purchase a Granada the decision is evaluated positively, the evaluative criteria and the consumer's attitude toward the Granada will be reinforced. The postpurchase evaluation of this decision may, however, cause the consumer to reorder his evaluative criteria or change his attitude toward the auto.

The complexity of the postpurchase evaluation process can vary substantially. The evaluation might involve nothing more than a casual comment to a friend about the purchase decision. For example, in the purchase decision described in the previous paragraph, a friend's comment as to the Granada's appearance might reinforce the consumer's evaluation of the car on that criterion. The superficiality of this postpurchase evaluation is markedly different from the evaluation involving careful monitoring of gas mileage and continuous comparison to available alternatives.

The managerial implications of postpurchase evaluations are becoming increasingly apparent. The Ford Company has indicated that it conducts thousands of interviews with Ford owners to determine what they do and do not like about their Fords. This information then assists Ford executives in identifying consumer priorities with respect to product modifications. Such information can also provide direction for promotional efforts. If, for example, consumers evaluate the product low on an important evaluative criterion, promotional efforts might be directed at changing consumer's evaluations of the product on that basis. Similarly, if the information suggests that consumers rank high a criterion on which this product is rated low, the promotion campaign might attempt to modify the ranking of that evaluative criterion.

FACTORS CAUSING POSTPURCHASE EVALUATION

Postpurchase evaluation that is triggered by new purchase-related information can occur for a number of reasons, the most important of which are: (1) unconfirmed expectations, (2) postpurchase attitude change, (3) misunderstanding of product-related information, and (4) the availability of desirable alternatives.

Unconfirmed Expectations

Prior to the purchase act, consumers develop expectations regarding the consequences of the purchase act, and the input of information after the purchase serves to either confirm or reject these expectations. When the purchase confirms the consumer's expectations, the information is fed back to the consumer's CCU, and the expectations are reinforced. However, when the expectations are not confirmed, the consequences are somewhat more complex. The failure of a product to provide the expected satisfaction can generate a state of cognitive inconsistency. Cognitive inconsistency is an uncomfortable condition that the consumer is motivated to overcome, that is, the consumer is motivated to restore balance.[4] The importance of consumer expectations is such that there is some indication that unconfirmed expectations will be evaluated negatively, regardless of whether experience exceeds or falls short of the expectancy.[5]

The evidence to date suggests that promotional messages need to create realistic expectations. Promotional efforts that create unrealistic expectations for products can result in consumer dissatisfaction with the purchase and use of the products. The importance of developing realistic consumer expectations is

[4]J. M. Carlsmith and E. Aronson, "Some Hedonic Consequences of the Confirmation and Disconfirmation of Expectancies," *Journal of Abnormal and Social Psychology*, 66 (1963), pp. 151–156.

[5]W. A. Watts, "Predictability and Pleasure: Reactions to the Disconfirmation of Expectancies," in *Theories of Cognitive Consistency*, R. P. Abelson, et al., ed. (Chicago: Rand McNally, 1968), pp. 469–478.

evident in a recent Ford Motor Company advertising campaign. The campaign compares the Ford Granada to two more expensive luxury cars (the Mercedes 280 and the Cadillac Seville) on two evaluative criteria. The advertisement reports that the Granada consistently ranked first or second on one criterion but was always second on the other criterion. The ad, of course, stresses that this performance is achieved despite the substantially lower price of the Granada. The promotional campaign is obviously designed to convince the audience that the Granada performs about as well as two luxury cars on certain dimensions but is lower in price. If the promotion asserted product superiority on every dimension, the likelihood of unconfirmed expectations might be great.

The potential consequences of unconfirmed expectations suggest that marketing communications should be designed to create expectancies that will be fulfilled by the product insofar as is possible.[6] Similarly, product designers should be keenly aware of the way in which a product fits into the consumer's life-style; that is, what does the product mean to the consumer? How will the product be used? The product should be designed and promoted so that performance will be satisfactory under conditions actually experienced by the consumer. For example, many consumers use electric toasters for English muffins, rolls, and other forms of baked goods besides bread. If the toaster cannot handle these items satisfactorily, disconfirmed expectancies and, consequently, buyer dissatisfaction will probably result.

Many consumers become quite vocal when they are dissatisfied and do not hesitate to spread unfavorable word-of-mouth communication. One low-priced brand of automobile seems to have been particularly damaged in this fashion by product performance that failed to meet the expectations established in advertisements. When consumers receive unfavorable word-of-mouth communications about a product, they tend to screen out advertisements about that product, seriously prohibiting the opportunity to convert these people into prospects. In June 1975

[6]R. E. Anderson, "Consumer Dissatisfaction: The Effect of Disconfirmed Expectancy on Perceived Product Performance," *Journal of Marketing Research,* 10 (February, 1973), pp. 38–44.

the Chevrolet Division of General Motors extended the warranty on 1975 Vega engines from 12,000 to 60,000 miles. There is some indication that this drastic step was undertaken to combat rumored difficulties with the Vega engine.

Postpurchase Attitude Change

The purchase and use of a product provides the consumer with new experiences and new information that can produce attitude change. The information acquired from using the product can be inconsistent with a consumer's existing attitudes. Information that is inconsistent with existing attitudes can create an uncomfortable state, motivating the consumer to restore consonance or balance.

Suppose that a consumer has a favorable attitude toward suede coats and for some time has intended to purchase one. When this consumer purchases a suede coat and uses it, she will acquire new information about the product. The information acquired may be discrepant with preconceived attitudes. The consumer may find, for example, that suede requires substantial care to maintain its appearance. Because the consumer has committed herself to the purchase, she will typically be reluctant to admit having made a mistake. The more likely course of action is to change the attitude toward the effort required to care for the suede coat.

Thus, it might appear that inducing people to engage in attitude-discrepant behavior is a valid marketing goal. For example, the offer of a free coupon might induce a consumer to try a previously avoided brand of toothpaste. If this consumer were strongly committed to another brand and if the free brand was used, liked, and purchased voluntarily, then cognitive inconsistency would result. The likely method of eliminating the discomfort caused by this inconsistent cognition would be to change one's brand preference. The change in brand preference resulting from this product trial would probably not occur if the behavior advocated were perceived as nonacceptable. For example, if the consumer had reservations about the decay preventative capabilities of this brand, he might decide that the toothpaste will never be used by his children. If this were the case, the consumer would probably not use the free coupon and, thus, would avoid the advocated behavior.

Different results can occur if the marketer use a free sample. A consumer might use the sample without giving the product an actual trial; that is, the consumer might not want to waste a free sample but is not willing to actually evaluate the sample because such an evaluation would pose a challenge to the preferred brand.

For some time consumer analysts have contended that the effect of product purchase on attitude change was only operative for major purchases. In recent years, however, research has indicated that postpurchase attitude change can result from the purchase of minor products. The underlying basis for attitude change may be consumer commitment.[7] While the purchase of a minor product might not involve the large financial commitment of a major product, it can very well involve a psychological commitment.

Misunderstanding of Product-Related Information

Postpurchase evaluation can result from a misunderstanding of product-related information. This is especially true for products that are somewhat technical in nature. For example, a consumer can obtain information on the memory capabilities of an electronic calculator prior to purchase. However, since every electronic calculator must have some type of memory capability, the consumer might have misunderstood product information vital to product use. The consumer's inquiry as to the calculator's memory capability might have been with respect to a secondary memory that is used to store data that has been processed, such as the sums of squares. Such a misunderstanding of the product's capabilities can trigger postpurchase evaluation. If the product-related information that was misunderstood is important to the consumer's satisfaction, the consumer might replace the product.

Misunderstanding purchase-related information, whether due to careless prepurchase evaluation by the consumer or decep-

---

[7]F. W. Winter, "The Effect of Purchase Characteristics on Postdecision Product Evaluation," *Journal of Marketing Research,* 11 (May, 1974), pp. 164–171.

tion by the seller, has been an area of concern for many consumer advocates. State and federal legislative bodies have been concerned enough about such misunderstandings that numerous bills have been introduced to help alleviate this problem. The cooling-off laws are an example of such legislation. These statutes take various forms but are basically directed at providing a "cooling-off period" during which a consumer may rescind a contract to purchase goods or services when the sale is transacted at a place other than the seller's place of business.[8] Such legislation permits a consumer to thoroughly evaluate a purchase decision and, if so desired, rescind the purchase decision without financial loss.

Availability of Desirable Alternatives

Extensive external information search and alternative evaluation can result in the consumer's having to chose from among several attractive alternatives. The consumer must chose the one alternative perceived to be the most desirable. Selection of the most desirable alternative, however, is not an easy task because available information seldom eliminates all uncertainty. Consequently, when a consumer selects the alternative perceived to be most desirable, other desirable alternatives must be foregone. Information on desirable alternatives, particularly new information, can trigger postpurchase evaluation.

Suppose that a consumer recognizes the need to purchase a dishwasher. After considering the numerous alternatives, the consumer reduces the number of alternatives under consideration to three, all of which appear equally desirable. After several weeks of evaluating alternatives, the consumer selects Brand A. Five days after the purchase, the consumer becomes aware of a *Consumer Report* which contains the results of tests of the five major brands. Brand B was evaluated superior to Brand A (the brand purchased) on nearly every relevant product feature. This new information about an available alternative can cause postpurchase evaluation that can affect the satisfaction the consumer derived from this purchase.

[8]O. C. Walker, Jr. and N. M. Ford, "Can 'Cooling-off Laws' Really Protect the Consumer," *Journal of Marketing,* 34 (April, 1970), pp. 53–58.

MANAGERIAL IMPLICATIONS OF POSTPURCHASE EVALUATION

The preceding sections focused on the nature of postpurchase evaluation and the factors that produce such behavior. This section focuses on the results of consumer postpurchase evaluation and the managerial implications of such.

Postpurchase evaluation will typically result in some change in the consumer. The change may be limited to a broadened purchase experience and consequent reinforcement of purchase behavior. However, the result may be a major change in the purchase process. The effect postpurchase evaluation has on the consumer's behavior depends on the type of feedback that is transmitted to the CCU. The information transmitted to the CCU can range from complete satisfaction with the purchase to complete dissatisfaction with the purchase. The complete satisfaction, complete dissatisfaction conditions represent the two ends of a continuum that encompasses varying degrees of partial satisfaction and partial dissatisfaction.

If the feedback to the consumer's CCU is complete satisfaction, similar purchase behavior will be reinforced and repeated to solve a similar problem in the future. Similar purchase behavior will, of course, not occur if the behavior was solving a one time problem. For example, the selection of a university to get a B.A. degree is, if the institution provides a completely satisfactory solution, a one time problem. This can be contrasted with the purchase of Goodrich radial tires which produced a completely satisfactory type of feedback to the CCU. Because auto tires are typically purchased several times in a consumer's lifetime, this feedback will reinforce the consumer's decision and, thus, increase the likelihood that Goodrich tires will be purchased when the need for tires arises again.

The managerial implications of this postpurchase evaluation outcome are rather apparent. The marketing analyst must regularly monitor consumers' evaluation of the product to be certain the product continues to receive favorable evaluations on the evaluative criteria. The activities of Ford Motor Company relative to the Granada provide an illustration of how one major corporation uses postpurchase evaluation information.

If the postpurchase evaluation results in complete dissatisfaction being transmitted to the CCU, two types of outcomes can result. First, the consumer can discontinue this type of purchase behavior. Discontinuance of purchase behavior can result when the current solution is unsatisfactory and no other acceptable solution is available. For example, a consumer with a strong preference for Italian food might, after unsatisfactory experiences at all available restaurants, simply discontinue his purchases of Italian food. The second type of outcome that can result is a change in purchase behavior: The consumer might continue his search for a satisfactory solution in other locations, reevaluate the alternative solutions, or redefine the problem to increase the likelihood of locating a satisfactory solution. Thus, the connoisseur of Italian food referred to previously might decide to experiment with Italian restaurants outside his immediate area, change his evaluation of one of the available restaurants, or decide that a 24-hour heartburn is not a valid indicator of the quality of Italian food.

If the feedback to the consumer's CCU is partial satisfaction, the outcome might be discontinuance of the purchase behavior, continuance of the purchase behavior but with some reservations, or modification of the purchase behavior.[9] If the partial satisfaction was experienced with respect to the solution of a one-time problem, the purchase behavior will, of course, be discontinued. A consumer might be only partially satisfied and yet continue the same purchase behavior because the product is an inconsequential one or because the best available alternative is presently being used. A postpurchase evaluation that results in partial satisfaction for the consumer may cause a modification in purchase behavior. The modification can result from a change in the consumer's problem recognition or from the alternatives available to the consumer.

Postpurchase evaluations that result in partial satisfaction or dissatisfaction present particularly appealing opportunities to the marketing analyst. A method of identifying and subsequently

[9]C.G. Walters, *Consumer Behavior: Theory and Practice,* 2nd ed. (Homewood, Illinois: Richard D. Irwin, Inc., 1974), p. 560.

converting consumer dissatisfaction and partial satisfaction into marketing opportunities has been suggested by the director of research for Batten, Barton, Durstine & Osborn, Inc.[10] This executive made the following observation:

> If you ask consumers what they want in a canned dog food, they tell you they want a food the dog will eat and it should be good for the dog. If you ask a housewife what problems she has with canned dog food, she will tell you that it is too expensive and smells bad.

The statement was made to illustrate the difference between *benefit research,* which focuses on consumers' evaluations of the benefits provided by a product, and *problem research,* which focuses on the features of a product that bother consumers. Problem research can be of considerable value in identifying a partially satisfied or dissatisfied consumer and converting that consumer into a marketing opportunity. The Problem Detection System, developed by BBD&O, has consumers list all possible problems associated with the use of a particular product.[11] This enables the researcher to identify those problems that can be converted into marketing opportunities. Once the marketing analyst has identified the consumer problems, new product concepts must be developed to solve these problems.

In 1970 General Motors made the decision to call back 4.9 million cars to check for safety defects. GM's decision, estimated to have cost the company $50 million, might have been influenced by proposed warranty legislation.[12] Regardless of GM's motivation, the decision underscores the urgent need for manufacturers and distributors to devote adequate attention to postpurchase considerations. Adequate attention to postpurchase considerations provide substantial profit opportunities to business organizations—opportunities that only a few firms currently recognize.

[10]"Light Says Problem Research Will Give More Benefits Than Benefit Research," *Marketing News,* 9 (September 26, 1975), p. 12.

[11]"Light Says Problem Research Will Give More Benefits Than Benefit Research," p. 12.

[12]G. Fisk, "Guidelines for Warranty Service After Sale," *Journal of Marketing,* 34 (January, 1970), pp. 63–67.

Summary

The consumer decision process does not culminate with the purchase decision. Postpurchase processes follow and can result in one of two types of outcomes: further purchase-related behavior and postpurchase evaluation. Further purchase-related behavior that is significant to the marketer is of three types: (1) purchase-related financial outlays, (2) recognition of interest in related products and services, and (3) product installation and use considerations. The marketer can make use of this purchase-related behavior to improve profitability by such things as: (1) having simple financing arrangements for purchases, (2) having available related products and services, and (3) having available proper installation and use instructions for products.

Postpurchase evaluation is the process by which a consumer assesses the result of a purchase decision. It serves the functions of enabling the consumer to appraise the astuteness of his decision making in the marketplace and providing vital feedback to the CCU as to the extent to which a purchase serves to reduce a problem. This chapter relates the most important factors that cause postpurchase evaluation. First, expectations of a product or service that are unconfirmed prior to purchase cause consumers to carefully evaluate the product following the purchase. Second, a consumer's postpurchase change in attitude, however caused, can stimulate postpurchase evaluation. Third, misunderstanding of product-related information can also cause postpurchase evaluation. The final cause is the availability of more than one desirable alternative.

Managerial implications can be drawn from this study of postpurchase evaluation. Managers should attempt to cause the consumer's evaluation of their product to be positive. If the consumer transmits dissatisfaction to the CCU, the purchase behavior will be either discontinued or changed. Marketing opportunities are created when partial satisfaction or dissatisfaction arise from the postpurchase evaluation process.

1. What is the distinction between "further purchase behavior" and "postpurchase evaluation?"
2. Some consumer analysts believe that an understanding of "further purchase behavior" can provide considerable opportunities to the astute marketing manager. Explain how this might be the case.
3. How might an understanding of further purchase-related behavior benefit marketers in the following areas:

   a. Women's clothing store
   b. Major department store
   c. Chevrolet Division of General Motors
   d. United Airlines
   e. Wilson Sporting Goods.

4. Evaluate the following statement: "Marketing managers of all types are well advised to undertake research that leads to an understanding of the total *purchase act.*"
5. Postpurchase evaluation frequently follows a consumer's purchase decision. Why does postpurchase evaluation occur?
6. What functions does postpurchase evaluation serve? How do positive and negative postpurchase evaluations effect the CCU?
7. Charlie Bass, an avid fisherman, recently purchased a new fishing rod because of the rod's durability, light weight, and moderate price. After using the product for three weeks, Charlie becomes aware of a comparable fishing rod at a lower price. What is likely to happen to Charlie's evaluative criteria? Would the results have been the same if Charlie had been only a casual fisherman?
8. Megan Coffman purchased a new compact auto expecting to get about 20 miles per gallon in city driving and about 30 miles per gallon on the highway. What is the likely postpurchase evaluation if Megan actually gets 15 in the city and 24 on the highway? What are the marketing implications of this postpurchase evaluation?
9. Research indicates that consumers were very surprised to discover the quality of sound output of a particular stereophonic system. Is this finding necessarily favorable? Explain.

10. What are the implications of postpurchase evaluation providing a partially satisfactory feedback to the CCU? Will a consumer continue to purchase a product that regularly receives a partially satisfactory postpurchase evaluation?

SITUATIONAL PROBLEMS

Case 1.

The Johnson Company, a small producer and distributor of ski equipment, has experienced declining sales for the past three years. This decline in sales has occurred while the ski equipment industry as a whole has experienced substantial sales increases. In an effort to determine the reason for declining sales, Johnson's management submitted their major product, skis, to rigorous testing by expert skiers. The experts reported that Johnson skis were slightly more difficult to break in, but after the break in period they rated them comparable to the best skis available. Such a rating was indeed encouraging since Johnson skis were less expensive than most of those of its competitors. In addition to the evaluation by expert skiers, the Johnson Company conducted a market research study in which they elicited the evaluations of current users of their skis. The study revealed considerable variation in the evaluation of Johnson skis. One of the more interesting findings of the study is presented in the accompanying table.

Based on your experience with Johnson skis would you recommend them to a friend?

Type of Skier	Yes	No	Undecided	Total
Beginner	30	50	20	100
Intermediate	60	25	15	100
Advanced	80	10	10	100

Based on your understanding of postpurchase processes, how might you explain Johnson's declining sales?

How might an understanding of postpurchase processes, particularly further purchase-related behavior, aid Johnson's management in overcoming their disappointing sales performance?

Case 2.

Clark Incorporated, developer of the radar oven, recently completed an internal audit which indicated that although sales of Clark radar ovens have continued to increase, market share has declined in recent years. Alarmed about the declining market share, K. C. Clark, President of Clark Incorporated, instructed the marketing department to carefully evaluate the situation and determine what changes might be required. In compliance with K. C. Clark's request, the marketing department conducted an extensive research study to understand consumer decision making relative to radar ovens. The research indicated that the most important evaluative criteria in order of importance are: (1) time required to cook food, (2) price, (3) appearance, and (4) safety. The research further indicated that consumers planning on purchasing a radar oven evaluated the Clark radar oven as follows: (1) time required to cook food—very satisfactory, (2) price—satisfactory, (3) appearance—very satisfactory, and (4) safety—very satisfactory. The research also included the evaluation of the Clark radar oven by consumers who had used the oven for approximately six months. The evaluation of these consumers was as follows: (1) time required to cook food—unsatisfactory, (2) price—satisfactory, (3) appearance—satisfactory, and (4) safety—very unsatisfactory. The marketing director felt the unsatisfactory evaluation of the oven's safety was due to the concern voiced by some consumer groups regarding the safety of all radar ovens. The marketing director was, however, perplexed by the evaluation of the Clark radar oven relative to the time required to cook food.

How might an understanding of postpurchase evaluation aid the management of Clark Incorporated?

What changes, if any, would you suggest with respect to the Clark radar oven or the manner in which it should be promoted?

PART V

DIRECTIONS IN CONSUMER ANALYSIS

OUTLINE

Market Segmentation
Meaning of Market Segmentation
Identifying Markets
Evaluating Market Segments

Product Development
Product Life Cycle
New Product Development

Summary

Questions and Issues for Discussion

Situational Problems

Selected
Applications of
Consumer Behavior

Understanding consumer behavior, although an intriguing subject in its own right, is fundamental to the development and execution of effective marketing programs in a developed economic system. Consider the following marketing programs:

BMW thinks that their luxury car, which sells for between $14,000 and $18,000, has not achieved the market penetration it could in the United States. As a result, BMW recently kicked off a national media campaign in those U.S. magazines with high-income readerships. The U.S. subsidiary of the Bavarian company hopes to experience a 20 percent increase in unit sales of the car they refer to as the 'ultimate' car.[1]

Morton Foods, a small potato chip and salad dressing producer in Dallas, has developed a marketing program that combines old-fashioned service with country music. Morton Foods, recently purchased by a group of Dallas businessmen, experienced considerable difficulty under its previous owners, W. R. Grace & Co. Morton's new president attributes the difficulties to Grace's decision to discontinue business to small outlets in rural Texas that were buying less than $15 worth of merchandise per week. These small outlets were the core of Morton's business before Grace bought the company, and the new owners have developed a marketing program featuring door-to-door service and country music to attempt to regain their business.[2]

The Gulf Oil Company has adopted the slogan 'where the automotive run-around ends' for its new auto parts and service centers. The Gulf stores will handle a complete line of auto parts, tires and accessories and complete mechanical service but no gasoline. Each outlet will handle an $80,000 inventory and operate seven days a week. The firm's objective is to satisfy all the motoring public's automotive repair and service needs in a single outlet.[3]

Ten religious denominations in Atlanta, Dallas, Kansas City, Los Angeles, and Philadelphia are participating in a project whereby a member can authorize that his church contribution be made automatically through his checking account, or debited against his credit card (BankAmericard or Master Charge). The church member must simply authorize his bank to make a regular transfer of funds or make

[1] "Marketing Observer," *Business Week* (August 4, 1975), p. 66.
[2] "Marketing Observer," p. 66.
[3] "Marketing Observer," *Business Week* (June 16, 1975), p. 84.

a charge against his credit card. The objective of the new service is to provide the churches involved with a more stable cash flow.[4]

These four illustrations, albeit quite varied, have a common element—they all illustrate the importance of developing marketing programs that are based on an understanding of consumer behavior. The widespread adoption of the marketing concept that includes as its basic precept a consumer orientation has had a subtle yet pervasive impact on marketing decision making. The result has been that virtually every decision made by marketing strategists includes an analysis of consumer behavior. The analyses range from subjective judgments to comprehensive market study, but the consumer's behavior is almost always a key consideration.

The remainder of this chapter focuses on the manner in which consumer behavior affects two key marketing strategist concerns—market segmentation and product development. These two areas will be considered in detail and illustrated to demonstrate how an understanding of consumer behavior facilitates decision making in each area.

Market Segmentation

A hundred years ago when markets were geographically limited by existing transportation and communication systems, the marketers could identify the distinctive needs of their consumers. Once identified, the marketing strategist could adjust his marketing effort to meet the distinctive needs of the market. However, the twentieth century, characterized by increased urbanization, improved transportation, and advanced communication systems accentuated the benefits of product uniformity. The widespread acceptance of product uniformity is illustrated by the following comment frequently attributed to Henry Ford: "They can have any color they want, so long as it's black."[5]

[4]"Marketing Observer," *Business Week* (August 4, 1975), p. 66.
[5]G. S. George, *The History of Management Thought* (Englewood Cliffs, N.J.: Prentice-Hall, Inc., 1968), pp. 86–99.

Improved transportation and communication systems, careful planning and scheduling techniques, as well as the increased affluence and education of consumers have resulted in a substantial change in this philosophy in the past 25 years. Marketing analysts now recognize that profits are increasingly contingent on the development and distribution of products and services in a manner consistent with the variation in consumer needs. Although not a universally appropriate approach, marketing strategists have found that considerable benefits can be achieved by identifying the distinctive characteristics of consumer segments and focusing product developments and marketing efforts on those distinctive characteristics.

MEANING OF MARKET SEGMENTATION

Market segmentation is based on the premise that all marketing activity should start with the identification of distinctive consumer needs or interests. Before market segmentation can be considered, a market must be identified; that is, a firm must have a clear understanding of which group of consumers is likely to be interested in and can afford to buy its products and/or services. For instance, there is a specific market in "Braillegram," a new Western Union telegram service for the blind and visually impaired. This market is made up of all those who are likely to be interested (or could be encouraged to be interested) in and who can afford the use of braille via Western Union telegraph services.

It might be that this market is not homogeneous, that is, not very similar throughout. For example, it may be useful to divide the market between blind persons and those nonblind persons who may have a need to communicate with the blind or those with impaired vision. If this kind of division is meaningful, that is, if it helps the firm better serve each of these two groups, then these become two market segments.

Thus, *market segmentation* is the "subdividing of a market into homogeneous subsets of customers, where any subset may conceivably be selected as a market target to be reached with a distinct marketing mix."[6] In other words, if the marketing strate-

---

[6]P. Kotler, *Marketing Management* (Englewood Cliffs, N.J.: Prentice-Hall, Inc., 1972), p. 166.

gist can divide the market into segments having distinctive preferences and adjust his product offering and efforts to the preferences of a particular segment, the opportunity to achieve consumer satisfaction is increased. An effective segmentation strategy can result in a satisfied consumer and increased profits for the firm.

The effective use of market segmentation requires that two conditions be met. First, the marketing analyst must be able to identify adequate market segments with distinctive preferences or behavioral patterns. Second, the market segment must be accessible by differential media distribution, product, or some aspect over which the marketing strategist has control. Although the effectiveness of adjusting marketing efforts to a particular market segment varies considerably, the boundless creativity of marketing strategists seems to always provide some means of responding differentially. As a result, the issue that has plagued marketing analysts is the identification of marketing segments. The following section considers those bases for segmenting markets that consumer analysts have identified as useful.

IDENTIFYING MARKETS

Marketing strategists have identified three strategies for dealing with markets: (1) *undifferentiated marketing*—satisfying the needs of the mass market with a single product and single marketing program, (2) *differentiated marketing*—satisfying the distinctive needs of the various segments by developing distinctive products and perhaps marketing programs, and (3) *concentrated marketing*—satisfying the distinctive needs of a single segment of the market by designing a product and marketing program that focuses specifically on those needs.[7] The appropriateness of a particular strategy depends upon product, organizational, competitive, and consumer considerations, meaning that it is not possible to indicate that one strategy will be more effective in all instances. There is, however, growing evidence that suggests that the strategy of adjusting products and marketing programs to the various segments within a market can result in the greatest sales in most instances. However, whether this strategy also

[7]P. Kotler, pp. 182–187.

results in the greatest organizational profit remains to be determined.

As indicated previously, the issue that has troubled market analysts has been the identification of market segments. The primary methods that consumer analysts have used to identify consumer segments fall into the following classes: geographic, demographic, psychological, and consumer usage. The appropriateness of a particular consideration varies among products and markets. For example, while demographic considerations might be particularly effective in identifying the various segments for ski equipment, it might be an ineffective consideration for segmenting the market for automobiles.

Geographic Segmentation

Geographic segmentation can be an appropriate strategy if the consumer analyst has identified distinctive consumer preferences among various geographic areas. Geographic considerations serve as the basis for developing distinctive marketing programs for products such as ski equipment, boating equipment, warm clothing, and numerous other products. The Ford Motor Company, for example, has recently started selling its small cars in California with added options at no extra cost. This is a deliberate attempt by Ford to respond to the distinctive buying patterns of the California market where imports constitute about 40 percent of all auto sales.[8]

Geographic differences in consumer preferences have also served as the basis for a segmentation strategy implemented by the Procter & Gamble Company. Procter & Gamble observed that consumers residing in the western part of the United States had distinctive preferences for coffee. In particular, these consumers preferred stronger coffee, and a significantly higher proportion of them drank their coffee black. Procter & Gamble responded to these distinctive consumer preferences by developing a special blend of Folger's coffee and developed a promotional strategy focusing on this segment that produced high consumer acceptance for their product.[9]

[8]"Quite a Difference From Last Year," *Business Week* (October 27, 1975), pp. 25–26.

[9]D. T. Kollat, R. D. Blackwell and J. R. Robeson, *Strategic Marketing* (New York: Holt, Rinehart and Winston, Inc., 1972), p. 189.

Demographic Segmentation

Demographic variables such as age, income, sex, and level of education are perhaps the most frequently used bases for market segmentation. The popularity of using demographic variables is attributable to the observed relationship between the consumption of certain products and certain demographic variables. The consumption of pipe tobacco is highly related to sex, whereas the consumption of furs is highly related to income. Yardley of London, using age as a segmentation variable, developed a marketing program that focused on the distinctive preferences of the youth segment. As a result, they experienced a marked increase in sales and assumed a dominant position in the youth market. The youth market has also yielded substantial profits to a number of life insurance companies that recognized the distinctive preferences of these consumers and developed their marketing programs to satisfy these preferences.

Demographic variables can be used to identify the segment that is more likely to purchase a certain product or respond to certain marketing efforts. For example, homeowners are more likely to purchase house paint; households with babies are more likely to purchase baby food; and people over 55 are more likely to purchase condominiums. Even though demographic variables can, of themselves, indicate some market differences in consumer preferences and purchase behavior, demographic variables considered separately are of limited value to the marketing strategist.

Psychological Segmentation

Psychological segmentation involves the use of such variables as personality, attitudes, and life-styles to identify distinctive segments on which to focus marketing efforts. Attempts by consumer analysts to identify useful relationships between consumer behavior and standardized personality inventories have not produced encouraging results. However, as suggested in Chapter 7, personality variables can, when appropriately used, be of considerable benefit.

Life-style—a conceptualization of a consumer's attitudes, interests, and opinions—has added a rich dimension to consumer analysts' efforts to identify useful bases for market segmentation. Life-style is the orientation to self, others, and society that the consumer develops. Consumer analysts typically identify consumer life-styles by means of attitude, interest, and opinion (AIO) inventories that include the following types of questions: "I like parties where there is lots of music and talk" and "A good mother will not serve her family TV dinners." The life-style concept was very effective in identifying two distinct segments for ready-to-eat, carry-out fried chicken.[10] The two segments consumer analysts identified were the "young, active, working housewife" segment and the "older mother with children" segment. Once these segments have been identified, the marketing strategist can develop promotional programs that focus specifically on these segments.

Consumer Usage Segmentation

Consumer usage has been a particularly effective basis for segmenting markets. Market segments have been effectively identified on the basis of variations in quantity used and in benefits derived. The Quaker Oats company, for example, found that the heavy users of its dry breakfast cereal had a number of distinguishing characteristics. The identification of distinctive characteristics of various volume segments enabled the company to specifically identify the target market and more accurately focus its marketing efforts on those target markets.[11]

Consumer analysts have determined that market segments can also be identified by the benefits that consumers derive from a particular product. Benefit segmentation requires that the marketing analyst identify the various benefits that consumers seek from a particular product. For example, the benefits consumers seek in toothpaste might be taste, bright teeth, low price, and decay prevention. After identifying the benefit segments, the marketing analyst must determine if any demographic, geographic, or psychological differences exist between the various segments. There is, for example, some indication that consum-

[10]D. J. Tigert, R. Lathrope, and M. Bleeg, "The Fast Food Franchise: Psychographic and Demographic Segmentation Analysis," *Journal of Retailing,* 47 (Spring, 1971), pp. 81–90.
[11]P. Kotler, p. 174.

ers concerned with bright teeth are frequently single and that those concerned with decay prevention have large families.[12]

Benefit segmentation proved to be particularly valuable for Beecham's marketing program for Macleans toothpaste.[13] In the early 1960's Crest and Gleem had 70 percent of the toothpaste market, the remaining 30 percent shared by all other brands. Beecham's analysis of the market indicated that virtually all brands emphasized the decay preventive benefit of their toothpaste. Furthermore, their research indicated that decay prevention was the benefit preferred by the overwhelming majority of consumers. There was, however, a sizable segment that was interested in the bright teeth benefit. The identification of this segment and the fact that Macleans rated high on the bright teeth product feature caused Beecham to adopt a new marketing strategy. The strategy adopted, which focused on the market segment concerned with bright teeth, resulted in a substantial increase in market share for Macleans.

EVALUATING MARKET SEGMENTS

Market segmentation provides the marketing strategist with considerable direction in his efforts to increase consumer satisfaction and firm profit. An understanding of consumer decision processes is essential to the development of effective marketing programs that focus on particular market segments. As illustrated in the preceding section, an understanding of consumer behavior enables the marketing analyst to identify market segments with distinctive preferences or behavioral patterns and then develop marketing programs that focus on those segments.

The decision to adopt a particular segmentation strategy toward the market or the decision to focus on a particular market segment must encompass a number of considerations in addition to the identification of distinctive consumer preferences. The marketing strategist must also consider the implications any segmentation strategy has with respect to firm resources, other firm

[12]P. Kotler, p. 173.
[13]D. T. Kollat, R. D. Blackwell and J. F. Robeson, p. 191.

products, and firm competitors. The impact that these consider-ations have on the firm's ability to provide consumer satisfaction while earning a satisfactory profit must be evaluated prior to implementing any segmentation strategy.

Product Development

Marketing managers are in general agreement that product de-velopment decisions, particularly new product decisions, have a tremendous impact on organizational profit. Several studies have indicated that many firms earn as much as 50 percent of their profit from products developed in the last decade.[14] Product decisions are particularly important because these decisions commit the firm's resources to a specific direction that affects every aspect of the marketing function. Product decisions pro-vide the basis for the decisions made regarding price, promotion, and distribution. Consequently, product decisions must be made with a clear understanding of the firm's objectives and with a thorough understanding of consumer behavior. An under-standing of consumer behavior is vital to product decisions because marketing strategists now recognize that the sociopsy-chological dimensions of products are frequently as important as the product's physical characteristics.

PRODUCT LIFE CYCLE

The product life cycle concept has been developed by marketing analysts to describe the generalized pattern of sales and profit that products follow over time. This generalized pattern of sales and profit has been described as distinct stages in the life of a product. Each stage provides the marketing strategist with differ-ent opportunities and problems. Identifying the stage a product is in enables the marketing strategist to focus marketing efforts to assure consumer satisfaction and firm profit. Such adjustment

[14]R. W. Van Camp, "Essential Elements for New Product Success," in *New Product Development*, J. O. Eastlack, Jr., ed. (Chicago, American Marketing Association, 1968), p. 3.

of marketing efforts is only possible if the marketing strategist understands the distinctive consumer preferences that emerge in each stage.

The product life cycle is typically characterized as consisting of four stages: introduction, growth, maturity, and decline. The sales and profit patterns for these four stages are presented in Figure 15.1. The exact shape and length of the product life cycle varies substantially, but most products actually go through such a cycle. Examination of the product life cycle, as illustrated in Figure 15.1, suggests that marketing managers would prefer to get a product through the introductory stage as fast as possible and to prolong the growth and maturity stages as long as possible. The efficiency with which a marketing manager can do so depends upon factors such as the competition, technology, promotional efforts, and understanding of consumer behavior.

The minicalculator provides an excellent example of a product life cycle characterized by a short introductory stage and prolonged growth and maturity stages. Minicalculators were introduced in the consumer market less than five years ago. The introductory stage was characterized by high prices, high promotional expenditures, and few competitors. However, well-focused marketing efforts and some technological improvements pushed minicalculators through the introductory stage and into the growth stage in a few short months. The minicalculator's growth stage was characterized by high prices, high promotional expenditures, increases in the number of competitors, major production improvements, and development of other market segments. The

FIGURE 15.1.
The Product Life Cycle Concept

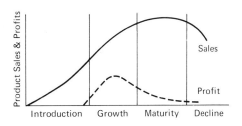

maturity stage for minicalculators is now characterized by excess supply capabilities, falling prices, private brands entering the market, declining margins, and some reduction in the number of brands carried by middlemen. The future in producing minicalculators depends on the firm's ability to adjust to the product life cycle in one of the following ways:[15]

1. Generating more frequent usage of the minicalculator among present users
2. Developing more varied usage among present users of minicalculators
3. Identifying and nurturing new users of minicalculators
4. Identifying and encouraging new uses for minicalculators.

The effectiveness with which a firm implements any of these strategies is directly dependent on its understanding of consumer decision making. For example, many a household financial officer would willingly spend $20 for a minicalculator to expedite the check-balancing process. Developing this market, however, may require a specially designed calculator and well-focused promotion efforts.

NEW PRODUCT DEVELOPMENT

New products have a profound impact on corporate profit and growth and, consequently, are of primary importance to the marketing strategist. A product's profit margin declines early in the product's life cycle (growth stage), meaning that profits can be sustained only by continuously introducing new products. In other words, a company must systematically introduce new products to maintain or increase profits. Furthermore, as the product life cycle continues to shorten, profits can be sustained in the long run only by a continuing flow of successful new products not only to sustain sales volume but also to sustain and increase profits. Continuous innovation of new products, however, is extremely risky because of the high incidence of new product failures. The estimates of new product failures range from 33

[15]T. Levitt, "Exploit the Product Life Cycle," *Harvard Business Review* (November–December, 1965), p. 93.

percent[16] to 89 percent[17] and can involve millions of dollars. For example, in the late 1960's seventeen new brands of household cleaners were introduced in a nine-month period. Brands like Easy-off, Clean & Kill, Whistle, Power-on and others produced an estimated loss of approximately $17 million.[18] About this same time several new brands of mouthwash, including Fact, Vote, Cue, Reef, and others, resulted in a combined loss of over $40 million.

Despite the frequency and magnitude of losses resulting from new product development, marketing strategists continue to espouse the importance of continually developing new products. This view is typically supported by long lists of successful new products that contribute substantially to firm profits. The dilemma that the high failure rate–high profit rate creates has stimulated considerable interest in a research tradition known as *diffusion of innovations,* the premise being that an understanding of the diffusion of innovations would enable the marketing strategist to enhance the success of new products introduced to the market.

Diffusion of Innovation

Consumer's responses to new products follow a somewhat predictable pattern frequently referred to as the *diffusion process.* The diffusion of innovations refers to "the spread of an idea from its source of invention or creation to its ultimate users or adopters."[19]

The central concept of the diffusion process is that of innovation. *Innovation* has been defined most frequently as any idea or product that is perceived by the potential innovator to be new. Marketing strategists consider an innovation to be any product that has been recently introduced into a market. Thus, the following would all be considered innovations: (1) the new model cars, (2) a new deodorant, (3) an existing deodorant in a new package or with a different scent, (4) the minicalculator in an untapped

[16]"Management of New Products," 4th ed. (New York: Booz, Allen & Hamilton, Inc., 1965), p. 11.

[17]B. Schorr, "Many New Products Fizzle, Despite Careful Planning, Publicity," *Wall Street Journal* (April 5, 1961), p. 1.

[18]T. L. Angeleus, "Why Do Most New Products Fail?" *Advertising Age* (March 24, 1969), pp. 85–86.

[19]E. Rodgers, *Diffusion of Innovations* (New York: Free Press, 1962), pp. 12–20.

market, and (5) cable television in a new geographic area. As is apparent from the preceding examples, the opportunities to innovate new products and services are nearly boundless.

The marketing strategist's innovations vary substantially in terms of impact. Some innovations, such as cigarettes and soft drinks, have little impact on the existing consumption patterns of consumers, whereas some new products and services, such as minicalculators and automatic dishwashers, can result in a modification in consumption behavior. A few products, such as television and air travel, can produce major adjustments in consumer purchase patterns. The appropriate marketing strategy for any new product depends on the disruption that product will have on existing consumer purchase patterns.

The Consumer Adoption Process

Consumer analysts' efforts to achieve an understanding of how consumers decide to adopt a new product have resulted in the conceptualization of this decision as a series of stages. A variety of conceptual schemes have been developed and tested to accurately characterize the adoption process. The following stages and definitions are common to most conceptualizations of the consumer adoption process:

1. *Awareness.* The consumer knows about the new product but lacks sufficient information about it.
2. *Interest.* The consumer becomes interested in the new product and begins to seek information about it.
3. *Evaluation.* The consumer makes a mental assessment of whether or not the new product will benefit him or her now or in the future and decides either to try it or not try it.
4. *Trial.* The consumer purchases the new product to determine whether or not it provides the anticipated benefit.
5. *Adoption.* The consumer accepts the new product and commits himself to using it regularly.

The adoption decision-process model presented in Figure 15.2 reflects the current conceptualization of consumer analysts. This model is based on the information-attitude-behavior conceptualization and reflects the most widely accepted view of how

FIGURE 15.2.
Summary Adoption Decision-Process Model.

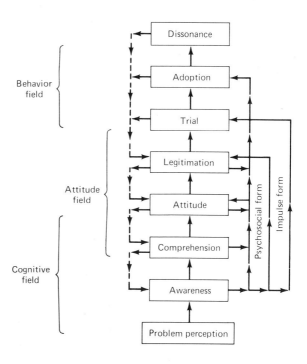

Source: T. S. Robertson, "A Critical Examination of Adoption Process Models of Consumer Behavior," in *Models of Buyer Behavior,* J. N. Sheth, ed. (New York: Harper & Row, Publishers, 1974), p. 290.

promotion functions.[20] The *problem perception* stage is not the typical beginning of the adoption process but can at times initiate the process. For example, a consumer's recognition of a problem with his or her current tennis equipment can produce the search and alternative evaluation that can result in awareness of graphite rackets. The typical beginning of the adoption process—consumer *awareness*—is the point at which a product stimulus

[20]T. S. Robertson, "A Critical Examination of 'Adoption Process' Models of Consumer Behavior," in *Models of Buyer Behavior,* J. N. Sheth, ed. (New York: Harper & Row, Publishers, 1974), pp. 271–295. Reprinted by permission of publisher.

penetrates the consumer's filtration system and registers with the consumer. In other words, the consumer recognizes that the product exists. The information processing stages—awareness and comprehension—comprise the cognitive field of the adoption process. *Comprehension* is the consumer's understanding of what a product is and how it performs. The manner in which a consumer processes information is determined by that consumer's abilities. Certain consumers assimilate information more rapidly and thoroughly than do others.

The *attitude* stage refers to the consumer's predisposition to evaluate a product in a favorable or unfavorable manner. Although some exceptions can occur, normally a consumer must have a favorable evaluation of a product for the adoption process to continue. However, a favorable attitude toward a product does not assure that product trial will occur. In order for trial to occur, the consumer must have a favorable attitude toward the product and must be convinced that purchase of the product is the appropriate course of action. Thus, the *legitimization* stage requires that the consumer be convinced that the new product is socially appropriate, properly priced, and, in general, meets the basic evaluative criteria. As is evident from Figure 15.2, the comprehension, attitude, and legitimization stages make up the attitude field of the adoption process.

The behavior field includes the legitimization, trial, and adoption stages of the adoption process. *Trial* is the actual use of a product on a rather limited scale. Thus, the initial use of a new product might indicate that the consumer has evaluated a product by means of first-hand experience or an actual commitment to a product. In the final stage—*adoption*—the consumer has evaluated the product favorably and has decided to purchase and/or use the product on a regular basis. In certain instances the decision to adopt a particular product requires the consumer to choose from several desirable alternatives. Because the consumer has decided to adopt one alternative in lieu of several others, he or she might experience *cognitive dissonance,* which is psychologically uncomfortable. Normally, consumers attempt to reduce this dissonance by obtaining information supporting their decision, obtaining social support, or in some other manner reestablishing consonance.

This model emphasizes the fact that the adoption process can take many different forms. The rational decision-making form of the adoption process would include all the stages from awareness to adoption. The impulse form refers to the adoption process that goes directly from awareness to trial, thereby omitting the comprehension, attitude, and legitimation stages. The adoption process can also take a third form—psychosocial—in which the consumer skips the comprehension and attitude stages. Numerous factors such as social characteristics, personality characteristics, and the perceived characteristics of the innovation determine the form the adoption process will take.

Knowledge of the form the adoption process will take can be of substantial benefit to the marketer of a new product. For example, if the marketing strategist knows that the adoption process that consumers or a particular segment of consumers would engage in was the impulse form, marketing efforts can be allocated accordingly. In other words, marketing strategy could exclude any efforts designed to promote comprehension, attitude change, or legitimization. On the other hand, if the rational decision-making form prevails, marketing efforts will have to focus on moving the consumer through all stages of the adoption process.

Using the Consumer Adoption Process

An understanding of the consumer adoption process can facilitate the marketing manager's decision making substantially. For example, consider the marketing manager's difficulty in predicting sales: Does a substantial early adoption of a product mean that sales will be great or does it mean that a particular segment, perhaps a small one, is highly interested in the product? Conversely, low sales of a new product might indicate low potential sales or an ineffective promotional program. These difficulties can be overcome by using the adoption process.[21]

Consider the classification of consumers by stage of the adoption process for an actual product as summarized in Table 15.1. A comparison of the adoption figure from January (3 percent) to June (10 percent) suggests that the new product being considered will be extremely successful. However, if the progress for all

[21]T. S. Robertson, p. 293.

TABLE 15.1

Classification of Consumers by Stage of the Adoption Process

Cumulative Percentage of Consumers

Adoption Stage	January 1976	June 1976	Change (January–June)
Adoption	3	10	7
Trial	10	14	4
Legitimation	16	18	2
Favorable Attitude	25	30	5
Knowledge	45	70	25
Awareness	55	85	30

Source: Adapted from T. S. Robertson, "A Critical Examination of 'Adoption Process' Models of Consumer Behavior" in *Models of Buyer Behavior,* J. N. Sheth, ed. (New York: Harper & Row, Publishers, 1974), p. 293. Reprinted by permission of publisher.

stages of the adoption process are examined, the situation is not nearly as favorable. During this six-month period, the level of awareness and knowledge has been increased substantially. Unfortunately, the firm's marketing efforts have been relatively unsuccessful in developing favorable attitudes and in advancing legitimation. This indicates that sales will soon level off because the firm's marketing efforts are not moving the consumer toward adoption. This stabilization of sales could be the result of ineffective or poorly focused promotional efforts. An alternative explanation might be that the market for this new product is small but quickly penetrated. Regardless of the actual reason, the marketing manager can correctly anticipate the progress of a new product and make the necessary changes in marketing effort.

Identifying Innovativeness
Consumer analysts have for some time attempted to identify consumers who adopt new products and services early. Interest in identifying innovators is based on the premise that such information would permit the development of new products that are compatible with the preferences of innovators. In other words, even though all consumers pass through the stages of the adop-

tion process, some consumers adopt the product much sooner than do others.

The diffusion is typically depicted as a cumulative normal distribution such as that shown in Figure 15.3. Initially a product is adopted by a few consumers, and then the number of adopters increases rapidly. Finally, the number of adopters reaches a peak and then diminishes as fewer individuals remain in the nonadopter category. Typically, the first 2.5 percent of consumers to adopt a product are called innovators, the next 13.5 percent are called early adopters, and so on.

Considerable effort has been expended to identify variables that are associated with these consumers. The groups of variables that have been identified as having a particularly pronounced effect on the adoption rate are consumer characteristics and product characteristics. The efforts of consumer analysts to associate innovativeness with consumer characteristics have produced several useful results. In particular, innovativeness has been found to be positively associated with education, income, level of living, aspirations for children, attitude toward change, knowledge of the world and events in general, social status, mobility, and venturesomeness.[22] For example, a study of the diffusion of a new automobile service found that the

FIGURE 15.3.
The Diffusion Process

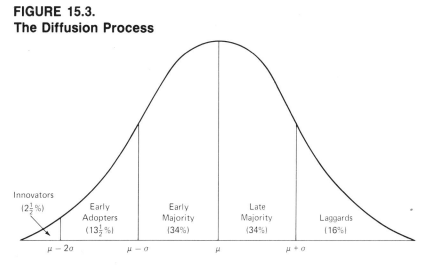

[22]T. S. Robertson, *Innovative Behavior and Communication* (New York: Holt, Rinehart and Winston, Inc., 1974), Chapter 5.

earliest adopters, compared to the population as a whole, were found to be:[23]

1. Much more willing to experiment with new ideas
2. More likely to buy new products (in general) earlier
3. Less likely to switch brands because of a small price change
4. Less interested in low prices per se
5. Less likely to try new convenience items if the innovation represented only minor changes.

Furthermore, innovators were the best-informed segment of the population and engaged in considerable planning before purchasing new products. An understanding of the characteristics of innovators enables the marketing manager to direct the firm's communications to those consumers who are likely to adopt the innovation, thus increasing the effectiveness of promotional efforts.

Consumer analysts have also determined that the acceptance of a new product by innovators is determined to a large degree by the characteristics of the product itself. The product characteristics that seem to have the greatest effect on the adoption rate of a new product are:[24]

1. *Relative advantage.* The greater the relative advantage of a new product—the more superior it is to the product it replaces—the more quickly it will be adopted.

2. *Compatibility.* The compatibility of a new product is the degree to which the product is consistent with the existing values and experiences of consumers. The more compatible products are with favorably held values, the more quickly they will be adopted. A new product's color, design, packaging, and related promotional materials act as a symbol to the consumer, communicating to him the compatibility of the new product with his existing values.

3. *Complexity.* The complexity of a product is the degree to which a new product is difficult to understand and use. New

[23]R. J. Kegerris, J. F. Engel, and R. D. Blackwell, "Innovativeness and Diffusiveness: A Marketing View of the Characteristics of Earliest Adopters," in *Research in Consumer Behavior,* D. Kollat, R. D. Blackwell, and J. F. Engel, eds. (New York: Holt, Rinehart and Winston, Inc., 1970), pp. 671–689.

[24]E. M. Rodgers and F. F. Shoemaker, *Communication of Innovation* (New York: Free Press, 1971), pp. 137–157.

products that require detailed personal explanation, for example, are likely to diffuse slowly. Marketing managers introducing complex new products must develop a means of stimulating product trial in order to increase the rate of consumer acceptance.

4. *Communicability.* Communicability is the degree to which the benefits of product use can be communicated to others. Products that are visible in social situations or that lend themselves better to demonstration or description are likely to have a faster rate of adoption.

The preceding generalizations suggest that the marketing manager can affect the rate of new product adoption. For example, the marketer can design a new product to specifically enhance its relative advantage over existing products, maximize compatibility with consumer values and experiences, and maximize the communicability of product benefits while minimizing product complexity. Typically the marketing manager must be willing to make certain concessions with respect to product design. For example, transacting banking business by means of consumer-computer interaction (e.g., Automatic Teller Machines, Point-of-Sale Terminals) provides communicable advantages over existing products but is somewhat inconsistent with consumers' values and experiences. Consequently, the adoption of computer-based consumer banking transactions is likely to be slow.

The generalizations regarding the effects of product characteristics on the adoption rate of new products can also provide considerable direction for the innovating firm's promotional efforts. Promotional efforts must be designed to effectively communicate the product's relative benefits. These benefits must be communicated in a manner that reflects the target market's values and that deemphasizes the product's complexity.

Summary

This chapter demonstrates how an understanding of consumer behavior facilitates decision making in two selected applications—market segmentation and product development. Kotler refers to market segmentation as the "subdividing of a market into homogeneous subsets of customers, where any subset may conceivably be selected as a market target to be reached with a distinct marketing mix." The primary consumer market segmentation methods are geographic, demographic, psychological, and consumer usage. Geographic segmentation is appropriate when distinctive consumer preferences can be identified among various geographic areas. Segmentation using demographic variables such as age, income, and sex is useful when consumption of certain products can be associated with one or several of these variables. When the marketer uses variables such as personality, attitudes, and life-styles to identify portions of the market on which to focus her or his efforts, she or he is using psychological segmentation. Consumer usage segmentation is effective for particular products when variations are identifiable by quantity used and benefits derived. The marketing segmentation strategy chosen must be evaluated in view of the firm's resources, other products, and competitors.

An understanding of consumer behavior is vital to product development decisions. An important factor in the marketer's ability to prolong the growth and maturity stages of the product life cycle is the understanding of consumer behavior during these periods. Also, because of the combined high profit–high failure rate characteristics of new product development, increased emphasis has been placed on the area known as *diffusion of innovations.* Rodgers refers to the diffusion of innovations as "the spread of an idea from its source of invention or creation to its ultimate users or adopters." The summary adoption decision-process model reflects current thought in the area via cognitive, attitude, and behavior fields. Understanding this process and the several forms that it can take can substantially benefit the new product marketer. Identifying the innovators in new product adoption enhances the marketer's ability to develop products compatible with the innovators and also to increase the effectiveness of promotional efforts.

1. What is market segmentation? What factors have contributed to the increased use of market segmentation strategies by marketing managers?
2. Which of the three strategies for identifying markets (i.e., undifferentiated, differentiated, and concentrated) would seem to be most appropriate for each of the following products:

   a. Automobiles
   b. Women's casual clothes
   c. Banking services
   d. College education
   e. Cigarettes
   f. Sporting equipment

3. Consider the appropriateness of the various means of identifying consumer segments for each product in Question 2.
4. Evaluate the following statement: "Geographic, demographic, and psychological considerations are intellectually gratifying, but benefit segmentation is the only useful basis for segmenting the market."
5. Describe the four stages of the product life cycle. What are the implications of each PLC stage for the marketing manager? What are the implications for the Consumer Product Safety Commission?
6. Which stage of the PLC are the following products currently in:

   a. Electric car
   b. Cable television
   c. Window home air conditioning
   d. Digital watches
   e. Wire eyeglass frames

6. Identify the implications the stage of PLC has for the marketing manager for each of these products.
7. Describe in detail how an understanding of the diffusion process might help the product manager for G & D radar ranges.
8. Explain the consumer adoption process. What are the particular strengths and weaknesses of the summary decision-process model presented in Figure 15.2?

9. The Solar Company has recently developed a home heating system that stores solar energy for home heating. Describe the diffusion process for this product. Develop a marketing strategy that will enable the company to accomplish the diffusion.

10. A large manufacturer of drug and personal grooming products has recently introduced a new men's hair conditioner. The conditioner must be applied immediately after shampooing while the hair is still wet. The manufacturer recommends that the conditioner be rinsed out between 3–8 minutes after application. Who would you identify for the company as the most likely innovators of this product? What appeals would you suggest be used in promoting the product?

SITUATIONAL PROBLEMS

Case 1

In 1966 Duncan McClure, music enthusiast, owner of a valuable record collection, and basement scientist, set out to develop a better method of cleaning phonograph records. The methods available left oil residue on the records which reduced the sound quality, shortened the record's life expectancy, and ultimately damaged the cartridge. After numerous attempts, McClure developed a procedure involving a chemical solution and plastic applicator that had none of the limitations of other cleaning methods. During the following ten years, McClure marketed the product to exclusive record shops throughout the world. The record cleaner, which retailed for $55, was well received by record collectors and music enthusiasts concerned about quality sound. McClure, although surprised by the product's initial success, adjusted his life-style to the financial success he experienced. Understandably, then, McClure became quite concerned when sales declined markedly in mid 1976. Determined to reverse the sales decline, McClure hired a marketing consultant who, after careful analysis, reported that the segmentation strategy adopted in 1966 had ceased to be appropriate. He recommended that McClure identify alternative market segments and design variations of his record cleaner to appeal to these segments.

What type of segmentation strategy did McClure initially employ? Was the strategy appropriate?

How might McClure identify distinctive consumer preferences in order to focus on alternative market segments?

Case 2

American Mopeds, a company formed in 1975 to produce and distribute motorized bicycles, is currently developing a marketing program which they hope will make them the leader in the moped industry. Unlike motorcycles, mopeds must be pedaled in order to get started, but once started they can easily attain speeds of 30 miles per hour. Mopeds weigh between 50 and 100 pounds, get 200 miles per gallon, and cost between $300 and $500. Mopeds are also quieter than motorcycles and automobiles. Mopeds have been extensively used in Europe, Bermuda, and the Caribbean but only became legal for sale in the U.S. in 1975. Prior to 1975 mopeds failed to meet the federal government's safety standards. American Moped's management have identified the following as the primary reasons for the optimism surrounding the introduction of mopeds: (1) the energy shortage, (2) the economic recession, (3) inflation, particularly in the area of private transportation, and (4) the concern for clean air. So far, only ten states have legalized the moped for use on their highways, but American Moped's management is optimistic that the remaining 40 states will soon approve their use. Research has indicated that 50 percent of the American work force live within five miles of work, a fact that American Moped's management contends will virtually guarantee immediate success.

How might an understanding of the consumer adoption process aid the management of American Mopeds?

Who are the likely innovators and early adopters of mopeds? How might the management of American Mopeds affect the rate of adoption of mopeds?

The Future of Consumer Behavior

After having covered a considerable number of topics and issues, we will take the opportunity in this last chapter to again bring into perspective the total thrust of consumer behavior as an area of study and to identify the new directions in which the discipline is moving. With these two objectives in mind, we have divided the chapter into three major parts. The first pays specific attention to consumer behavior as a field of study—the directions it has taken and the prospects for the future. The second part of the chapter presents a number of examples of emerging applications of consumer behavior analysis. These include two issues of special interest—consumerism and shopping as a behavioral pattern—and two markets that offer unique opportunities—the youth market and the black middle class. The third and last part of the chapter discusses what appears to be the most promising approach to furthering the understanding of consumer behavior.

Consumer Behavior as a Field of Study

The objective of consumer behavior is to understand, explain, and predict actions taken by individuals or small groups, such as the family, in their consumption of goods and services. A great deal of progress has been made in realizing this basic objective. Admittedly, no general or grand theory of consumer behavior exists; consequently, individual buyer behavior is not fully understood. Therefore, much work remains to be done, and considerable numbers of talented analysts will be needed. It is likely that a major share of this further study of consumers will be done by business.

CONSUMER BEHAVIOR AS A SCIENCE

Despite existing shortcomings, consumer behavior has gained considerable respectability and has even been called a science by some. In relation to this latter point, note that the field has centered around empirical research that for the most part has been carried out using scientific methods. The field of consumer behavior also meets the requirements that differentiate a science from other kinds of investigations. These include the following:[1]

1. A science is general and conceptual. Many consumer analysts have sought to study fundamental behavioral issues that have wide applications. These have included topics such as information search, decision making, and postpurchase evaluation.

2. A science is founded on controlled observation. By using carefully designed studies, the consumer researcher can identify and analyze individual behavioral patterns. These are illustrated by ad readership studies and the analysis of specific product purchase patterns, such as seasonal buying, multiple purchases, and the study of brand switching.

3. A science is oriented toward prediction. Any field of inquiry that has been closely related to business practices would quite naturally be oriented toward prediction. Because of their interest in generating profitable sales, business managers are very concerned with forecasting the consequences of particular actions. For example, they are likely to want to know the consequences of increasing their sales force by 10 percent, changing a package design, increasing a product's price, or shortening a warranty period. As a result of these interests, consumer analysts have often attempted to predict consumer reaction to changes in certain business tactics.

4. A science seeks causal connections. Throughout this book, the concern for determining interrelationships among key variables has been stressed. This has included knowing how learning influences consumer behavior and how cultural differences shape one's evaluative criteria.

5. A science strives for explicit explanations of events as well as closure. In consumer behavior, explanations are sought for various behavioral patterns with specific emphasis on the completeness of these. The use of models such as those developed by Engel, Kollat, and Blackwell and Howard and Sheth is an example of the interest in obtaining a comprehensive view of the purchasing process.

[1]T. S. Robertson and S. Ward, "Consumer Behavior Research: Promise and Prospects," in *Consumer Behavior: Theoretical Sources,* S. Ward and T. S. Robertson, eds. (Englewood Cliffs, New Jersey: Prentice-Hall, Inc., 1973), p. 7.

In explaining how scientific inquiry has been used to study the behavioral patterns of consumers, a number of examples have been used throughout the book that focus on the experiences or behavior of individual consumers in a given market setting. Nevertheless, consumer behavior must deal with aggregates; that is, it is important to keep in mind that any individual consumer is only relevant as a unit of analysis insofar as that person is representative of the individuals who make up a larger market.[2] In day-to-day transactions, business, government, and nonprofit organizations should be very interested in the welfare of each individual consumer with whom they deal, but in their strategy development, these organizations must focus on behavioral patterns that are common to members of various groups. For example, the purchase pattern followed by a particular family in buying a new home is only of interest to the consumer analyst and marketing manager if this pattern is reasonably similar to those of a sizable number of other families making a comparable purchase.

The dominance of marketing interests in the systematic analysis of consumer behavior is evident throughout the book. The following section explores the circumstances that have nurtured this interest.

THE MARKETER'S INTEREST IN CONSUMER BEHAVIOR

As early as Chapter 1, it was noted that even though the study of consumer behavior has much to offer other fields, the greatest interest in it has come from those in marketing. It is appropriate at this time to give some further indication as to why this has been true and what the prospects are for the future. There appear to be three primary reasons why marketing practitioners take an active interest in consumer behavior.[3] These are summarized below.

1. Some view marketing itself as a relatively advanced art and see the study of consumer behavior as a means of "fine tuning" marketing practices. If, for example, added information about

[2]F. Hansen, *Consumer Choice Behavior* (New York: The Free Press, 1972), p. 6.
[3]T. S. Robertson and S. Ward, p. 8.

consumer behavior is useful in marketing strategy decisions that result in only a one or two percentage point shift in market share, such study could be a very meaningful contribution to profit. To illustrate this, think of the $2.6 billion soft drink market in the United States. Coca-Cola and Pepsi account for 55 percent of the market, followed by 7-Up (7 percent), Royal Crown (6 percent), and Dr. Pepper (5 percent). Coke and Pepsi together spend over $130 million annually for advertising in an effort to maintain their dominant positions. Both of these firms have taken seriously Dr. Pepper's objective of being number one by the year 2000 and appear to be intent on preventing even small inroads into their respective market shares.[4]

2. Increasingly more often firms are being called on by various critics and regulatory bodies to explain the bases and implications of their actions. Information gained through an analysis of consumer behavior can be used to meet these demands. For example, some critics may challenge Kraft Foods' claims for their new Golden Image imitation colby cheese. Reportedly retail shelf pamphlets say that "Golden Image . . . looks, cooks and tastes just like natural colby cheese. . . . "[5] The proof of claims such as this one comes only through consumer analysis.

3. In a dynamic environment business firms are finding traditional descriptive marketing research less and less useful. What is being sought more often is an understanding of market events, which can only be obtained through a full explanation of such events. For instance, it is not enough to know that a recent study showed that 69 percent of 3,800 women interviewed in five market areas ate at least one evening meal in a restaurant every month. Or that only 18 percent of these women chose a restaurant in their own neighborhood for these outings, while 55 percent always made a point to eat outside their neighborhood.[6] It is the underlying explanation of these circumstances—what led to these behavioral patterns—that will be most helpful in management decision making.

[4]"Dr. Pepper: Pitted Against the Soft-Drink Giants," *Business Week* (October 6, 1975), p. 70.

[5]L. Edwards, "Kraft testing first imitation colby cheese," *Advertising Age,* 46 (September 15, 1975), p. 1.

[6]"Adbeat," *Advertising age,* 46 (September 22, 1975), p. 70.

Although marketing practitioners have shown the greatest interest in consumer behavior, there appears to be a trend toward wider usage. The next section identifies three areas of application that support the observation that there is a broadening of the horizons of consumer behavior taking place.

FURTHER APPLICATIONS ARE LIKELY

There appears to be a growing realization of the need for undertaking the study of consumer behavior as it relates to public policy development and implementation, social and environmental problems, and cross-cultural interests.[7] Each of these applications holds considerable promise and is described in the next few paragraphs with an explanation of why it is a likely prospect for consumer analysis.

Public Policy Development and Implementation

One of the most pressing reasons for studying consumer behavior in this context is the growing dissatisfaction with the use of microeconomic concepts to guide regulatory processes. These traditional economic concepts and their accompanying models do not offer much insight into consumer actions, consequently, without further assistance, considerable regulation will be founded on little more than intuitive judgment as to how it will affect consumers.

As some agencies attempt to move away from a case-by-case procedure in carrying out their duties, operational guidelines are being developed and imposed on businesses. The market consequences of these actions must be evaluated in terms of their effect on the consumer. Former FTC Commissioner Mayo Thompson made some specific comments with respect to his displeasure concerning one such situation.

The case in point was an industry-wide investigation of growers, wholesalers, and retailers of indoor and outdoor plants in which Thompson called upon the Commission to think in terms of the economic costs and benefits that could be expected from issuing guidelines for product information. Recognition of this

[7]J. N. Sheth, *Models of Buyer Behavior: Conceptual, Quantitative, and Empirical* (New York: Harper & Row, Publishers, 1974), pp. 400–402.

need for guidelines arose as the Commission sought to determine if the distributors involved were in violation of the FTC Act because of their failure to provide toxicity and care information concerning the plants they sell. In a dissenting statement, Commissioner Thompson said:

> This is not a case of deceptive advertising or one involving any of the various other varieties of economic rustling that our law and public policy so rightly condemn. . . . In substance, this agency has decided that the level of agricultural education among home gardeners is not sufficiently high to permit successful gardening. . . . We are going to tell the country's greenthumbers how often their plants need watering, how much and what kind of fertilizer they need, the kind of soil they require, the amount of sunshine they thrive best on, and—one trembles to say it—perhaps the kind and amount of personal "talking to" they would find most pleasant and gratifying.[8]

Social and Environmental Problems

Some believe that the area of social and environmental problems is one of the most promising for application of consumer behavior because of the possible contribution to societal welfare. One example of such an application includes the study of population control through an understanding of issues such as family decision making regarding the number of children to have and underlying attitudes toward birth control and family planning.

Another pressing world problem is malnutrition, and contributions to its resolution can be made by consumer behavior. For instance, some revolutionary new foods have been developed specifically for use in underdeveloped countries. Their impressive nutritional qualities and simple availability do not assure acceptance however. The consumption patterns of the people living in underdeveloped countries must be studied to determine their food preferences in such terms as the texture or consistency of the food, its color, and aroma. Information on the food's availability, quality, and use also must be distributed. Therefore, it is critical to gain insight into consumer information processing and decision making in these environments. Population control

[8]"FTC's Deficiencies as Seen by a Commissioner, or Ham on Wry with Mayo," *The 4A Newsletter,* 15 (July 24, 1975), pp. 7–8.

and the reduction of malnutrition are only two examples of possible applications; other areas of interest include environmental pollution and the delivery of public services such as education and health care.

Cross-Cultural Interests

Historically cross-cultural research has focused on the differences that exist in behavioral patterns from one country to another. At times this has even resulted in the fostering of certain stereotypes such as the two proposed by Dichter: "Only one Frenchman out of three brushes his teeth, four out of five Germans change their shirts but once a week."[9]

With the increased multinational character of many large corporations, management has shown a growing interest in identifying similarities between countries. They are understandably eager to use marketing expertise that has been developed in one country on an international basis. In other words, wherever possible firms would like to market their products to similar markets in other parts of the world using their domestic strategy. So far, there has been little encouragement that such direct transplantation of marketing efforts will succeed.

For example, one recent exploratory study was specifically designed to determine the extent to which such similarities exist. It investigated the behavioral patterns and attitudes of working and nonworking wives in the United States and France. Attention was given to four areas: (1) grocery purchase behavior; (2) women's clothing purchases; (3) life-style and attitudinal characteristics; and (4) background characteristics.[10] The intent was to identify similarities within each of the two groups of women across these two national boundaries, that is, to determine the extent to which the behavior and attitudes of United States working wives are similar to those of French working wives and to make the same comparison between the nonworking wives' groups. The results of this limited study were not encouraging to

[9]E. Dichter, "The World Customer," *Harvard Business* Review, 40 (July–August, 1962), p. 113.

[10]S. P. Douglas, *Cross-cultural Comparisons: The Myth of the Stereotype* (Cambridge, Massachusetts: Marketing Science Institute, May, 1975), p. 3.

those interested in developing universal marketing strategies. The results appear to further uphold the significant impact of cultural factors. Two of the findings are identified below.[11]

1. Differences between the two countries overwhelmingly dominate differences between working and nonworking women. Thus, the specific national environment appears to play a major role in shaping the behavior patterns of consumers, and any attempt to develop a cross-national marketing strategy will require a two-tier design, involving a country-by-country approach.

2. The significance of the differences observed both between countries and between demographic groups varies with the product class. The variation was greater in relation to grocery products than clothing. This suggests that the relative importance of cross-national differences and subcultural factors varies from one product to another and should be investigated before developing multinational strategies.

These and similar findings from other studies suggest that substantial investigation of behavioral patterns is necessary if firms are considering entering foreign markets.

Examples of Emerging Applications

This section contains a potpourri of topics that illustrate the variety of issues of special interest to the consumer analyst and presents examples of markets that deserve attention because they offer unique opportunities.

ISSUES OF SPECIAL INTEREST: TWO EXAMPLES

Any number of topics could have been singled out here for use as examples of the challenges that confront the consumer analyst. The two selected give some indication of the diversity. First, contemporary consumerism is explored, followed by an examination of shopping as an activity other than the purchase of particular goods or services.

[11]S. P. Douglas, p. 20.

Contemporary Consumerism

The term consumerism has no precise, widely agreed on definition; however, most of those interested in the subject would probably concede that it includes a high level of concern for issues related to consumer welfare.[12] This encompasses such broad topics as truth-in-advertising, the protection of the health and safety of consumers through product evaluation and control, improving the quality of repair services, equitable pricing, improving product durability, and keeping the interests of the consumer before the government.

Instead of trying to trace the historical development of modern consumerism, the next few pages will focus on the characteristics of contemporary consumerism. Attention will also be given to ways in which business management can adequately respond to these issues.

Dimensions of Modern Consumerism. Consumerism today has three fundamental dimensions:[13]

1. Action taken to protect consumers from deceptive and misleading practices, hazardous products, monopolistic activities of business, and other abuses stemming from tactics—This dimension has taken shape through the establishment of new state and federal agencies charged with consumer protection, such as the Consumer Product Safety Commission, and the enactment of numerous bills that deal with various consumer matters. The following partial list of such federal acts passed during the last decade illustrates the extent of these actions.[14]

Child Protection and Safety Act
Product Safety Act
Odometer Tampering Act
Automobile Bumper Act

[12]N. Kangun, K. K. Cox, J. Higginbothan, and J. Burton, "Consumerism and Marketing Management," *Journal of Marketing,* 39 (April, 1975), p. 4.
[13]F. E. Webster, Jr., "Does Business Misunderstand Consumerism?" *Harvard Business Review,* 51 (September–October, 1973), p. 90.
[14]G. G. Udell, "A Call for a Philosophy of Consumer Rights," in *1974 Combined Proceedings,* R. C. Curhan, ed. (Chicago: American Marketing Association, 1975), p. 336.

Lead-based Paint Poisoning and Prevention Act
Public Health Cigarette Smoking Act
Egg Products Inspection Act
Interstate Land Sales Full Disclosure Act
Consumer Education Act

2. Noticeable changes in consumer attitudes and value orientations toward specific goods and services, consumption in general, affluence and materialism, and the environment— Numerous attempts have been made to measure consumer interest in and attitudes toward various aspects of consumerism. One recent study sought to identify the relative importance that three different groups place on several key issues that have generally been associated with contemporary consumerism. The exploratory research was conducted in a large southwestern city, and attitudes among university business students, nonemployed women, and businessmen were compared. Of the seven issues studied, the two that were considered most important among the students and women were product "repair and servicing" and "health and safety." The businessmen also considered product "repair and servicing" to be extremely important, but placed supplying consumer "information" and "product quality" ahead of "health and safety."[15]

According to T. L. Jones, president of the American Insurance Association, changing consumer attitudes toward such issues as those just mentioned might have an unexpected economic impact. Reportedly, Jones said that ". . . in their quest for real happiness, people have become 'lawsuit happy' and that could wreck the property and casualty insurance industry." Furthermore, ". . . a consumerist attitude that any injury should be compensated, no matter what the cause, has manifested itself in a series of government regulations and a spate of court actions that make experience—the hallmark of insurance operations— no longer a guide."[16] This can be illustrated by considering the fact that product liability suits in the United States have risen from about 50,000 in 1960 to an estimated one million in 1975.[17]

[15]N. Kangun, et. al., p. 6.
[16]" 'Lawsuit Happy' Public Called Economic Threat," *St. Louis Post Dispatch* (October 14, 1975), p. 69.
[17]" 'Lawsuit Happy' Public . . .," p. 69.

3. The political force that has developed as a result of the factors identifed above—This dimension of contemporary consumerism has taken a number of forms, for example, consumer boycotts have become a reasonably common means of expressing displeasure with business practices, and there has been an emergence of various local and state consumer organizations. Some of these consumer groups have been single purpose (e.g., the banding together of citizens to work for more adequate housing for the poor or the discovery of a common interest in their frustration with increasing food prices). A number of these organizations have generated considerable support and, consequently, have been able to bring more equity to certain markets. There has also been an increased willingness among some to support consumer advocates such as Ralph Nader.

One of the most significant factors contributing to modern consumerism is a better educated consumer. One executive summed this up at a gathering of marketing managers by reminding them that ". . . the consumer isn't some dummy, she is your wife." The significance of contemporary consumerism takes form when one realizes that better education is just one of several factors, including greater purchasing power, more discretionary income, and more sophisticated tastes, that characterize the modern consumer. Also, more than ever before, the consumer has the necessary knowledge, skills, and willingness to speak out and seek redress when treated badly in the marketplace.[18]

Business Response to Consumerism
Businesses' responses to consumerism have been mixed at best. According to one recent survey of 156 companies of the Fortune 500, ". . . planned, coordinated programs of response to consumerism are the exception, not the rule. More common are defensive, isolated responses to specific problems."[19]

One of the exceptions identified in the above study is worth noting because it illustrates what can be done. Although historically Eastman Kodak has been customer-oriented, the emergence of modern consumerism has brought about their

[18]F. E. Webster, Jr., p. 90.
[19]F. E. Webster, p. 89.

development of new programs and the upgrading of others. Several examples of their responses follow.[20]

1. A product design philosophy that tries to anticipate the customer's difficulties and to design them out.
2. A consumer information service supported by a staff of 23 people who answer over 150,000 letters per year.
3. Thirty-nine customer service centers throughout the country that offer free advice and minor equipment adjustments and repairs.
4. A wide variety of pamphlets and books on picture taking made available through a nonprofit publication program.
5. The establishment of a high level position—Assistant Vice President and General Manager, Customer Equipment Services Division—with the responsibility for providing customer service for all product divisions.

It is essential that management become familiar with the implications of contemporary consumerism and respond accordingly. Constructive positive action such as that undertaken by Kodak will be needed.

Progress is being made toward fulfillment of the rights that John F. Kennedy proclaimed for the consumer in 1962:[21]

1. The right to safety
2. The right to be informed
3. The right to choose
4. The right to be heard.

But must this progress come so slowly? As E. B. Weiss said in commenting on a speech made by a former president of a large publishing firm, "Who could disagree that 'some degree of responsibility must rest on and with the consumer'? Who could disagree that it is foolish to regard the consumer as a 'pitiable imbecile'? Yet we (as businesspersons) err in going on to insist not only that the consumer has a right to be wrong, but that marketing must make sure he exercises that right!"[22]

[20]F. E. Webster, p. 93.
[21]Consumer Advisory Council, *First Report Executive Office of the President* (Washington, D.C.: United States Government Printing Office, October, 1963).
[22]E. B. Weiss, "Marketers Fiddle While Consumers Burn," *Harvard Business Review,* 46 (July–August, 1968), p. 47.

Shopping—There Is More to It than Buying

It has been suggested that consumer behavior be divided into three broad areas including shopping, buying, and consuming.[23] It is also the opinion of some that the analysis of consumer behavior has essentially focused on buyer behavior and virtually has neglected shopping and consumption. In this context, shopping refers to going to a store or shopping center and is an action performed for a number of reasons in addition to that of making a purchase. Exploratory research has identified several reasons for shopping.[24] Discussed here are three that pose attractive opportunities for retailers.

Role Playing.   Shopping is sometimes engaged in because it is part of a specific role pattern; that is, it is expected behavior on the part of individuals who assume a given role. For instance, historically, grocery shopping has been a customary activity of the homemaker. It apparently has some appeal beyond the purchase of food and related items because a number of attempts to eliminate the need to physically engage in shopping in the typical way have met with failure. Illustrating this result are the modern computerized services that permit filling grocery needs through telephone ordering and home delivery that have generally been unsuccessful.

Diversion.   The act of shopping offers an opportunity for varying the daily routine and represents a form of recreation. To some it can provide nearly free family entertainment without the necessity of formal dress or advanced planning. The common use of the term "browsing" and the readily observable strolling of people through shopping centers substantiates the suggestion that shopping is a national pastime. Innovative shopping center managements have encouraged this form of shopping through the use of atmospherics and the use of the center as a flexible display area for such products as boats, campers, and automobiles.

Sensory Stimulation.   Retail establishments offer many sensory benefits to their shoppers. People browse through a

---

[23]E. M. Tauber, "Why Do People Shop?" *Journal of Marketing,* 36 (October, 1972), p. 47.

[24]E. M. Tauber, pp. 46–49.

store looking at merchandise and at each other. They also enjoy handling the goods on display and either trying an item on or trying it out. Sound and scent are being used increasingly in a creative way to develop ambience for shoppers.

Each of the foregoing reasons for shopping offers an opportunity to the marketer. For example, stores or whole centers can be differentiated on the basis of the moods they create and offer to the public. It might be possible to segment consumers in a particular geographic market on the basis of what shopping atmospheres appeal to them. Some evidence already exists to support the proposition that background music can affect the way consumers shop in a given store. If this is further substantiated, it might be possible to change the tempo of the background music during the business day and to be able to control the efficiency of space usage by leveling out traffic flows. For instance, supermarkets might attempt to move people through the store somewhat more quickly during peak periods by increasing the tempo of the background music and then encourage a more leisurely pace at other times by slowing the tempo.

MARKETS OFFERING UNIQUE OPPORTUNITIES

There are several markets of such size and dynamism that they require special attention. Two are the focus of this section. The first is called the "kaleidoscopic" youth market because of its many contrasts. The second is the black middle class, which is included because it illustrates that the black market, like the white, is not homogeneous and that some segments offer considerable sales potential.

The Kaleidoscopic Youth Market

The youth of this country make up a sizable portion of the population and, consequently, are of considerable interest as a target market. Today those 15–19 years old number over 20 million. It is certainly not a homogeneous group, but members share some common interests and behavioral patterns that deserve special attention from any firm or other organization interested in reaching the youth segment.

Various analysts attribute different dollar values to the expenditures of youth. These range from a conservative $21 billion to a more generous $43 billion annually.[25] What makes this particularly attractive is its discretionary nature; that is, most youths have considerable flexibility over what they buy and where they purchase it. Furthermore, there is mounting evidence to show that some modes of behavior and living styles are passed from the more youthful segments of the population to the less youthful. In addition, teenagers can have a substantial influence in some family purchase decisions. For example, one study found the following pattern: Of the families studied, the influence of their children was present in 79 percent of the car purchases, 37 percent of their food product purchases, and 24 percent of their vacation plans.[26]

There are indications that what contemporary youths value is at some variance with what older adults value. Such differences have been reflected in varied life-styles and consumption patterns. One study conducted in 1971 compared the value orientations of college seniors toward business and society with those of individuals who had been out of school ten years. A few of the differences are identified in Table 16.1.

If the orientations of the seniors prevail, behavioral patterns significantly different than those of their predecessors are likely to emerge. There is reason to believe that some such changes will occur. A number of firms are already taking advantage of market opportunities that have arisen among the youth of the early 1970's. For instance, the wine industry found a willing market for sweet wines among a generation weaned on soft drinks. The fashion industry took note of the attractiveness of the army-navy surplus look and capitalized on the interest in casual dress and reintroduced denim.[27]

[25]H. N. Windeshausen and P. A. Williams, *Sacramento Metropolitan Teenage Market Study,* Occasional Paper No. 2 (Sacramento, California: Center for Research, School of Business and Public Administration, California State University, 1975), p. 4.

[26]C. B. Axford, "How Banks Can Relate Their 'Thing' to Youth," *Burroughs Clearing House* (June, 1970), p. 81.

[27]S. Ward, et. al., p. 374.

TABLE 16.1
Comparison of Value Orientations

Ten Years Out Of School	*College Seniors*
1. The System works, with reservations.	The System does not work, but it used to.
2. Material success is desirable and attainable.	Material success is questionable and no longer attainable for everyone.
3. Material success and status go together.	Material success and conventionally defined success are questionable values.
4. Personal self-fulfillment comes with material success.	Personal self-fulfillment might have no relation to material success.
5. Whatever cuts the incentive to work hard is dangerous for the System and its values.	Working too hard and devoting too much attention to work is dangerous for the individual.

Source: Adapted from S. Ward, T. S. Robertson, and W. Capitman, "What Will Be Different About Tomorrow's Consumer?" in *Combined Proceedings 1974 Spring and Fall Conferences,* F. C. Allivine, ed. (Chicago: American Marketing Association, 1972), pp. 372–373.

More recently there appears to be evidence of a move back toward an acceptance of the value orientations of the 1950's— a time when materialism was in full bloom. The extent of this movement is unconfirmed, but there are some indications as to its strength. One is the renewed interest in the songs of the post-World War II years. A more vivid illustration of the return to conspicuous consumption is evident in the attention given the van as a status symbol.

Just a few years ago, vans were considered unglamorous, utilitarian vehicles driven by plumbers and delivery men. Today some analysts contend that vans have become the centerpiece of a rapidly growing subculture, complete with its own set of values, magazines, and clubs. For many youths aged 16–21, the van is a status symbol and an expression of personality. The custom interiors tend to have the character of a well-planned bachelor pad—expensive sound system, crushed velvet walls, subdued lighting, and beds with fake fur bedspreads and even satin sheets. The conversion process has reached such a stage of complexity and stylization that in its most lavish form, a van is no less than an art form.[28]

It appears that in addition to the initial price of $4,000 to $15,-000 asked for such a vehicle, those involved must have enormous amounts of time to invest. Owners of a true show van often wash them daily and wax them by hand at least three times a week to protect their expensive paint jobs. Such a purchase and devotion is hardly representative of a lessening interest in material goods or hard work.

To those planning to focus on the youth market, it is essential that it be viewed as a dynamic entity. Furthermore, just as it is frequently appropriate to segment the older market to realize its full potential, such an approach might be necessary in marketing to the youths of this country. The consumer analyst can be of great assistance in identifying various behavioral differences that have major implications for segmentation. For instance, there might be significant identifiable differences in groups of youths in terms of the media to which they are exposed or their behavioral patterns might vary noticeably from one major geographic area to another.

The Black Middle Class: A New Market

To many American businesses, blacks as a segment of the total consumer market have not represented sufficient potential to make pursuit of them with a unique marketing strategy worthwhile, or they have been assumed to have behavioral patterns similar to those of the white majority.[29] However, recently there has been increased interest shown in what is being called the black middle class. Although this group can be defined in a

---

[28]"The Van: Latest Status Symbol for Youth," *The Columbia Daily Tribune* (September 26, 1975), p. 16.

[29]D. P. Gibson, *The $30 Billion Negro* (New York: The Macmillian Company, 1969), pp. 11–13.

number of ways, several characteristics have proven most helpful. These include family income, family composition, number of
wage earners, occupations, and the attitudes that characterize
its members.

In terms of income, the black middle class earns from $8,000
to $15,000 and includes somewhat less than 25 percent of all
black households. Nevertheless, it accounts for over 40 percent
of the blacks' $54 billion annual spending power. The family
composition of this middle-class segment is summarized in Table
16.2.

There is an employed woman in over 60 percent of the black
families that include a husband and wife. This compares to only
about 40 percent among white families with the same composition. The black middle-class family distinguishes itself from its
white counterpart on the basis of several other dimensions as
well.[30]

> Only 24 percent of middle class black family heads have white-collar
> occupations as compared to 47 percent of the whites.
>
> Sixty per cent of the black middle class work at blue-collar jobs
> versus 51 percent of the whites.
>
> Many of these black family heads work at jobs that are not ordinarily
> associated with middle-class status: bus drivers, social workers,
> postal workers, policemen, and city sanitation workers. However,

TABLE 16.2
Family Composition: All Blacks and the Black Middle Class[31]

Family Composition	All Black Families	Black Middle-Class Families
Husband-wife	61.4%	80.8%
Female head	34.6	14.4
Other male head	4.0	4.6

Source: Adapted from T. C. Taylor, "Black Middle Class: Earn, Baby, Earn,"
Sales Management: 1974 Survey of Buying Power, 113 (July 8, 1974), p. A-6.
Reprinted by permission from *Sales Management,* The Marketing Magazine,
copyright 1974.

[30]T. C. Taylor, p. A–11.

the money contributed by the second family wage-earner often accounts for the middle-class income level.

In terms of personal interests and orientations, there has been a noticeable movement away from the characteristics often used to represent poorer blacks. For instance, among these families there is increasing concern for self-improvement and a strong desire for gaining higher self-esteem. Family cohesiveness is also highly valued. Aspirations often include a better place to live, college for the children, and a home of their own. These changing interest patterns are likely to have considerably more influence on black purchasing patterns than will the upward movement of their incomes.[31]

Some emerging purchasing patterns deserve particular recognition. Firms marketing big ticket items should pay special attention to the black middle class. Historically, blacks as a group have been said to spend proportionately more on food, alcoholic beverages, soft drinks, and clothing than do whites. However, as the figures in Table 16.3 indicate, blacks are an increasingly attrac-

TABLE 16.3
Black Buying Index

Product Type	Index Value
Automobiles	
New	77
Used	107
Washing machine	125
Kitchen range	160
Refrigerator, freezer	133
Black and white television	243
Color television	103
Radio, phonograph, hi-fi equipment	155
Furniture	153

T. C. Taylor, "Black Middle Class: Earn, Baby, Earn," *Sales Management: 1974: Survey of Buying Power* 113 (July 8, 1974), p. A–11. Reprinted from *Sales Management,* The Marketing Magazine, Copyright 1974.

[31]T. C. Taylor, p. A–6.

tive market for many more expensive items—those that are often considered symbols of the "good life."

Using 1968–1972 census data, Sales Management has constructed what they call the "black buying index." This index adjusts comparative black and white spending to allow for income differences. When the index is over 100, it shows that the typical black family is outspending the white family when its lower income is taken into account. It shows rather dramatically that the growing discretionary buying power of the emerging black middle class is being used to purchase products such as television sets, stereos, and furniture. Of course, one explanation for these differences lies in the fact that many white families already have these products, whereas numerous blacks do not. As household ownership of such items grows among black families, the differences reflected in this buying index can be expected to be reduced. However, this may take considerable time.[32]

The importance of the black middle class to marketing managers can be summarized as follows:[33]

1. This group may have a long-term catalytic effect on the black consumer market generally similar to that which the white middle class had following World War II. Some contend that the consumption patterns that emerged in the postwar years had a considerable impact on what has come to be known as the affluent society.

2. Viewing blacks as a homogeneous market of 23 million people with essentially uniform behavioral patterns is no longer appropriate. It might need to be segmented when attempting to market certain products such as travel, for example. The black travel market has grown from $541 million to $1 billion in about five years.[34] It is reasonable to assume that the better educated black professional has more time and money to travel. However, blacks generally are traveling more and often spend considerably more on accommodations and food than does a comparable white family.

[32]T. C. Taylor, p. A–11.
[33]T. C. Taylor. p. A–5.
[34]D. P. Gibson, p. 214.

3. Because the black middle class is a relatively new phenomenon, it is still not well understood, and it will require substantial
research to identify its full dimensions. For example, a variety of
black-oriented media are available in some major markets; however, the question still remains as to whether or not it is more
economical to use the mass market media to reach the black
middle-class consumer. The appearance of some new black
magazines such as *Essence* for black women, *Encore,* a news
magazine, and *Black Creation* for the arts lover, suggests a
growing interest in the special media.

4. The black middle class is considerably more susceptible to
the impact of economic hard times. A great deal of the potential
growth of this emerging market depends on the economic health
of the United States. If, for example, there were extended periods
of high unemployment, the consequences would likely be substantial for this group of black families.

Sources of New Insights into Consumer Behavior

New insights and theories that are offered as a means of furthering the understanding of consumer behavior can come from a
number of sources using varied approaches. Despite this fact, it
appears that the problem-solving approach is likely to contribute
the most to furthering the understanding of consumer behavior
in the foreseeable future.[35] This is based on the assumption that
those interested in marketing issues will continue to give substantial attention to consumer analysis. The problem-solving approach is outlined in the diagram shown in Figure 16.1. It is
explained briefly in the following paragraphs.

The problem-solving approach has several major phases.[36]
These include recognition of a situational marketing problem,
identification of the consumer behavior dimensions, development of a behavioral analysis plan, review of existing knowledge
from the behavioral sciences generally and from consumer behavior specifically, development of testable propositions and a

[35]T. S. Robertson and S. Ward, pp. 17–18.
[36]T. S. Robertson and S. Ward, p. 18.

FIGURE 16.1
Problem-Solving Approach to
the Analysis of Consumer Be-
havior

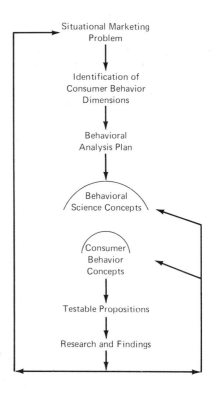

method of investigation, and finally, carrying out of the research. It should be noted from the diagram that feedback serves two major purposes. First, it provides management with information to assist them in making decisions with respect to specific problems at hand, and it also serves to facilitate understanding of consumer behavior, leading to the development of more complete theories.

A short example will be presented here to illustrate how the problem-solving approach can evolve. Assume that the T. R. Value Company is in the final planning stage before the introduction of a new nail polish remover called Nail-Renew. The new product is said to work faster, easier, more neatly and completely than existing brands.

A decision will need to be made soon as to how to introduce Nail-Renew so that the consumer will try it. Two alternatives are under serious consideration. One is that the product be heavily advertised using magazine ads that include a coupon good for a free bottle. The other alternative tactic being proposed is that free samples of the product be mass mailed to all prospective users in several major market areas.

One issue of vital concern to the Value Company management is the extent to which these two alternative marketing tactics can induce consumer innovators to use and adopt this product. To investigate this issue, a plan is developed to use two cities in the Midwest as test locations for determining the relative value of each tactic. These cities are representative of the total market and are reasonably similar in terms of those factors that appear to be important in marketing nail polish remover: number of women, age distribution, education, and life-style characteristics.

After a two-month period, the extent of success of market penetration in each area will be measured. This setting provides the consumer analyst studying the problem with the opportunity to assist management with a specific problem and also to further the knowledge of consumer behavior in general. Under the circumstances surrounding this problem, all the information that can be obtained about the adoption of innovations must be reviewed. Once this has been done, testable propositions should be formulated that focus on the major issue of interest to the firm's management.

One such proposition might be framed in the following manner:

> The probability of new product trial increases as the amount of initiative necessary on the consumer's part is reduced.

This proposition can be tested by comparing the number of consumers who had tried the new nail polish remover in each of the two test markets. If the rate of trial is significantly greater in the city where the free sample was mailed to the home, the proposition would be accepted, that is, found to be consistent with the behavior observed. In this situation, the firm's management is supplied with critical information concerning the introduction of its new product. In addition, consumer behavior theory is advanced by the results of the findings. These research results become most helpful if they are shared through publication or discussed at a professional meeting so that other analysts can learn about the findings.

The extent to which the field of consumer behavior is nurtured and grows depends on the dedication of its analysts and the willingness of business, government, and those organizations that make up the nonprofit sector to share their findings. As the field is advanced, it will facilitate more efficient use of our natural resources and assist in raising the level of living for everyone. Furthermore, there is no evidence to show that people can be manipulated through this added knowledge, but there is evidence to show that consumer needs and wants can be better served with it.

Summary

The final chapter attempts to again bring into perspective the total thrust of consumer behavior as an area of study and to identify new directions in which the discipline is moving. The objective of consumer behavior is to understand, explain, and predict actions taken by individuals or small groups such as the family in their consumption of goods and services. Consumer behavior today is actually a science in that it is general and conceptual, founded on controlled observations, oriented toward prediction, seeks causal connections, and strives for explicit explanations of events as well as closure. Marketing practitioners are taking an active interest in consumer behavior to "fine tune" their actions and to gain an increased understanding of market events through a full explanation of such events. Further consumer analysis applications are likely to occur in the significant areas of: (1) public policy development and implementation —primarily because of growing dissatisfaction with the use of microeconomic concepts to guide regulatory processes, (2) social and environmental problems—population control and the reduction of malnutrition, for example, (3) cross-cultural interests such as the identifications of consumer similarities between countries.

Two issues of special interest are considered—contemporary consumerism and shopping as something other than a purchase activity. Consumerism has three dimensions: (1) action taken to protect consumers from deceptive and misleading practices, hazardous products, monopolistic activities of business, and other abuses stemming from business tactics: (2) noticeable changes in consumer attitudes and value orientations toward specific goods and services, consumption generally, affluence and materialism, and the environment; and (3) the political force that has developed as a result of the first two factors. It is essential that business management become familiar with consumerism and its implications and respond with constructive positive action. Shopping is frequently engaged in for nonpurchase reasons, such as playing an expected role (e.g., homemaker), diverting from a daily routine, or attaining stimulating sensory benefits from the shopping experience.

The youth and the black middle class markets are viewed as those offering unique opportunities. The youth market is a very substantial one made up of relatively independent consumers who are having a significant influence on older markets as well as on family purchase decisions. The marketer must be aware that the black middle class market (1) might have a long-term catalytic effect on the entire black consumer market, (2) is not a homogeneous composition of 23 million people, (3) is still not well understood and will require substantial research to identify its full dimension, and (4) is considerably more susceptible to the impact of economic hard times than is its white counterpart.

The problem-solving approach appears to be the most likely to contribute to new insights in consumer behavior in the near future. The advancement of consumer analysis must complement any relevant findings. The willingness of all sectors to share important results will further the discipline of consumer behavior and benefit the consumer through better need fulfillment.

1. If consumer behavior is a science, shouldn't it have universal application? Consequently, should it not be possible to use the same appeals to consumers no matter what part of the world they live in?
2. A wealth of information on consumer behavior is generated every year by business firms doing research for their own use. However, most of this is maintained as proprietary information. What practical means could be suggested for sharing this information without giving away competitive secrets?
3. How is a general increase in the level of education likely to affect the following:

   a. the purchase of national brands versus private store brands
   b. the buying of convenience foods
   c. the selection of homes
   d. the amount of time spent searching for purchase-related information

4. Is it reasonable to assume that the youth market as an entity remains rather stable and that different groups just pass through it? Explain your answer.
5. To what extent is it possible to characterize the youth market as a state of mind or set of attitudes rather than as a particular age group? If this is true, it is then possible to have youthful 50-year-olds and nonyouthful 22-year-olds. Comment.
6. Some have contended that consumer behavior as it exists today deals with product purchases and has little or nothing to say about how or why people buy services. Is this an accurate statement?
7. As businesspeople become more knowledgeable in their understanding of consumer behavior, by what means can consumers improve their skills in buymanship in order to maintain some balance in the marketplace?
8. Is it fair to say that consumerism exists because business generally has been too much concerned with short-run profit and has not given enough attention to long-term social responsibility? Discuss.
9. If you were a marketing manager, how would you go about keeping yourself informed about the changes that were taking place in the consumer behavior field? Be specific.

10. Who should study consumer behavior? Is it appropriate to expect all marketing students to take a course in consumer behavior? Is this also true for all business students generally? What specific groups of people should keep well informed about consumer behavior?

Case 1.

A new compound for use in filling teeth was developed recently by a major university's chemical engineering department. In extensive laboratory tests, it has proven to be substantially superior to any existing material. However, despite these findings, great difficulty has been experienced in getting dental supply houses to carry the material. The supply firms who sell to dentists say that there is no demand for the product. The engineering school faculty involved feel that this is a revolutionary new product that should have a wide appeal. The dean of the school has considered asking a journalism school faculty member for some assistance in generating public awareness and interest in the new material.

What consumer behavior patterns are of interest?

Of what good is it to generate consumer awareness and interest in this new product?

Case 2.

Hear Perfect is a brand of hearing aid produced by Health Products Diversified. The company has been in business for 20 years and sells its products exclusively through franchised dealers. The parent company has sponsored national television advertising encouraging people to see their local Hear Perfect dealer for a free hearing check. They have also featured testimonials from satisfied customers. The following is a typical statement: "I had a hearing problem for years until I got my Hear Perfect hearing aid. Now I know what I was missing all those years. If you have a hearing difficulty, see your local Hear Perfect dealer. He is as concerned about your hearing as you are."

Although these ads have been very effective in generating dealer office traffic, the company has recently been accused of deceptive advertising by two different local consumer groups.

Is this testimonial deceptive?

What criteria should be used in determining whether an ad is deceptive?

How would you advise HPD's management to respond to these recent charges?

Glossary

Abstract elements   Term which refers to that aspect of culture which includes the values, attitudes, ideas, and personality types that can be used to characterize some large groups of people.

Accultration   The learning of another culture or subculture different than the one in which the person was raised.

Actual state   Refers to the way the consumer perceives his existing state of affairs.

Adjustment function   The adaptive tendency of consumers to develop favorable attitudes toward products, brands and retail outlets that provide the expected level of satisfaction and to develop unfavorable attitudes toward those that do not provide the expected level of satisfaction.

Adoption   A stage in the consumer's acceptance process—the consumer adopts the new product and commits himself to using it regularly.

Affective component   Refers to the consumer's overall feeling of like or dislike for an attitude object.

AHA Experience   Refers to a problem solving situation where there is perceived to be one correct or acceptable response. This solution may be recognized after some trail and error.

Analogue model   A model which portrays various properties of something by a different set of properties, e.g., a road map.

Analysis for pertinence   Further processing to determine a stimulus' pertinence to a consumer, after the initial response.

Atmospherics   The conscience designing of space and its various dimensions to create certain environmental effects in the buying situation.

Attention   A phase of consumer information processing, refers to taking special note of something among a number of possibilities.

Attitude   (1) The assessment a consumer makes regarding the ability that a product, brand, or store has to satisfy his or her expectations, which in turn, have been defined by his evaluative criteria.

(2) A consumer's assessment of the ability of an alternative to satisfy his purchasing and consumption requirements as expressed in his evaluative criteria.

Autonomic Decision making   Refers to specific family purchasing decisions made most often by either the wife or husband.

Awareness   A stage in the consumer's acceptance process in which a product stimulus penetrates the consumer's filtration system and registers with him.

Bachelor state—Family life cycle   A category of the family life cycle; it is a nonfamily household and includes one young single person not living at home.

Behavioral component   Refers to the consumer's action tendency or expected behavior.

Benefit segmentation   Identification of the various benefits that consumers seek from a particular product and using this information as a basis of market segmentation.

Black buying index   This index adjusts comparative black and white spending to allow for income differences. It was developed by *Sales Management*.

CAD   A scaling technique developed for the measurement of personal orientation and behavioral tendencies.

Central control Unit (CCU)   A component of the decision-process model. It consists of significant psychological variables which help explain a consumer's motivation and behavior.

Centrality of attitudes   Attitudes that are closely related to the consumer's self concept and basic values.

Clarifiers   Consumers characterized by their behavioral pattern used to reduce perceived risk. When confronted with some confusion, individuals who follow this pattern seek additional information in order to better understand the context in which a decision can be made.

Classical conditioning   A learning process in which the relevant action follows some triggering event.

Classical Psychological model   A model which maintains that attitudes are made up of three components: (1) cognitive, (2) affective, and (3) behavioral.

Closure The process of bringing consumers to the point where the evidence before them conclusively suggests that the product or service being offered should be bought. That is, it is showing that the product fully meets all their needs and wants.

Cognitive component Refers to the manner in which a consumer perceives information about a product, service, advertisement or retail outlet.

Cognitive dissonance A psychologically uncomfortable condition experienced by a consumer after a purchase decision.

Communicability The degree to which the benefits of product use can be communicated to others.

Communication (Comes from the Latin word *communis,* which means common) The effort to establish commonness with someone or a group.

Comparative function Refers to the means by which the individual uses a group of people to establish his or her framework of reference for value formation and decision making.

Compatibility Refers to the degree to which a new product is consistent with existing values and experiences of consumers.

Complexity The extent to which a new product is difficult to understand and use.

Complicated problem recognition Refers to the problem recognition process characterized by the investment of considerable time, many influencing factors and typically intense consumer attitudes.

Comprehension A phase of consumer information processing which refers to understanding the stimulus that is noted.

Concentrated marketing Satisfying the distinctive needs of a single segment in the market by designing a product and marketing program that focuses on those needs.

Conflict models of man Describes human behavior as the result of the struggle between good and evil or at least between opposing forces. One of the earliest models of human behavior.

Conscious motive Reasons for action that a person is readily aware of and, therefore, need not be aroused by a sales person or advertisement, e.g., planning to purchase a new winter coat because last year's is no longer fit to wear.

Consumer behavior The acts of individuals directly involved in obtaining and using economic goods and services, including the decision processes that precede and determine those acts

Consumerism An orientation to the study of consumer behavior which includes a high level of concern for issues related to consumer welfare.

Covert involvement The internal responses to stimuli, e.g., a mental or emotional feeling. By this means a consumer may experience some of the benefits from a product or service by simply thinking about it.

Crosscultural analysis The comparison of similarities and differences among countries in the behavioral and material aspects of their cultures.

Cue Stimuli which occur externally to the individual and can emanate to the individual from any environmental source.

Culture The complex set of values, ideas, attitudes, and other meaningful symbols created by man to shape human behavior all of which are transmitted from one generation to the next.

Daily life routine The pattern of behavior each family develops to cope with the day-to-day demands placed upon it.

Decision-process approach (1) An approach which views a purchase as simply one stage in a particular course of action undertaken by a consumer.
(2) A way to study consumer behavior empirically by describing the way consumers actually make decisions, including the impact of various influences on the purchase process.

Demarketing The effort directed toward the orderly reduction of demand among consumers for selected goods or services.

Demographic factors Variables such as age, education, income, and geographic area of residence.

Demographic segmentation The use of demographic variables such as age, income, sex, and education as the basis for market segmentation.

Differentiated marketing Strategy for dealing with specific markets by satisfying the unique needs of its various segments through distinctive products and specific programs.

Diffusion of innovation The spread of an idea from its source of invention or creation to its ultimate users or adopters.

Direct questioning A series of inquiries that ask in a rather straight forward manner upon what basis the person being questioned makes a particular buying decision.

Distributive approach A way to study consumer behavior empirically by focusing on behavioral outcomes, that is, on the purchase act rather than the purchase process.

Dormant motive A motive which is hidden from self awareness and must be aroused. What these are frequently will vary from one consumer to another.

Drive A strong internal stimulus that impels action. It is a force that arouses an individual and keeps him ready to respond and thus it is the basis of motivation.

Ego Functions to control and direct the id's impulses so that gratification can be achieved in a socially acceptable manner.

Ego defensive function The human tendency to avoid situations or forces inconsistent with one's ego or self image.

Emotional motives Motives which are often assumed to include pride, status, pleasure, uniqueness and showiness. Sometimes considered subjective in nature.

Empty Nest I—Family life cycle A category of the family life cycle, includes older married couples who have no children living with them, but where the household head is employed.

Empty nest II—Family life cycle A category of the family life cycle, includes older married couples with no children living at home with the household head retired.

Encultration The process of absorbing or learning the culture in which one is raised. Also referred to as socialization.

Evaluation A stage of the consumer's adoption process —refers to the mental assessment of whether or not the new product will provide benefit now or in the future.

Evaluative criteria (1) Internalized standards used by consumers to assess and compare alternative products, brands, stores, and other consumption alternatives.
(2) A group of product features or performance characteristics such as price and dependability that consumers value and expect to find in a particular product, brand, retail outlet, or other organization that they anticipate dealing with during some reasonable period of time.

Evoked set Also called consideration group; this is the range of brands of some product group assembled by the consumer that can feasibly be looked upon as true alternatives. For example, if you only consider three brands of ball point pens before purchasing, these three brands are your evoked set.

Exposure A phase of information processing in which the person comes in contact with external stimuli from various physical and social sources.

Extended decision process behavior Most comprehensive type of consumer decision making represented by the complete Engel, Kollat, and Blackwell model.

Extended family Includes the nuclear family plus other relatives such as grandparents, uncles, aunts, cousins, and in-laws.

External search The act of seeking information from any source outside the individual who is engaged in the search process.

Family A group of persons who are related by blood, marriage, or legal adoption.

Family life cycle Changes in family composition over time which may substantially alter the family needs, its decision-making process and its market behavior.

Family of orientation The family that one is born into or adopted into.

Family of procreation The formation of a new family unit capable of existence as a separate entity.

Family role structure Refers to the behavior of nuclear family members at each stage in the decision-making process.

Fear appeals Organization of message content so as to arouse the anxieties or fears of the consumer.

Ferber's model A simplified decision-making framework which shows that both financial and nonfinancial decisions are affected by the available financial resources of the family, by the objectives or goals of the family and the attitudes of the family members.

Filter Component of the consumer's CCU that permits what appear to be the most relevant information for the consumer to be transmitted to the other variables in the CCU.

Formal group A group characterized by an explicit structure, specified membership requirements, and typically, a specified goal.

Full nest I—Family life cycle A category of the family life cycle, includes young married couples with the youngest child under six.

Full nest II—Family life cycle A category of the family life cycle, includes young married couples with the youngest child six years or older.

Full nest III—Family life cycle A category of the family life cycle, includes older married couples with dependent children.

Further behavior An outcome of the purchase which takes the form of further action.

Gatekeeper A concept which refers to an individual who acts as a valve or filter affecting the flow of information coming into the family or other decision-making unit.

Generalization The process that enables the individual to respond to a new stimulus as he has learned to respond to a similar, but somewhat different one in the past.

Geographic segmentation Identification of distinctive consumer preferences among various geographic areas.

Habitual decision process behavior A variation of the consumer decision process generally involving repetitive action. In this behavior, external constraints may still operate to halt the decision or delay its culmination, but their affect is likely to be minimal.

Highly complex problem recognition Refers to those infrequent, unprogrammed types of processes that involve a considerable period of time, are affected by a large number of factors and include strongly held attitudes.

Household Refers to a living unit or entity for consumption purposes. It may consist of one or more persons.

Howard/Sheth model An integrative model of buyer behavior that attempts to explain brand choice behavior over time.

Id Related to Freud's conceptualization in defining man's personality. The id is considered the genetically implanted component containing basic cravings or instincts.

Indirect questioning Probing questions that nurture the discussion of deeply held ideas and notions.

Informal group A group which usually develops on the basis of proximity, interests, or similar circumstances and has explicit structure or membership requirements.

Information processsing Refers to all the means by which a sensory input is transformed, reduced, elaborated, stored, recovered and used by a consumer in decision making situations.

Innovation Any idea or product perceived by the potential consumer to be new.

Instrumental conditioning A process of learning in which the response or action sought precedes the conditioning stimulus. It has been referred to as trial and error learning.

Interest A stage in the consumer adoption process—the consumer becomes interested in the new product and begins to seek information about it.

Internal search The conscious recall and consideration of specific information and experiences that appear to be relevant to the recognized problem that the consumer faces.

Interpersonal attitudes The predisposition of family members toward interactions among themselves as well as toward those outside the family.

Knowledge function The function of attitudes which provides consistency and stability in the way an individual perceives the world around him.

Learning Changes in responses and response tendencies due to the effects of experience.

Legitimization stage Stage of the adoption process in which the consumer becomes convinced that the new product is socially appropriate, properly priced, and meets evaluative criteria in general.

Lewin's formula A conceptual view of human behavior which is portrayed as the result of the interaction among components of what is viewed as one's life space.

Life space Consists of the total "facts" that psychologically exist for an individual at a given moment in time.

Limited decision process behavior A variation of the consumer decision process; the consumer has adequate information about feasible alternatives, yet lacks adequate information to select the best alternative.

Logic trap The fallacy of relying upon intuitive reasoning and simple logic as a substitute for empirical investigation as a means of understanding consumer behavior.

Machine models of man Models of man which view a person as simply a physiological machine which responds to genetically implanted drives and environmental stimulation. Often referred to as the S-R model.

Macromarketing problems Problems a society faces meeting the needs of its people as an aggregate.

Market segmentation Refers to the subdividing of a market into homogeneous subsets of customers where any subset may conceivably be selected as a market target to be reached with a distinct marketing mix.

Marketing concept Organizing resources toward the fulfillment of unmet needs; often described as a consumer orientation.

Material elements Those objects that are employed by a large group of people in meeting their various needs, such as automobiles, buildings and computers.

Mathematical model A model which uses mathematical relationships to represent something else.

Medium image The perception of the source, or medium, which can influence its impact. For example, what consumers in a given target market think of television as a mode of communication is the image of television as a medium.

Mental completing The human tendency to remember incomplete patterns better than those that are complete.

Metamarketing The broad application of marketing knowhow. Frequently associated with the application of marketing technology to problems facing the not-for-profit sector, particularly on a micro basis.

Micromarketing problems The problems of a marketing nature encountered in administering specific units or entities in an economy, e.g., a hotel, supermarket, amusement park, or consumer goods manufacturer.

Middle majority Refers to the lower-middle and upper-lower social classes which comprise the largest group of consumers in America.

Model Any simplified representation of some occurence or phenomenon.

Motive A term which was used early in marketing to explain consumer behavior. It was defined as an internal urge which often assumed the entire burden of explanation for a consumer's actions.

Multiattribute model A model which considers attitudes to consist of two components—(1) beliefs about the attributes of an object, and (2) an evaluation of the beliefs.

Multimediation A term used to convey the fact that many processes intervene or mediate between exposure to a stimulus and the final outcomes of behavior —applies to the decision-process model of consumer behavior.

Myopic view of behavior The tendency to define the behavior of others in terms of one's own personal experiences.

Newly married couples—Family life cycle A category of the family life cycle, it includes husband and wife with no children.

Nicosia model An integrative-comprehensive model of consumer behavior which makes use of a flow chart to designate the basic elements of the decision process and the relationships that exist among these elements.

Norm A statement or belief by the majority of group members defining what the activities of group members should be.

Normative function A function performed by a reference group; refers to a group having a consensus of opinion with which the individual agrees and in which the person seeks to gain or maintain acceptance.

Nuclear family The immediate kin group of father and/ or mother and their offspring or adopted children who ordinarily live together.

Open-system model A model of human behavior which views man as being essentially purposive, as interdependent with the physical and social environment, and as actively involved in transactions with that environment as goals are pursued.

Other directed A term used by Reisman to indicate that some people rely more on immediate social stimuli as behavioral cues than they do on other sources of stimulation.

Oversimplification The tendency toward isolating one particular characteristic to explain the purchasing behavior of a consumer.

Patronage Refers to the reasons for selecting a store or other source from which a product or service may be purchased.

Permanent memory A component of the information handling process; this is the source of affects upon consumer behavior. It is also called long-term memory.

Personality Individual uniqueness which is observable in the form of rather consistent modes of behavior.

Postpurchase attitude change Attitude change which may be produced from new experiences and the information obtained from the purchase and use of a product.

Postpurchase evaluation Refers to the consumer's evaluation or assessment of the purchase decision that was made.

Preattentive processing The triggering of an initial response when a consumer is presented with a new stimulus.

Preliminary search The external search that is initiated by an individual after it is recognized that internal search has not provided adequate information.

Primary buying motives A motive that leads to the purchase of a general class of products or services, e.g., the purchase of candy or potato chips.

Primary drives Drives essentially based upon innate physiological needs such as thirst, hunger, pain avoidance, and sex.

Primary group An aggregate of individuals small enough and intimate enough so that all members can communicate regularly with each other on a face-to-face basis.

Problem recognition A stage of the consumer decision process; it occurs when an individual perceives a difference between an ideal or desired state and an actual state.

Problem solving approach Recognition of a situational marketing problem, identification of the consumer behavior dimensions, development of a behavioral analysis plan, formulation of testable propositions and a method of investigation, and finally the carrying out of research.

Product life cycle   Generalized pattern of sales and profit that products follow over time. This pattern has been described as including distinct stages in the life of a product.

Product motives   The reasons for selecting a particular good itself, e.g., why a consumer buys a new garden hose.

Psychoanalytic theory   Also known as Freudian theory, indicates that personality is composed of three interdependent forces—the id, the ego, and the superego.

Psychographic inventories   Inventories that attempt to describe the life styles of select consumer market segments through the use of activity, interest and opinion statements.

Psychological field   Another term for life space.

Psychological segmentation   The use of such variables as personality, attitudes and life styles to identify distinctive segments on which to focus marketing efforts.

Purchase intentions   The intervening variable between attitudes and behavior that is operative when a problem is recognized.

Purchase probability scale   A technique which provides an accurate measure of problem recognition for numerous product categories; groups consumers with different purchase intentions by requesting that they estimate their probability of purchasing a particular product or brand within a designated time period.

Purchasing processes   The purchase act itself and those encounters which are part of the circumstances which make up the immediate surroundings of the act of buying.

Rational motives   Motives which usually include economy, efficiency and dependability.

Reference group   A group to which one aspires to belong and to conform to its perceived norms.

Reinforcement   The matching of consequences or outcomes of a response with the anticipated benefits.

Reminder techniques   Attempts made by the merchant or one who wishes to influence consumer purchasing, that the consumer actually needs or wants some particular product.

Response   Refers to the outcome or what occurs as the result of the interaction among drive, cue, the variables of the CCU, and environmental forces.

Retention   (1) The final information processing stage which refers to those impressions from consumption related stimuli that are stored in the consumer's conscious memory.

(2) The remembering of learned material and experiences over time.

Role dominance   Refers to the extent to which one member of the family has greater influence in the family decision-making process than other members.

Role specialization   Refers to the tendency for the husband or the wife to assume greater responsibility in making certain decisions because one is more knowledgeable in particular decision areas.

Search   The purposeful attention given to the gathering and assembling of information related to the satisfaction of some perceived need, want, or desire.

Secondary drives   Learned drives; that is, those that are acquired over time through experience.

Secondary group   A group to which people belong, but have relatively little face-to-face exchange with its members; these include such groups as professional associations, university classes, and many community service organizations.

Selective buying motives   Those motives associated with the purchase of one brand over others, e.g., why a consumer buys a Maytag washing machine instead of some other brand.

Selective exposure   Part of information processing in which the consumer restricts his exposure to various sources.

Self-concept   Those more or less discrete perceptions an individual has of himself which he regards as part, or characteristic of his being. (5–154)

Self-perception   The way one thinks or perceives of himself. This has been found to vary by social class.

Semantic generation   The process of establishing meaning for words that essentially have no meaning.

Semantic satiation   Refers to the fact that continued use of a meaningful word can make it less meaningful.

Sensory memory   A component of the information handling process, it receives all information to which it is exposed.

Social aggregates   A collection of persons occupying the same approximate space. Members of aggregates may have common attitudes and behavioral patterns even though they do not purposefully meet and exchange information.

Social class   A relatively permanent and homogeneous division in a society within which individuals or families share similar values, life styles, interests and behavior.

Social class determinants   Refers to those characteristics that differentiate the members of one social class from another.

Social exchange theory Theory which is based upon the premise that the behavior of one individual responding to another is more or less reinforcing or punishing to the behavior of that individual.

Social factors These include family, peer groups, social class norms, as well as other group influences that come to bear upon the individual.

Social psychological theory Contends that social variables, not biological, are the most important determinants of personality.

Socialization The process in which a new member of a group learns the value system, the norms, and the required behavior patterns of the groups or organizations he or she is entering.

Society A collection of individuals who share a particular set of symbols and conduct their interpersonal and collective behavior according to the prescriptions of that group of people.

Solitary survivor—Family life cycle Actually two different categories of the family life cycle. One includes a single surviving spouse still in the labor force. The other includes a single surviving spouse who is retired.

Sheth's model of family decision making A comprehensive model of family decision-making in consumer behavior.

Short-term memory A component of the information handling process; it retains content somewhat longer than sensory memory before it is lost.

Simple problem recognition Those strongly learned, highly programmed and automatic types of comparisons of desire with actual states of affairs.

Simplifiers Consumers characterized by their behavioral pattern used to reduce perceived risk. When confronted with some confusion, individuals who follow this pattern selectively screen out information that is not consistent with their predisposition, thus simplifying the context within which a decision can be made.

Store image A composite of the impressions which consumers have with respect to a particular store or service establishment.

Stored information and experience An element of the CCU, includes stored information from prior consumption experiences and enables the consumer to respond to stimuli more directly because previously processed information is available.

Subculture A smaller group of people within a larger culture who have modified the way they deal with their environment.

Superego The internal representation of society's norms and values; acts to inhibit the impulses emanating from the id that would be contrary to social norms.

Syncratic decision making Refers to family decisions of a particular type which are made by both husband and wife exerting equal influence.

Target markets Specific groups of consumers within the broader consumer market that have the greatest interest in certain products or services

Theory An explanation of a set of phenomena. It includes the identification of important variables and an indication of their interrelationships.

Total purchase process Refers to all aspects of the consumer-store-environment interaction.

Trait factor theory Considers an individual's personality to be composed of a set of traits or factors that are relatively enduring and distinctive.

Trial A stage in the consumer's adoption process—the consumer purchases the new product to determine whether or not it provides the anticipated benefit.

Triple appeal A concept developed by Lasswell; in applying this to advertising, an effective message would arouse id impulses toward basic drives, while appeasing the superego by suggesting that the impulses are justified. Also the ego would be reached by emphasizing the logic of a proposed action.

Unconfirmed expectations A condition that occurs when a product fails to provide the expected or anticipated satisfaction.

Undifferentiated marketing A strategy of segmenting markets by satisfying the needs of the mass market with a single product and single marketing program.

Value expressive function Those attitudes which reflect a consumer's values, that is, attitudes that express to society those values that are consistent with the consumer's self image.

Values Fundamental principles to which individuals subscribe; they can vary across social classes.

Variable A factor or influence that enters into the measurement and prediction of consumer behavior.

Vehicle image The perception of a specific source, or vehicle, such as the *Wall Street Journal* that can influence its impact upon consumer behavior.

Vicarious practice Referred to as observational learning, the object of attention is seen in use. This concept is closely related to the concept of covert involvement.

Warner's six class system A representation of the distribution of the United States' population by dividing population into six classes.

Author Index

Subject Index